*Ron Jackson Suresha*
*Pete Chvany*
*Editors*

# Bi Men:
# Coming Out Every Which Way

*Bi Men: Coming Out Every Which Way* has been co-published simultaneously as *Journal of Bisexuality*, Volume 5, Numbers 2/3 2005.

*Pre-publication*
*REVIEWS,*
*COMMENTARIES,*
*EVALUATIONS . . .*

"A MUST-READ, THIS BOOK IS SURE TO BE THE STANDARD FOR YEARS TO COME. . . . A rich and eclectic compilation of personal stories. Editors Suresha and Chvany explode many myths and extend the basic library on gender and sexuality studies with this groundbreaking anthology of coming-out and coming-to-terms stories."

**Les K. Wright, PhD**
*Independent Scholar, Author,*
*and Gay Activist*
*Editor of* The Bear Book *and* The Bear Book II
*Founder of the Bear History Project*

*More pre-publication*
*REVIEWS, COMMENTARIES, EVALUATIONS...*

"**B**isexual men coming out of gayness, Mormons, Pennsylvania Dutch, Celtics, Canadians, Aussies, Southern Californians, New Orleans decadents, bicultural Bears, incarcerated bis, married dads, swingers and cross-dressers, female-to-male trans men; so many beautiful bi guys–wow and oh my! Not since *Male Lust* have I found a men's book I so enjoyed. The high school youth touched my heart most; I wish they were my sons! *Bi Men* is AN IMPRESSIVE COLLECTION that brings together many new voices describing their most intimate experiences as bisexual men as well as excellent reprinted material from classic sources. The sum total is A MAGNIFICENT ANTIDOTE TO BI-HATRED AND IGNOR- ANCE, especially as has been seen lately in the mainstream media."

**Loraine Hutchins, PhD**
*Co-editor of* Bi Any Other Name: Bisexual People Speak Out

"**I**n my work as a psychotherapist in private practice for over twenty-five years I have come to believe that bisexuality, though often latent, is far more prevalent than ever believed with truly homo- and hetero-oriented people being small minorities at opposite ends of a long spectrum. Sexual orientation is more fluid than we like to think and is much more complex than simple genital arousal. THIS BRAVE ANTHOLOGY PRESENTS BISEXUALITY IN DAZZLING ARRAY, with many diverse points of view well articulated. It is valuable not only in its own right but as a tool to question basic cultural assumptions not only about sexuality but about the very nature of intimate relationships."

**Franklin Abbot, LCSW**
*Editor of* Men and Intimacy *and* Boyhood: Growing Up Male

Harrington Park Press

# Bi Men:
# Coming Out Every Which Way

*Bi Men: Coming Out Every Which Way* has been co-published simultaneously as *Journal of Bisexuality*, Volume 5, Numbers 2/3 2005.

# Monographic Separates from the *Journal of Bisexuality*™

For additional information on these and other Haworth Press titles, including descriptions, tables of contents, reviews, and prices, use the QuickSearch catalog at http://www.HaworthPress.com.

*Bi Men: Coming Out Every Which Way,* edited by Ron Jackson Suresha and Pete Chvany (Vol. 5, No. 2/3, 2005). *"A must-read, this book is sure to be the standard for years to come." (Les K. Wright, independent scholar, author, and gay activist; editor of* The Bear Book *and* The Bear Book II; *founder of the Bear History Project)*

*Plural Loves: Designs for Bi and Poly Living,* edited by Serena Anderlini-D'Onofrio, PhD (Vol. 4, Nos. 3/4, 2004). *"Heartful, insightful, provocative, and stimulating. . . . In these pages, polyamory provides a context for many kinds of complex relationships that simply refuse to be pigeonholed into neat and exclusive little boxes." (Oberon Zell-Ravenheart, DD, MA, President, TheaGenesis LLC; Founder, Church of All Worlds; Former Publisher,* Green Egg *magazine; Author of* Grimoire for the Apprentice Wizard)

*Current Research on Bisexuality,* edited by Ronald C. Fox, PhD (Vol. 4, Nos. 1/2, 2004). *"Finally, the subdiscipline of bisexual studies has moved forward. This book represents a greater breadth and depth of empirical research on bisexuality than any other work to date. It contributes greater insight into issues ranging from better understanding of the bisexual identity formation process, to friendship patterns, intimate relationships, and mental health. The reader's guide alone is worth the purchase price." (Michele J. Eliason, PhD, Associate Professor, College of Nursing, University of Iowa)*

*Bisexuality and Transgenderism: InterSEXions of the Others,* edited by Jonathan Alexander, PhD, and Karen Yescavage, PhD (Vol. 3, Nos. 3/4, 2003). *The first book devoted exclusively to exploring the common ground–and the important differences–between bisexuality and transgenderism.*

*Women and Bisexuality: A Global Perspective,* edited by Serena Anderlini-D'Onofrio, PhD (Vol. 3, No. 1, 2003). *"Nimbly straddles disciplinary and geographical boundaries. . . . The collection's diversity of subject matter and theoretical perspectives offers a useful model for the continued development of interdisciplinary sexuality studies." (Maria Pramaggiore, PhD, Associate Professor of Film Studies, North Carolina State University)*

*Bisexual Women in the Twenty-First Century,* edited by Dawn Atkins, PhD (cand.) (Vol. 2, Nos. 2/3, 2002). *An eclectic collection of articles that typifies an ongoing feminist process of theory grounded in life experience.*

*Bisexual Men in Culture and Society,* edited by Brett Beemyn, PhD, and Erich Steinman, PhD (cand.) (Vol. 2, No. 1, 2002). *Incisive examinations of the cultural meanings of bisexuality, including the overlooked bisexual themes in James Baldwin's classic novels* Another Country *and* Giovanni's Room, *the conflicts within sexual-identity politics between gay men and bisexual men, and the recurring figure of the predatory, immoral bisexual man in novels, films, and women's magazines.*

*Bisexuality in the Lives of Men: Facts and Fictions,* edited by Brett Beemyn, PhD, and Erich Steinman, PhD (cand.) (Vol. 1, Nos. 2/3, 2001). *"At last, a source book which explains bisexual male desires, practices, and identities in a language all of us can understand! This is informative reading for a general audience, and will be especially valuable for discussions in gender studies, sexuality studies, and men's studies courses." (William L. Leap, PhD, Professor, Department of Anthropology, American University, Washington, DC)*

# Bi Men:
# Coming Out Every Which Way

Ron Jackson Suresha
Pete Chvany
Editors

*Bi Men: Coming Out Every Which Way* has been co-published simultaneously as *Journal of Bisexuality*, Volume 5, Numbers 2/3 2005.

**HPP**

Harrington Park Press®
An Imprint of The Haworth Press, Inc.

New York • London • Victoria (AU)
**www.HaworthPress.com**

Published by Kerry E. Mack

Harrington Park Press®, 10 Alice Street, Binghamton, NY 13904-1580 USA

Harrington Park Press is an imprint of The Haworth Press, Inc., 10 Alice Street, Binghamton, NY 13904-1580 USA

*Bi Men: Coming Out Every Which Way* has been co-published simultaneously as *Journal of Bisexuality*, Volume 5, Numbers 2/3 2005.

The development, preparation, and publication of this work has been undertaken with great care. However, the publisher, employees, editors, and agents of The Haworth Press and all imprints of The Haworth Press, Inc., including The Haworth Medical Press® and Pharmaceutical Products Press®, are not responsible for any errors contained herein or for consequences that may ensue from use of materials or information contained in this work. Opinions expressed by the author(s) are not necessarily those of The Haworth Press, Inc. With regard to case studies, identities and circumstances of individuals discussed herein have been changed to protect confidentiality. Any resemblance to actual persons, living or dead, is entirely coincidental.

Cover design by Kerry E. Mack

**Library of Congress Cataloging-in-Publication Data**

Bi men : coming out every which way / Ron Jackson Suresha, Pete Chvany, editors.
    p. cm.
    "Bi Men: Coming Out Every Which Way has been co-published simultaneously as Journal of bisexuality, v. 5, no. 2/3 2005."
    Includes bibliographical references and index.
    ISBN-13: 978-1-56023-614-6 (hard cover : alk. paper)
    ISBN-10: 1-56023-614-0 (hard cover : alk. paper)
    ISBN-13: 978-1-56023-615-3 (soft cover : alk. paper)
    ISBN-10: 1-56023-615-9 (soft cover : alk. paper)
    1. Bisexual men. 2. Bisexuality. 3. Coming out (Sexual orientation) I. Suresha, Ron Jackson. II. Chvany, Pete. III. Journal of bisexuality.
HQ74.B525 2005
306.76′5′081–dc22
                                                                 2005008520

# Indexing, Abstracting & Website/Internet Coverage

This section provides you with a list of major indexing & abstracting services and other tools for bibliographic access. That is to say, each service began covering this periodical during the year noted in the right column. Most Websites which are listed below have indicated that they will either post, disseminate, compile, archive, cite or alert their own Website users with research-based content from this work. (This list is as current as the copyright date of this publication.)

(continued)

(continued)

*Special Bibliographic Notes related to special journal issues*
*(separates) and indexing/abstracting:*

- indexing/abstracting services in this list will also cover material in any "separate" that is co-published simultaneously with Haworth's special thematic journal issue or DocuSerial. Indexing/abstracting usually covers material at the article/chapter level.
- monographic co-editions are intended for either non-subscribers or libraries which intend to purchase a second copy for their circulating collections.
- monographic co-editions are reported to all jobbers/wholesalers/approval plans. The source journal is listed as the "series" to assist the prevention of duplicate purchasing in the same manner utilized for books-in-series.
- to facilitate user/access services all indexing/abstracting services are encouraged to utilize the co-indexing entry note indicated at the bottom of the first page of each article/chapter/contribution.
- this is intended to assist a library user of any reference tool (whether print, electronic, online, or CD-ROM) to locate the monographic version if the library has purchased this version but not a subscription to the source journal.
- individual articles/chapters in any Haworth publication are also available through the Haworth Document Delivery Service (HDDS).

# ABOUT THE EDITORS

**Ron Jackson Suresha** authored the groundbreaking men's studies book, *Bears on Bears: Interviews & Discussions*, which the *Village Voice* acclaimed as "required reading for anyone interested in gender studies." He has edited several fiction anthologies including *Bearotica* and *Bear Lust*, both from Alyson Publications. Suresha is editor, with Pete Chvany, of the nonfiction anthology *Bi Men: Coming Out Every Which Way*, copublished as a double issue of the *Journal of Bisexuality*; and sole editor of *Bi Guys: Firsthand Fiction for Bisexual Men and Their Admirers*, both from Haworth Press. His fiction and nonfiction writing appears regularly in GLBTQ periodicals and anthologies. He resides in New London, Connecticut, with his husband, Rocco, and his online presence dwells at <http://www.suresha.com>.

**Pete Chvany** is a longtime bisexual activist from the Boston area. A former head of fund-raising for the Bisexual Resource Center, he has also presented at LGBT conferences ranging from the Fifth and Eighth International Conferences on Bisexuality to the first Gay Men's Health Summit in 1999, and the first LGBTI Health Summit in 2002. He served in the US Air Force in the late 1980s and holds a doctorate in English and American Literature from Tufts University. Along with paid work as a computer system administrator for a prominent university, he spends his time as a writer, musician, and photographer. He lives in the Boston area with his chosen family and several cats.

Dedicated to
Alfred C. Kinsey
1894-1956
who steadfastly dedicated himself
to listening to and telling the story
of the bisexual man

# Bi Men:
# Coming Out Every Which Way

## CONTENTS

PART THREE: INTERACTING IN EVOLVING GLBTQ
   COMMUNITIES

# About the Contributors

Virginia Woolf said that writers must be androgynous. I'll go a step further. You must be bisexual.

–Rita Mae Brown

**Marc Anders** lives in Santa Barbara with his wife and son. He has published one piece of fiction. "Miniature Golf "is his first nonfiction publication. He is currently working on the third draft of a novel about bisexual married men who, Anders states, are everywhere.

**Ed Boland** is a frustrated maid and chauffeur to his insufferable partner, Bob. They are slowly growing to resent each other in central Kentucky. Bob thinks Ed should mention rehab or God, because "that always sounds good in a bio." In his spare time, Ed is also a musician working on the great gay-coming-of-age epic rock album.

**Chuck Greenheart Bradley** is a working-class, Bear-identified, bisexual man living in Everett, Massachusetts. A member of two druidic organizations, the Order of Bards, Ovates and Druids and the Henge of Keltria, Chuck seeks to swim in an Irish polytheistic stream traditional enough to invoke the gods, goddesses, nature spirits, and ancestors, and progressive enough to acknowledge that we live in an urban, technological, and pluralistic world.

**Arch Brown**'s produced and published plays include *Sex Symbols, FREEZE!, Pantheon, Brut Farce,* and his hit *News Boy,* which has seen eight productions around the country. His films include *The Night Before, Musclebound, Top Story,* and *Sir Real!* He is founder and president of the Arch and Bruce Brown Foundation. His biography of his life with Bruce appears in *Longtime Companions.*

**Wayne Bryant** is the co-founder of Biversity Boston, a mixed-gender support network, and is past President of the Board of the Bisexual Resource Center. He also chaired the Fifth International Conference on Bisexuality, held in Boston in 1998. He has programmed bisexual films for a number of conferences and festivals and has been writing about bisexuality, films, and politics for more than a decade, notably in *Bisexual Characters in Film: From Anaïs to Zee.*

**Patrick Califia** is a bisexual transman who is also a proud member of the leather community, a therapist in private practice in San Francisco, and a parent. His latest books include *Mortal Companion,* a vampire novel, and *Speaking Sex to Power,* a collection of essays. He can be reached at <himself@ patrickcalifia.com>.

**Alfred Corn** is the author of nine books of poetry, one novel, and a collection of essays. He has received Guggenheim and NEA fellowships, as well as awards from the Academy of Arts and Letters and the Academy of American Poets. He holds the Amy Clampitt residency in Lenox, MA, for 2004-2005.

**Raven Davies** is the author of *Between Here & There,* a fantasy about the spiritual and sexual awakening of a bi man and his gay lover, their children, friends, and families. With five Western Slash novels on her Website, Slash Horizon <www.quotetheravin.com>, Raven is currently promoting the release of her first novel, published by NightLight Books and available through Amazon.com, Barnes & Noble, and elsewhere. Raven is a Canadian author now living in Mexico.

**John Egan** is a Canadian activist and researcher whose interests include HIV/AIDS prevention, substance misuse, and anti-queer violence. He lives in Sydney, Australia, with his partner.

**J. "Mac" McRee Elrod** was born in Georgia in 1932. He has obtained a BA (magna cum laude), two MA degrees, and an MSLS. He has worked in Korea (helping to set up their first library school), Tennessee, Missouri, Ohio, and British Columbia, Canada. For a decade, he was Head of Cataloguing at the University of British Columbia. Since 1979, he has been Director of Special Libraries Cataloguing, a cataloguing service for special libraries, operating out of log structures on a mountain in rural Vancouver.

**Jim Fenter** is a 44-year-old man living in Jamaica Plain, MA. He has discovered the peace that comes from not being at war with one's sexuality and thought this essay was a good way to share some of that. This writing is his first published work, but probably not the last, as it has rekindled his dream of writing. Jim has three great kids who find him somewhat dorky, but love him anyway.

**Michael Gallardo** is a second-generation Latino male in his forties married for sixteen years. He did a lot of soul searching to write this piece and shared countless drafts with his wife, friends, co-workers, and supporters. He feels this topic is important enough to articulate and, in so doing, he hopes to support other bisexual married men, and to help families understand why their husbands, fathers, stepfathers, brothers, stepbrothers, brothers-in-law, uncles, or grandfathers may be this way.

**Woody Glenn**, along with Robyn Ochs and Alan Hamilton, was a co-incorporator of the Bisexual Resource Center in Boston. His careers include antiques dealer, social worker, and community activist. He lives in the Boston area with his chosen family.

**Stephen James** is a writer/actor who lives and works in Brighton, England. He has played bit part roles in numerous radio and television series, but is best known for his theatre work. He has toured the United Kingdom as both Romeo and Hamlet, as well as singing the lead role in several musicals. But it is his next theatre piece that will prove to be his biggest challenge. His semi-autobiographical show, *If You Knew Suzy . . . ,* will be opening at the 2005 Edinburgh Festival.

**Julz** is a longtime bisexual and polyamorous mischief-maker living in the suburbs with too many pets and people, including her gorgeous daughter, who claims not to be embarrassed by her mom. She moderates several bisexuality-related Internet discussion groups and has presented at the Fifth International Conference on Bisexuality and the First and Second Endless Possibilities conferences. She was a speaker at Philadelphia's first Dyke March. Her bisexual boyfriend of thirteen years and her bisexual girlfriend of one-and-a-half years put up with her antics and mood swings graciously.

**Fritz Klein, MD,** is a psychiatrist living in San Diego, California, editor of the *Journal of Bisexuality* published by Haworth Press, and Haworth's bisexuality series editor. His former positions include Clinical Instructor at the University of California at San Diego and co-leader of the Bisexual Forum in New York City, which he founded in 1974. He is the author of *The Bisexual Option* and co-editor of *Bisexualities: Theory and Research* and *Bisexual and Gay Husbands: Their Stories, Their Words* (all from Haworth Press).

**Jason Large** lives with his family in western Rhode Island.

**Larry Lawton** is a prisoner in a federal correction institute in North Carolina.

**Gregg Lind** writes and lectures on a wide range of queer, kink, and sexuality topics. He and his partner Charlie Cooper own Coppertone Studios, which specializes in intimate and portrait photography. Currently, Gregg is a graduate student in public health at the University of Minnesota. In his spare time, he does technical work on the *BiCities* television program in Minneapolis-St Paul. He lives in Minneapolis with his family of choice.

**Randy McDonald** is a 24-year-old Canadian who has completed his undergraduate education in Honours English at the University of Prince Edward Island and his Master's degree at Queen's University. He currently lives in Toronto.

**Andrew Milnes** is a queer journalist, writer, musician, and poet from a Catholic lower middle-class Australian background. He currently lives in Melbourne and has worked in community radio and newspapers. His interests include broad left politics, radical Christian and other spiritualities, songwriting, travel, and learning languages.

**Victor J. Raymond** is of Lakota, Scottish, and English heritage, and a longtime bisexual activist. He is currently a Ford Foundation Pre-Doctoral Fellow in the Sociology Department at Iowa State University. Perhaps most importantly, he is much more than the sum of his labels.

**Moss Stern** is a 42-year-old bi man living with his wife Karen and son Oliver in the Philadelphia suburbs. He has been doing various forms of bi activism for nearly 15 years. He is also an accomplished singer/songwriter whose CDs, *Scotch Tape and Spit* and *Sodomy*, are available under the name "Moss" at Amazon.com and elsewhere.

**Hiram Ed Taylor** has written thirty-seven plays and musicals. His New York credits include *Movie Buff, Teasers, Man of My Dreams, Bumps & Grinds, Fifth Avenue,* and *Buddies.* He won the Bultman Playwriting Award for his first gay play, *Members,* which was produced off-Broadway in 1974 and has since been produced by gay theatre companies worldwide. His book, *Louisiana Plays,* is a collection of plays about his home state. A second collection of his best-known gay plays will be published soon. He has also published short articles, short stories, and gay erotica in several national publications.

**Marco Vassi** authored more than a dozen books, including *The Metasexual Manifesto* and *The Erotic Comedies,* and hundreds of essays and erotic stories. Born in 1937 in New York City, Vassi studied in the 1970s with several spiritual masters in various communities. From 1976 to 1981, Vassi did research on contemporary erotic possibilities, "embodying and articulating the full range of metasexual forms, including heterosexual neo-monogamy, gay romance and promiscuity, male lesbianism, bisexual double-coupling, the triad, the swing, the orgy, and the sadomasochistic ritual." He died of AIDS in 1987.

**Angus West** was born in Worcester, Massachusetts, in 1975. Throughout high school and college he often visited and lived with the Old Order Amish and Old Order Mennonites. He attended graduate school in Massachusetts and New York City, and now works as a scientist and adjunct professor. Angus still has a significant interest in the Old Order Anabaptist groups, and still maintains contact with these groups and helps those interested in learning more about the Amish and Mennonites. He lives in Connecticut.

Our history is huge but scrambled;
the books that really represent us have yet to be written.
–Michael Ambrosino, "Choosing Not To"
In *Bi Any Other Name*, 1991

# Introduction

Ron Jackson Suresha

Available online at http://www.haworthpress.com/web/JB
© 2005 by The Haworth Press, Inc. All rights reserved.
doi:10.1300/J159v05n02_01

[Haworth co-indexing entry note]: "Introduction." Suresha, Ron Jackson. Co-published simultaneously in
*Journal of Bisexuality* (Harrington Park Press, an imprint of The Haworth Press, Inc.) Vol. 5, No. 2/3, 2005,
pp. 1-9; and: *Bi Men: Coming Out Every Which Way* (ed: Ron Jackson Suresha, and Pete Chvany) Harrington
Park Press, an imprint of The Haworth Press, Inc., 2005, pp. 1-9. Single or multiple copies of this article are
available for a fee from The Haworth Document Delivery Service [1-800-HAWORTH, 9:00 a.m. - 5:00 p.m.
(EST). E-mail address: docdelivery@haworthpress.com].

**SUMMARY.** The senior editor of this volume discusses how he came to the subject of male bisexuality through journalistic inquiries into Bear subculture, which attracts many older, previously married, mature gay and bisexual men. He describes his collaboration with bisexual activist Pete Chvany on this book in response to the lack of available narratives by bi men. Despite solid evidence pointing to the commonality of male bisexuality, heterosexuals and homosexuals are complicit in erasure of bisexual men in literature, media, and culture; several notable examples of bi male invisibility from August 2004 are cited. The four-part structure of this book and arrangement of stories stems from a distillation of the coming-out process itself from self-discovery, to spouse and family, and from community and world, to spirit and back to self. *[Article copies available for a fee from The Haworth Document Delivery Service: 1-800-HAWORTH. E-mail address: <docdelivery@haworthpress.com> Website: <http://www.HaworthPress.com> © 2005 by The Haworth Press, Inc. All rights reserved.]*

**KEYWORDS.** Bisexuality, bisexual men, gay men, bisexual identity, body image, GLBTIQA activism, Bear subculture

## *BY WAY OF BEARS AND BOOKS*

This book begins with its own coming-out story, a process of manifesting the previously invisible.

Although I've taken a personal interest in masculinity and men's studies since I can remember, only ten years ago did I begin to examine gender issues in general and the ongoing evolution of American masculinity in particular. While living in Boston and preparing my first book, *Bears on Bears: Interviews & Discussions*, I also began questioning the solidity of my own sexual identity as a gay man after nearly 30 years of exclusively homosexual activity.

Bear identity, at first, seemed primarily a gay male phenomenon. By the time I completed work on the book, however, I employed a broader definition of "Bear" that included bisexual-identified men, non-gay/non-bi identified men who have sex with men (MSMs), and, when convenient, female, transgender, and intersex Bears, Bear-lovers, and other folks active in the Bear community.

A significant number of gay-identified Bears whom I met while promoting the book admitted to previous sexual relations with women, sometimes still with female partners, families, grandkids, and male lovers. At readings for *Bears on Bears*, when asked about topics not covered in the book that I wished I could have included, I often raised the subject of married and bisexual Bears.

Bears queer, or subvert, traditional gay male life by diversifying erotic style from a youth-oriented, image-conscious, fashion-driven urban male beauty standard: hairy butch homos as opposed to the smooth femme homos. Bears present a softer-edged–furrier, if you will–more mature, and complex image of homomasculinity. Investigating Bear subculture led me to conclude that numerous masculinities exist–as many as there are individuals, perhaps.

My association with *Bi Men* co-editor and bisexual advocate Pete Chvany grew out of our contact through the Bear community in Boston. I contacted Pete to discuss the topic of "Bi Bears." At several fascinating and animated dinners at Mary Chung's restaurant in Cambridge, Pete and I analyzed, unpacked, debated, teased, and joked about complex issues around Bears, gays, bisexuals, communities, gay men's health issues, human rights, and gender politics. His insight into complex issues around bisexuality and what it means to be a bi man has illuminated and inspired me greatly.

## *TELLING TALES OUT OF THE BI MAN'S CLOSET*

This book aims to provide an editorial forum for men struggling to make sense of their masculinity in a furiously exploding American landscape of postmodern queer studies, postsodomy culture wars, and post-9/11 civil-rights struggles for GLBTIQA people (gay, lesbian, bisexual, transgender, intersex, queer, questioning, and allies).

Bisexual male readers require not merely an approach and perspective unique from bi women; bi men need to come out of the bisexual closet by telling other men the stories of their love. Yet our investigations into the field of men's writing on bisexuality produced an alarming absence of material. The vast majority of writing published and now available on bisexuality, nonfiction as well as fiction, is created by bisexual females.

Considering that Kinsey's research assessed a 2:1 ratio of male to female bisexuals, bisexual men are a vastly unrecognized and underserved population among GLBTIQA studies, men's studies, gender studies, fiction, and other literature, arts, and media in general.

The dearth of bisexual men's narratives is understandable perhaps when considering the huge personal risk involved in coming out as bisexual, gay, or queer. *The Joy of Gay Sex*, 3rd rev. edition (Dr. Charles Silverstein & Felice Picano) states: "Truly, bisexual men and women belong to one of the most persecuted groups in society. Both gays and straights find them confusing, and their very existence threatens widely held preconceptions."

Repression of male bisexuality is historically more severe than for bisexual women. Bi men are also made invisible by the disease-prevention medical field, who through their risk typology no longer even look at them as bisexual–whether gay, bi, or straight identified–but as MSMs. Strong cultural influences deeply affect many of these bisexually active men, such as married African-American men on the Down Low, and Hispanic/Latino men whose machismo prohibits men's submissive role in intercourse.

But these racial and ethnic considerations are secondary in examining bisexual invisibility, states Yale legal scholar Kenji Yoshino, author of "The Epistemic Contract of Bisexual Erasure," a 30,000-word article for *Stanford Law Review*. Yoshino reviewed the major sexuality studies and discovered that they all "uniformly showed that bisexuals existed in comparable or greater numbers than homosexuals. . . . [yet] politically and socially, gays are so much more visible than bisexuals in this society–by orders of magnitude." Straights and gays, due to different but overlapping interests, are complicit in the erasure of bisexual identity, which reinforces gender distinction as a silent but effective device of oppression.

My experience thus far is that calling myself bisexual doesn't require identity with some easily defined, marketable demographic–which may or may not even exist for bisexuals, at least yet. Calling myself bisexual doesn't mean that I can't also identify with aspects of gay and lesbian and straight culture and community, independently and together at times.

## BURYING THE B WORD

One need not dig deep to uncover evidence of media and cultural suppression of bisexuality: within a two-week period in August 2004, numerous examples presented themselves. Most sensational was politician Jim McGreevey, who appeared with his gorgeous, adoring wife to announce his resignation as governor of New Jersey apparently because he had one miserable, doomed affair with an Israeli man whom he says was blackmailing him. Standing with his wife, McGreevey affirmed their love for each other and said, "As a child I always felt ambivalent. . . . My truth is that I am a gay American." The announcement and ensuing media furor conspicuously avoided speaking "the B word," and no, the word isn't "beard." But the misnomer got better: the accused blackmailer's lawyer asserted that his client was not gay but heterosexual. *The Daily Show*'s Jon Stewart perhaps most accurately called him a "flaming extortionist."

I asked a famous physician-scientist whom I know if he could connect me with any celebrity bisexual men, such as Alan Cumming or Michael Stipe, for this book. He responded, "In Italy almost every man marries. I know lots of gay–and I mean very gay men–who are married and have sex with women. Bisexuality to me is not a reality." This is especially odd coming from a doctor: what is a gay man who is married and has sex with women but *bisexual*?

A longtime bi biker buddy from San Francisco, in a personal message declining to submit an essay for this book, commented, "I don't write about my own sex experiences or history. . . . Some women are deep down sexy and fascinating and indescribable in their complexity to me. Most are not . . . to me. Most *men* are, to me, a sexual blank. . . . I don't know if I would still call myself bisexual, merely open to sensations. My partner, John, is the only person to whom I'm constantly attracted. That said, good luck with what you're working on."

The following week brought the release of *A Home at the End of the World*, Michael Cunningham's touching new movie based on his novel, in which two boys develop a deeply emotional and sexual friendship in 1960s suburban Cleveland. After a sudden break, the two reunite in 1980s Manhattan with an older female friend, and their friendship deepens as they struggle with a father's death and unexpected pregnancy. With only their hearts to guide them, the three (and one half) move upstate to Woodstock as they struggle to create a form of home, family, work, and love for which they have no model, and apparently no word: "bisexual" is never used in the movie. Not only that, most of the reviews also omit the word, romantically referring to the relationship as a "love triangle."

In sharp contrast to the preceding series of "bisexual erasures," two historical movies released at year-end 2004, examining the lives and loves of famous bisexual men, have seized national attention with strikingly different narratives. Bill Condon's *Kinsey* examines the life and work of sex researcher Alfred Kinsey (portrayed by Liam Neeson), whose 1948 book, *Sexual Behavior in the Human Male*, introduced a completely new view of sexuality into American consciousness. Oliver Stone's *Alexander* reveals the bisexual nature of the great Greek king, played by Colin Farrell, who in the third-century BCE conquered much of what was then the civilized world. Perhaps this moment is a turning point for bisexuality–especially bisexual men such as the ones you are about to encounter.

## TAKE THE BI WAY TO YOUR FINAL DESTINATION

When Pete and I met Dr. Fritz Klein, the bisexual author who oversees editing of bisexual nonfiction works for Haworth, we were still at a loss to contrive an organizing principle for the anthology. We discussed the book's contents during the Eighth International Conference on Bisexuality held in Minneapolis in August 2004, the first bisexuality-focused meeting of any sort that I ever attended. Fritz suggested dividing the material into three parts: self, family, and world; this would perhaps reflect his triad of established principal categories of bisexual men: Bi-Gay, Bi-Bi, and Bi-Straight.

But I perceive four kinds of bisexual men, if I may be so brash as to introduce another element to the mix: Bi-Trans. We have included essays representing all four categories, and are especially honored with an essay from the noted bisexual transman author Patrick Califia, and contributions from gay men and bi-men-loving women on their experiences with bi men.

Many essays fit several categories, which reflects the complex interrelation of bisexual men's issues as well as the fluidity of personality that characterizes these men. Thus we affirm the innate fluidity of self, sexuality, family, and community, and the understanding of our sexual world as a diverse range of predispositions and choices.

As many of the stories inform us, coming out as bi is a process usually requiring several steps. Typically, for bisexual men, these stages include: coming out by admitting to oneself an undeniable attraction to men (if previously straight) or to women (if previously gay); coming out as bisexual to one's partner, or potential partner; coming out to one's family and children; and coming out to friends, neighbors, and coworkers, and the rest of the world.

The four-part structure of the book reflects this progression from coming-out themes of inner struggle, sexual exploration, and self-discovery, to issues surrounding marriage and family, leading through emergence in new community and cultural paradigms, and finally into aspects of religious and spiritual identity. The stories build upon each other, culminating in a realization of one's bisexual nature that returns us to selfhood. At the end, we may find that we have stepped forward together through these intimate stories to an expansive new vision of our masculinity—yet not so very different from the men who we were at the beginning.

Telling our coming-out stories, how we have learned to love more than one gender, is an essential part of the process required to reconcile our inner desires and outer identifications, to gain the perspective and power required to heal the violent split in our psyches. Not only as writers yearning to confess their deepest secrets, but also as readers, we yearn to hear the long-hidden stories of other proud bi men that reflect our actual lives.

## THE BI(G) ONE THAT GOT AWAY

This collection of nonfiction memoir essays cements a cornerstone of bisexual men's true-life stories. Its primary goal, as well as that of its companion fiction volume, *Bi Guys: Firsthand Fiction for Bisexual Men and Their Admirers*, is to reduce the invisibility of bisexual men by presenting powerful, proud bisexual men's voices. They reveal lively and moving personal coming-out accounts; emphasize thoughtful, accessible firsthand experiences; and show how bisexual men come to bi identity and create unique family structures and communities. The books also include non-bi-male perspectives that will enrich readers' understanding of bisexual male identity and community.

Authors include bisexual authorities as well as novice writers from diverse backgrounds across the USA, Canada, UK, Australia, and the Netherlands, ranging from queer to questioning. We widely circulated calls for submissions, repeating the request over several deadline extensions, in order to recruit contributions as diverse as possible. Suitable submissions on several topics, most conspicuously African-American bi men (despite recently published bestselling books by E. Lynn Harris and J.L. King), were not forthcoming. However, it is ultimately the editors' responsibility for any gaps in the books' coverage.

Many forms of biphobia and gender bias overtly and subconsciously drive men to claim all sorts of identity and behavior in denial of their true nature. Although names in essays by several contributors were changed to protect the anonymity of all concerned, their experiences are real. We encourage readers to continue their explorations into male bisexuality and other contemporary men's issues utilizing the concluding selected bibliography and resource list.

Bisexuality itself has infinite flavors–omnisexual, polyamorous, queer, pansexual, bi-curious, asexual, trisexual ("I'll try anything!"), bi-friendly, ambisexual, heteroflexible, transgendered, intersex, metasexual, and multisexual. Yet regardless of our male individual expressions of masculinity, together as bisexual men we struggle to live with conscious sexuality loving all. We release our grasp on the narrow and receive in return the most holy blessing of richness of experience.

May this book illuminate the mystery that is bisexuality and that manifests in the complex masculinity of bisexual men.

# Part One: Discovering a Bisexual Self

## Feed the Leviathan

Available online at http://www.haworthpress.com/web/JB
© 2005 by The Haworth Press, Inc. All rights reserved.
doi:10.1300/J159v05n02_02

[Haworth co-indexing entry note]: "Feed the Leviathan." Taylor. Hiram Ed. Co-published simultaneously in
*Journal of Bisexuality* (Harrington Park Press, an imprint of The Haworth Press, Inc.) Vol. 5, No. 2/3, 2005,
pp. 11-18; and: *Bi Men: Coming Out Every Which Way* (ed: Ron Jackson Suresha, and Pete Chvany) Harrington Park Press, an imprint of The Haworth Press, Inc., 2005, pp. 11-18. Single or multiple copies of this article
are available for a fee from The Haworth Document Delivery Service [1-800-HAWORTH, 9:00 a.m. - 5:00
p.m. (EST). E-mail address: docdelivery@haworthpress.com].

**SUMMARY.** New Orleans folklore tells of a gigantic subterranean serpent that lives and feeds on human sexual energy and activity aboveground, regardless of gender. From his native Louisiana hometown, the "Bi(g) Easy," to the "Big Apple," New York City, the author appreciates how he relates differently with men and women, and recounts his prepubescent, adolescent, and adult sexual explorations with both sexes. In an exotic yet familiar culture where little is forbidden and much is permitted, New Orleans residents and tourists alike break traditional sexual boundaries when they let the good times roll. *[Article copies available for a fee from The Haworth Document Delivery Service: 1-800-HAWORTH. E-mail address: <docdelivery@haworthpress.com> Website: <http://www.HaworthPress.com> © 2005 by The Haworth Press, Inc. All rights reserved.]*

**KEYWORDS.** Bisexuality, bisexual men, New Orleans, New York City, Mardi Gras, bisexual identity, sexual exploration, Southern Decadence, coming out

A local voodoo priestess once told me that New Orleans is controlled and protected by a reptilian swamp creature, a Leviathan that feeds on sexual energy. The Leviathan, or demon, does not care if the sexual activity is male-to-female, male-to-male, or female-to-female. As long as there are constant orgasms, the Leviathan is satisfied. Sexual labels are not important to the demon. Skin color is not important. Pleasure is very important. Maybe that is why the lines of sexuality blur here in New Orleans in our search for ultimate satisfaction.

New Orleans is a decadent sex town. Growing up here, I started having sex at a very young age–and I mean *very* young. My mother and aunt caught my cousin Tyler and I when we were only a few weeks old. They walked in and found we had pulled our diapers down and were sucking on each other's little peepees. They screamed and giggled and separated us immediately.

This is why, during college, when I told them I had fallen in love with a boy at school and "outed" myself, they smiled and said they knew when I was a baby and just wondered how long before I knew. How disappointed I was! I had hoped to shock them. I have learned that it is impossible to shock anyone in New Orleans.

What they did not know was that I had been fucking with both girls and boys since I was fourteen on a very steady basis. At twenty, I had finally "fallen in love" with the man to whom I wanted to be married for the rest of my life. We were both so excited we decided to tell our families. When it only lasted nine months, I went back to fucking girls and guys again.

How did this bisexual behavior happen? Well, cousin Tyler and I kept sucking each other's peepees throughout our childhood. By about eight years old, we were sucking other kids in the neighborhood too. So, I never stopped having gay sex from the time I was born.

My first experience with a girl took a little more time and trouble. I went through the usual school crushes that led to kissing when playing spin the bottle, or walking the girl to the door to say goodnight. My first time to actually try vaginal penetration, however, was quite an experience.

It was with a Baptist preacher's daughter who was sixteen, a year older than me. She had already had experiences with guys. She approached me one night at a school dance.

"You're cute," she said. "I want to see you naked. Does that shock you?"

"Uh no," I managed to mumble, completely shocked.

"You want to fuck me?" she asked. "You think you know how?"

"I know how," I lied.

"Don't I shock you?" she asked again. "It's hard to shock people here."

It didn't take us long to get at it, right outside in the azalea bushes behind the gym. That was only the beginning.

We started fucking two and three times a week. She liked for me to talk dirty to her while we were screwing. She also liked trying lots of different positions she had read about in a book. She liked the danger of fucking in forbidden places. We fucked in a tree at the park, at the beach, in the dressing room of the local mall, and all kinds of other places where we could have been arrested. The danger excited her and made her cum. It was good for me, too.

After several months of this, she announced she wanted to fuck another boy in my class who she said had a bigger dick than me. We were finished. At first, I was depressed but she told her girlfriends what a good fuck I was and soon I was in demand. I had become a seasoned fucker. Now, I knew what girls liked to do and I could do it. I became very popular. I also got a reputation as a ladies' man with the guys at my school.

During this period of time, however, I never stopped sucking dick. To me they were like grapefruit and grapes. Fucking pussy and sucking dick were two completely different sexual activities and I liked them both.

I liked the soft skin of a woman's body and the way a girl quivers when you run your hands over her lightly and barely touch her. Girls smell good when they sweat and as they reach orgasm there's sometimes a strong musk scent. I love that scent. They sigh and melt in your arms after they cum. They like to cuddle and hug and kiss deeply as they claw their nails in your back. It makes me feel strong and powerful, the way a man is supposed to feel when he is inside a woman.

I also love a man's fleshy cock down my throat. I like to feel the veins on the side of the dick with my tongue as it slides up and down the shaft. I feel excited that I have a man's most private part in my mouth and that I am giving him pleasure. Every dick is different in size and shape and taste. Some men are salty as they shoot their load, others are sweet, and some bitter from the taste of garlic. Men moan when they cum and their ball sac twitches against my chin. What's not to like? How does it have anything in common with fucking pussy?

How did I manage to keep my reputation at high school as a ladies' man while sucking dick at the same time? I had discovered a hole in the bathroom toilet at Sears one afternoon while my girlfriend was shopping. When a man stuck his hard dick through it, I knew what to do. I soon discovered there were lots of such holes all around town. All I had to do was sit and wait and soon I would have a dick to suck. It was easy. Nobody had to know. I kept it my little secret. I went through high school without anyone calling me queer. Everybody knew I was fucking a lot of pussy. What they did not know was that I was also sucking a lot of dick.

Sometimes I wonder if the fact that sex is always so readily available in New Orleans with either men or women is why I developed bisexual activity at such a young age. It would be years before I ever thought about it or analyzed it. I was having fun. It seemed natural and normal to me and I had no guilt about it. That would all change one night very quickly in college.

In the mid-1970s, I went to New York University on the Lower East Side of Manhattan and had a wild time. There were lots of holes in the bathrooms around New York City, so finding dick to suck was never a problem. I also met a hot Jewish girl, Jill, and started fucking her steady right away.

One night, we drank a lot of bourbon and smoked a lot of pot with her roommate, Nancy, and a guy, Wendell, whom Nancy had met at a bar. Soon, we were fucking next to each other on the floor of their living room. Jill and I finished first and she got up and ran to the bathroom. I lay on the floor watching the two naked bodies next to me and without really thinking I reached over and touched Wendell's ass. He looked over at me and we started kissing each other and soon he had pulled out of Nancy and we were sucking on each other's dicks. Nancy went ballistic. She started screaming. Jill came running out of the bathroom and Nancy told her we were cocksucking fags! That was the end of the relationship with Jill. She told me I was a real sicko. It was the beginning of a relationship, however, with Wendell. He told me I really knew how to suck cock.

Still, I was so distressed over the event that I ended up seeing a shrink. He was very interested in my story. He told me that I was a homosexual. He said that I only pretended to like girls because society made me think that I should. If I were true to myself and explored my true nature, he assured me, I would discover I was really a homosexual. That's how I became a homosexual. I bought the label, put it on, and wore it very proudly for years.

However, I never stopped having sex with women. I just didn't tell anyone about it. I became a "closet bisexual." I hid my pussyfucking from all my boyfriends and tricks. I went to all the discos and gay bars and leather clubs like the Mineshaft and the Anvil and had lots and lots of homosexual sex. I was totally gay in Manhattan.

But then, there were those out-of-town trips I often took. I would pack a suitcase full of "straight-looking clothes," outfits that no gay guy in Manhattan would be caught dead in. Tan pleated pants, brown Oxfords, and striped shirts–all from Kmart. Then I'd catch a train to Albany, Syracuse, Baltimore, or New Haven, check into the local Holiday Inn and cruise the lounge for women. I almost always scored. Women like sex as much as gay guys do, they just need a few more drinks and some tender words layered with respectful erotic implications.

Finally, my two worlds conjoined when I was invited to attend a secret underground sex club that everyone in Manhattan was talking about. At the time, it was about sixty percent straight couples and forty percent gay couples. But actually, none of us were one hundred percent either, we were all completely bisexual. Everybody did whatever with whomever they wanted. Nobody cared. Unexpectedly, being bisexual was "in." Everybody was trying bisexuality as if it were the newest dessert on the Manhattan menu. I was overjoyed.

Then AIDS erupted and the bisexual scene crashed to a halt. Straight couples just couldn't take a chance being with a gay guy. It wasn't safe. Everyone was scared. I was immediately labeled a homosexual again and purged from invitation lists. Doors closed, as sex was forbidden with gay men. Bisexuality became taboo in New York.

I moved back to New Orleans during this time for family reasons. I discovered that nothing had changed in New Orleans. People were still having lots of sex. They were being safer, but the sex demon demands his energy–and the tourists and locals keep him well fed. Bisexual activity here was more evident now than ever. Homosexuality had become even more open and accepted. Decadence reigned. Thank god I was home.

New Orleans' two biggest holidays, Mardi Gras in the winter and Southern Decadence weekend in the summer, are both about living one's fantasies. There are parades and parties at both, but most people come for the sex. Sex is everywhere. Out in the open streets, in the dark corners of bars, and in the motel bedrooms: fucking, sucking, and all kinds of S/M activity are being indulged in by both sexes and all ages.

It is very common at Mardi Gras for so-called straight married guys to wear drag and prance around at parties, kissing guys and patting their asses. Everyone knows it's just "playtime." So if, after a few too many drinks, the two men end up blowing each other in the bathroom . . . oh well, "It's Mardi Gras!"

During Southern Decadence, the action gets even wilder. The weather is so hot in August that everyone goes about as naked as possible. Sometimes, the only article of clothing is a pair of flip-flops. Every man, straight or gay, loves showing off his dick and having it played with. It's no wonder that what started off as a totally gay holiday has become a very bisexual affair. I have seen lots of my gay friends having their dick played with or sucked by women at Decadence. If you say something about it to one of them, he'll scream, "That was a real woman? I thought she was a drag queen!" That's Decadence!

Both holidays have become about exposed women's breasts. During Mardi Gras, it's a bead thing: "show your tits and get some beads." But at Decadence, it's "suck that tit, gay boy!" My friend says it is because gay men did not get enough tit in their childhoods. I think the truth is that Decadence gives them an excuse to break out of their sexual labels and identity patterns and step into the forbidden territory of bisexuality.

I always get into trouble for saying this, but I believe if it weren't for our sexual labels and social conditioning, we would all be bisexual. Fear keeps people from exploring outside of their comfort zone. Decadence and Mardi Gras present opportunities where everyone is free to explore. They actually promote and encourage exploration of sexual taboos.

I had dinner last night with a straight couple that I have known for years. They've been married since 1980. When her husband went to the bathroom, my friend leaned in and whispered to me.

"I finally did it, Ed. I had sex with another woman during Mardi Gras. Don't tell Randle, he wouldn't understand. But I kept thinking, I'm getting old and I've always wanted to try it and the opportunity came, so I went with it. Does that shock you?"

"No," I answered. "New Orleans expects people to escape the boundaries they have placed on themselves and step into their sexual fantasies."

"She's really good. We meet on Wednesday afternoons. Randle thinks I go to the garden club meeting. We get a hotel room on Airline Highway. It's so much fun. I think my marriage is actually better from it."

If only she knew how many friends I have who are doing the same thing! Only last week at the movies, I was standing next to a straight friend peeing. I glanced over and saw he had a huge dick.

"Good god," I said "No wonder Maureen is always smiling."

He stood back and played with it until it was hard. I pulled him into a stall and blew him right there. He came in a matter of seconds.

"She doesn't do *that*," he remarked as he zipped up and we went out.

While the three of us passed around a huge bucket of popcorn and watched Brad Pitt descend on Troy, I couldn't help but think how nice it is to share things with your friends.

Most cities condemn what New Orleans encourages. Marriages end in other cities when such activities occur. Here folks brush it off with a sigh. "That's New Orleans," they'll say, and go on with their lives as normal. Maybe that is why we are called the Big Easy. Perhaps we should drop the "g" and call the city the Bi-Easy.

One thing for sure, we will never drop the word *easy*. "Easy" is our motto here.

Life is easy. Sex is easy. And don't forget to feed the Leviathan.

# Walking the Shifting Sands

*Andrew Milnes*

Available online at http://www.haworthpress.com/web/JB
© 2005 by The Haworth Press, Inc. All rights reserved.
doi:10.1300/J159v05n02_03

[Haworth co-indexing entry note]: "Walking the Shifting Sands." Milnes, Andrew. Co-published simultaneously in *Journal of Bisexuality* (Harrington Park Press, an imprint of The Haworth Press, Inc.) Vol. 5, No.
2/3, 2005, pp. 19-25; and: *Bi Men: Coming Out Every Which Way* (ed: Ron Jackson Suresha, and Pete
Chvany) Harrington Park Press, an imprint of The Haworth Press, Inc., 2005, pp. 19-25. Single or multiple
copies of this article are available for a fee from The Haworth Document Delivery Service
[1-800-HAWORTH, 9:00 a.m. - 5:00 p.m. (EST). E-mail address: docdelivery@haworthpress.com].

**SUMMARY.** A young, gay-identified Australian journalist contemplates his bisexual attractions, questions of monogamy, intimate relationships, and community politics, and ponders the process of coming out to colleagues who view him as a gay man. *[Article copies available for a fee from The Haworth Document Delivery Service: 1-800- HAWORTH. E-mail address: <docdelivery@haworthpress.com> Website: <http://www. HaworthPress.com> © 2005 by The Haworth Press, Inc. All rights reserved.]*

**KEYWORDS.** Bisexuality, bisexual men, gay men, Australia, GLBTIQA journalism, GLBTIQA community advocacy, monogamy, biphobia, coming out

First of all, I have to confess that I don't much like the term "bisexual," certainly not as a major descriptor of who I am. "Bi" is marginally better, but I still feel more comfortable with the term "queer" to describe myself sexually. Some of this may be due to my background and history; some of this may, I admit, be due to internalized biphobia. I think some of it is just that I find the term both clunky and vague–and I hate the usage "hot bi babes" with a passion!

While my sexuality has been shifting sands in some ways–going from de facto straight to bisexual to gay to queer–and this has been worrying and quite traumatic, in other ways it has made little difference to the essential characteristics of who I am. Other labels that have been in some ways of more importance to me, like left wing, Christian, writer, musician, all of which preceded my sexual explorations, still remain.

Also, I have ambivalence towards bi culture (or that which I've encountered) but at the same time recognise the necessity of it, and activism in a world that's not only homophobic but biphobic and monosexist to boot.

My own sexual development has been long and drawn out in some cases–not unusual for people like me, I know, but certainly not as cut-and-dried as that of my heterosexual sisters, or as clean and simple as some of my gay and lesbian peers, who threw off the shackles of heterosexism with evangelical fervour and haven't looked back since.

I, on the other hand, knew from the time I was a teenager that I had attractions to both men and women, but not how to process that into a life and decide what I wanted, relationship-wise. Add in the fact that my attractions to men have been significantly more plentiful and intense, on the whole, than those to women, as well as coming from a loving but sexually conservative family, and dealing with societal homophobia, and you can see that I had a few issues to tackle.

At nineteen, after several pleasant and sweet crushes on girls, and some significant lusting after boys, I met my first "head-over-heels" obsession–a twenty-something counsellor by the name of Robert, with dreamy dark eyes and a sweet sad smile. I was smitten, and although my desires, while not totally unreciprocated, were never acted upon (not wise to sleep with your counsellor!), I knew that I had never felt this way about someone before, and that this would mean a huge change in my life and outlook.

There followed another several years in my twenties where I privately considered myself bisexual, though I really wasn't sexual at all, with the exception of a few furtive experiences with other men, some of which I enjoyed, some of which I didn't. But my desires seemed to be pointing me in the direction of men, and so when, at twenty-three, I met another gay man whom I felt physically and emotionally connected to, I decided it was time: time to come out to my friends, time to come out to my family, time to start exploring more fully the gay community and world.

Which I did, although with reservations–I never did get into a lot of the cultural politics of the community, not understanding why I should suddenly adopt a certain persona or certain interests because of my orientation. Why was I supposed to like Kylie and Hi-NRG music, popping pills and drag, I reasoned, when I preferred PJ Harvey and Sonic Youth, art house movies and reading George Orwell or Milan Kundera? So my relationship with the gay community was somewhat ambivalent, but it was still there. Like a child born into a somewhat dysfunctional family (my own birth one mercifully not), I alternated between fiercely protective, passionate, aloof, disappointed and at times angry in my feelings towards the gay community, but always connected by that link whether I liked it or not.

Something else got sidelined, however. When I came out, the attractions I had had to women, to Diane with her wonderful laugh, to Louey with her boyish airs and whimsical humour, got sidelined. "That was just because you hadn't worked out your sexuality," I told myself. "It was cultural programming, not what you really felt." Yet part of me knew I really had felt it, that it was not just imagining, but I couldn't process it. It wouldn't fit into the rest of how I understood my sexuality. I told myself because those attractions were only a small minority they weren't important, and sidelined them.

Years went by, I living the "gay life" (whatever that entails), having sex and relationships with men (or at least attempting to–I've had my own issues with male lovers that could probably make its own essay!), and being involved in the gay community. But a gnawing sense that I had put a lid on some of my desires was growing: whether it be meeting some lesbian women at venues and noting an attraction there, or getting turned on by heterosexual or lesbian sex scenes in movies or pornography, or realising that I was starting to fantasise about women as well as men, I was becoming aware that my sexuality was really quite complex, and that, just as I couldn't limit attraction on the basis of race (a significant number of my male lovers have been non-Caucasian), so I couldn't really limit it by gender either. I was also becoming aware that these attractions were becoming stronger: while I still feel more deeply and more often attracted to men, my attractions to women over the last few years have increased a noticeable degree.

And so where does that leave me? That is the question. There's a lot of things I've been mulling over in my head recently about this issue: how I feel about women and about men, how I feel about my identity and where I'm headed relationship-wise in my life.

I have had some contact with the organised bisexual community, at least what there is of it in Melbourne, over the last few years, but I have to say I have quite mixed feelings about it on a few levels. While not as dogmatic as the straight or gay scenes, there is a certain mindset amongst many people in the community about some things–an implicit assumption by many that polyamoury is more "open minded" than monogamy, for example, or a parroting of "sex-positive" rhetoric I find simplistic–that has distanced me, not to mention a nascent identity politics I'm wary of. I've had enough issues not fitting into straight or gay culture without worrying about not fitting into yet another club. I have also found few people, particularly men, who have come from my background (coming out bi from the gay world) as opposed to ones who have lived hitherto straight lives, therefore few people to really talk with about the specific issues I face. I know of quite a number of women who've come from lesbian backgrounds and then came out as bi, but while some of the issues are similar, some aren't. Many heterosexual men aren't nearly as threatened about bisexuality in women, it's kinda chic and even a turn-on for some of them, as straight women are about bi guys.

And there are significant issues. For a start, there's biphobia in the gay community and homophobia in the straight one. This doesn't concern me so much with friends, though I have some gay friends I have yet to "come out" to (the second time!), although I plan to. However, most of my friends don't really care how I define my sexuality, because our friendships are based on other commonalities. But it does concern me with partners. I wonder how comfortable some of my exes would have been if I had identified at the time as "bi," not "gay," while I wonder how comfortable and secure many straight women would be in dating men they knew had mostly had relationships with other men. I could of course just date other bi people, but in my experience they often come with partners already attached, and given that I'm of a fairly monogamous bent when it comes to relationships, that's not really what I want.

Aside from those concerns, there are other things I wonder about the dynamics of dating women. I'm so used to dating or cruising men, my knowledge about how to interact with women sexually, what expectations they have, or how relationships are supposed to develop, is very meagre. I must admit, while the thought of dating an individual woman or entering into a relationship, if I met one who I had a physical, intellectual and emotional connection with, doesn't daunt me, the expectations of "heterosexuality" as society frames it, with men and women falling into different roles in the relationship, does. As paranoid as it sounds, after years of "un-brainwashing" myself of all the conditioning our culture does about sex, gender, and relationships, part of me is scared to fall back into that heterosexual "trap."

And there is my whole history with men, which while not dreadful has left some problematic residue. I want to make sure if I have female lovers (as well as male ones) in future it's because that's how I feel about those individuals and where my sexuality is headed, not just "oh well, I'm over men, let's give girls a try!"

My work hasn't really helped with that either: I've been a journalist at a queer newspaper and thus "in the closet" there (ironically enough!) about that part of my sexuality. Not so much because the people are biphobic per se, but because I really didn't want to become the "token bisexual" in the office and have to explain what that meant for me and what my sexuality was about when I was only just working it out myself! But this is something that will change in the next year or so.

At times I still feel that it is probably more likely that my main relationships or love interests in my life will be men–my link with masculine sexuality is very intense and there is something very psychologically deep there for me, as well as having a bit of psychological work to do before getting to a stage of seriously dating women. I do know though there is an openness in me to explore sexually with women in the future as well as men, definitely physically and possibly emotionally, depending on whom I meet. I also know my link with the gay community will remain a very important one, even if only in terms of the political and social questioning it's given me. I may end up in relationships with women, but that will never make me straight, or my worldview heterosexual, in the sense of people who've never questioned their orientation and what it means.

There are times when I feel disheartened that at age 32 there are still many questions in relationships and sexuality I still haven't answers to, unlike others, but, if as they say in the film *The Matrix*, the test of any choice is that given the same situation again you'd make exactly the same choice, then I feel pretty satisfied with my choices in identity and sexuality and where they've taken me. And while life looms somewhat dauntingly with new sexual and emotional opportunities, it also promises to be enticing, intriguing, empowering, and certainly not boring; a great adventure, possibly, in fact. And you can't ask for much more than that.

# It's a Life

Eriq Chang/Jim

[Haworth co-indexing entry note]: "It's a Life." Chang, Eriq, and Jim. Co-published simultaneously in *Journal of Bisexuality* (Harrington Park Press, an imprint of The Haworth Press, Inc.) Vol. 5, No. 2/3, 2005, pp. 27-38; and: *Bi Men: Coming Out Every Which Way* (ed: Ron Jackson Suresha, and Pete Chvany) Harrington Park Press, an imprint of The Haworth Press, Inc., 2005, pp. 27-38. Single or multiple copies of this article are available for a fee from The Haworth Document Delivery Service [1-800-HAWORTH, 9:00 a.m. - 5:00 p.m. (EST). E-mail address: docdelivery@haworthpress.com].

**SUMMARY.** Two high school age men discuss coming out to friends and family in an oppressive community in the San Francisco Bay area. Sexuality and self-knowledge are important issues, but so is trying to decide what to do with one's life, and where and how to do it, when one's options are still limited by age and geography. Excerpts compiled from *In Your Face: Stories from the Lives of Gay Youth,* Mary L. Gray, editor, 1999. *[Article copies available for a fee from The Haworth Document Delivery Service: 1-800-HAWORTH. E-mail address: <docdelivery@haworthpress.com> Website: <http://www.HaworthPress.com> © 1999 by The Haworth Press, Inc. All rights reserved.]*

**KEYWORDS.** Bisexuality, bisexual men, San Francisco Bay area, bisexual/queer youth, adolescent sexuality, high school students, sexual exploration, coming out, body image

## *ERIQ CHANG*

I identify as bisexual, and have since I was about six or seven. It was pretty firm; I pretty much knew. I came out to myself when I was ten. I really didn't understand the whole thing. I sort of experimented when I was young. I pretty much knew that it wasn't normal.

At that time, I knew I wasn't supposed to like guys, that I was supposed to like girls, but I wasn't attracted totally to one sex. I guess I just found that I liked both. At that age, I was pretty comfortable with myself. I came out as bi two years ago, and in Pleasanton [California], that's fairly difficult. But it was eventual. It was a process that I did.

I really feel like I'm on my own now, and I'm open about who I am. Because, for me, if you're not comfortable with your own sexuality, then you're not going to be comfortable with someone else's.

I can never just hang out with straight guys. I've actually been able to hang out with a lot of straight guys, but I couldn't talk about sex and things that are less superficial. I have a lot of straight friends, and I have a lot of bi and gay/lesbian friends. But with straight guys, we're either looking at other women or else we're talking about sports or something. I don't feel like I can talk about my whole self. Ninety percent of my friends are girls.

I come from a very traditional Asian family. In our culture, being gay is not even really spoken about. So if my parents knew, I think it would cause a lot of problems for me. There would be a lot of difficulty adjusting. Especially for my grandparents.

I'm not the type of person to talk about whom I'm attracted to anyway. It's not something that I really worry about. But it is difficult sometimes. I plan on telling my parents after I graduate from high school.

I will be moving then, and I feel it's something that they should know. It's pretty grueling sometimes to think about it. They have their suspicions, I'm sure. My dad probably does, and he's already adjusting to the fact that I cross-dress for shows professionally. But, I know that if they knew that I was bi, that they would feel disappointed. I'm prepared for that.

In elementary school, it was very difficult because I would just be constantly called a sissy, queer, and confused. Junior high was a turning point because I sort of discovered my more artistic side, rather than my feelings for other people. That was when the teasing and jokes started.

When I was a freshman, a lot of people would talk behind my back. I remember one day I was in English class, and I did this video where I had a wig on and I had lipstick on or something. It was just supposed to be funny. People didn't take it as funny. They took it seriously: "He's queer." That was difficult for me because everyone in the class was just really a macho boy or femme girl. That was my freshman year. I could tell they were talking, and I just wanted to leave. Actually, I did leave at the end of the period, close to the end of the period, just to go to the bathroom; I didn't want to face it. That was something I'll always remember. I hated it. After I left the class, people started the rumors and stuff.

And in my sophomore year, this big rumor went around–I don't know where it started–that I went to San Francisco and sang at a gay bar and had sex, totally fucked like six different guys at once. And so I went through this sort of depression period. At lunchtime, I'd go on these walks and think about what was in my future. Was it wrong to like both boys and girls? How am I gonna deal with it? A lot of people would tell me that being bisexual is just a cover-up for being gay. If I were gay, I would simply come out and say, "I like men." But I have an attraction to both. At school, that's sort of a problem. They either think I'm one way or the other.

Basically, now that I have done drag, a lot of the jocks that used to make fun of me accept it. Or they want to go out and take pictures because they're very interested in it. I guess I could say, I sort of won a battle in high school. I don't want to sound egotistical or anything, but I feel I've sort of been a role model at school.

This one gay teacher I have really looks up to me because during high school, he would never have been able to do what I do now. I look up to him because in so many ways, he is so real. It's as if my teacher feels like he can be more open with himself with me. And he loves living alone; he loves being himself. He's forty-nine years old, but he's great because he's been able to live a perfectly content life. He acts like he's nineteen. I feel that, since I am gay, I'll able to keep my youth as he has. I look at other gay people who are his age who are just old and lazy and they feel like there's nothing to do. But he feels blessed, and that's what I like about him. He's really cool, and he's a good teacher. My freshman year, he sort of knew about me. It was funny because he wanted to talk to me. I want to go back to my freshman year and totally do things over.

A lot of people have come out to me at school. I know several people who are gay, several people who are bisexual, and ten lesbians. I would never have guessed; they just come up to me and will tell me. Telling people I'm bi has been successful for me.

I have a lot of gay friends. I mostly hang out with people outside of high school because I really don't like a lot of people in high school. I socialize a lot, but the people I mostly hang out with are college-type and just have all types of sexuality. I have friends who are gay, trans, just a whole bunch of different types of people.

I feel more open with gay kids than with other kids. I feel more comfortable, and it sounds corny and hokey and stupid, but I feel more brotherly. I feel like we know each other. I know several gay adults. I guess I just think of the person. I really don't know too many people who are around or under my age who are gay, bisexual, or lesbian. But I do know several people in college.

The gay community's a little too raucous for me! I saw my first gay magazine at Tower Records. It was pretty much pornographic. I was like, "Oh, hot, baby." My first impression was, "Omigod, the whole gay industry is all about sex." The gay community is very sexual; well, I would have to say as sexual as the straights. They're very aimed at the entertainment and the looks-type feel. Especially gay men.

I went to the Castro and thought, "This is so fucking trendy." Everyone has shaved heads and short hair and they're really butch-looking and they have leather "or else," and that was my impression. Just like there was no real relationship out there. I'm being totally honest. That's what I got. Now I know better than that. I know people who are gay and people who are bi, and they have relationships and they're totally content. They're just people. I don't call it a lifestyle either. I hate it when people say, "Oh, the bisexual and the lesbian and the gay lifestyle." It's not a lifestyle; it's a life. We're people. We shouldn't be labeled.

It felt strange at first. I saw these two guys totally like, "Oh, hi, honey, I haven't seen you in the longest time," and they pecked on the cheek. I thought, "Whoa!" because that's something I've wanted to do, not just in the Castro, but also in public. I see people holding hands, and it's something that I want.

When I was in the Castro, I just got the impression that everyone there knows who they are. Now I don't really think the Castro is that big of a deal. I think of it as sort of another club. When I go there, I feel like it's not just a gay street; it's almost a tourist attraction.

I haven't really done too much as far as getting involved in the community though. I really wanted to go to the Halloween Castro party thing. I really wanted to perform or something. I've been to several clubs; I've been to Universal and Club X in San Francisco and I went to the AIDS Dance-a-thon.

Since I live so far away in Pleasanton, I don't go to too many places. I've been to the gay bar, JR's, and I have snuck in. I walked in there, and I was like, "Oh, whoa." I've been to very, very few places where all men or all women hang out. I really just like to go to clubs in general. My first impression of JR's was that it was hot and I was sweating, and I wanted to take off all my clothes and go, "Omigod, take me!" It was fun; it was a lot of fun. I love dancing.

There are no gay support clubs at my school. Nothing at all. I think a club would be difficult to have in Pleasanton, and at the school that I go to, I think it would be totally a heated subject, and all the jocks would go hang out there and see who shows up so they know who's gay. That's the type of society it is over there.

I don't live in the city, but I know there's a lot of gay support groups there, but I don't go to any. Usually, I don't meet people who are my age who are gay or bi. I think a group in Pleasanton would be a good thing though. Yes, I do. I sort of have come to that for me, myself, personally–I don't feel like I really need to go to youth groups and stuff anymore–maybe to help other people.

I've had girlfriends and boyfriends, but I'm not a player. The longest relationship I've had was actually five or six months with my boyfriend Mark. He's nineteen. I usually like people who are around my age or a little bit older. We met at the mall. I approached him in a weird manner, because at the time I was working on the printing of a book of pictures, and I was looking for models. So I approached him, and I said, "Would you like to help me with my book?" I'm totally a stranger, I know, but this is the best way for me to get to know someone. He agreed, and we basically got to know each other. We went out, and we started getting into deep talk, as though we sort of knew each other well. I still love him. He's a great guy. He's cool and I related to him really well. I still do, but we had our differences.

The girls I have gone out with have been high school age or a little bit older. I went out with this girl Jennay, and with her, it was just total attractiveness. I got to know her on a different level, and we became lovers. It's funny to say it, but we didn't really relate emotionally. So we sort of became fuck buddies. This was actually going on at the same time I was going out with Mark, so it was kinda bad.

I think I'm attracted to strong women. I think I like men for different things. In men, I look for personality, looks, and stuff. For women, it's not even attractiveness; it's almost a power. I think women are like animals, they're powerful. They are the huntress, the seductress, but they can also be totally smart. They're a whole package. That's stereotyping men too. It's weird. It's hard for me to explain. I picture both as equal, but then each sex has its own characteristics individual to it. I don't know. I guess I have a checklist of what I'm looking for.

Last night, I went out with someone I was very interested in. His name is Matt. He goes to this school right here across the town. He's eighteen. We were just kinda hanging out 'cause he thinks we're just friends, but I really want to get to know him better. I know he's either gay or bisexual; I know he likes women, but no straight guy's gonna talk about men like he does. I'm interested, but the thing about him is he acts stupid even though he's really smart, and I don't like that.

I want to own a multimedia company like Disney. But before that, I want to direct movies; I would love to direct movies and act. So far, I've been able to do artwork for computer games, Lucas Arts in Marin County. But I'm really trying to get my foot into the entertainment field. That's really where I want to go. Theater—not theatre, but movie theaters. I think that's the most powerful medium that you can use because it's on all emotional levels.

I don't really want a family. I'd love to be in a relationship with someone who is interesting. I'm not picky, but I need someone who is there when I need them there, but gives me space to work. I think in the field that I'm going into, it's very difficult until you're actually established and famous. If you are famous and you're bisexual or gay, like Madonna, you can get away with it and people can look up to you. But you give a part of yourself away when you're famous. I don't know if I'd be able to have a family and settle down, because I love to be busy.

If I'm bisexual, I can't live in Oklahoma! I think I want to have an apartment in New York, a studio flat, and I want to have it lavishly designed by a top decorator. I'd love to live in Miami and LA. Three houses by the beach, and a flat in the city.

I'm looking at several different places for college. I really want to go to Full Sail, which is in Miami; it's an art school for recording, theatrical, and dramatic arts. Geena Davis and Madonna went there. It's an expensive school, but it's nice. They have the high-tech equipment, and they have contacts with the entertainment industry; UCLA, but it's difficult to get into the theater program; Cal Arts, which is a beautiful school too, right next to LA. LA is the center, the central place for entertainment–the place. I've heard terrible things about getting into the entertainment industry, "Blah blah blah." But I think that if you have talent and you can put it out there, that you can do it.

I'm scared about graduating. I'm really scared because I'm leaving a lot of people who are my friends, not really personal, personal friends, but people who have been there for me. I think the scariest thing is actually moving on with my life, finding out what I am gonna do, finding colleges and stuff. And that's scary. I really want to do all these things, but it's hard for me to get the will power to actually apply somewhere. I'm afraid I won't be accepted. But I think that comes along with the territory about fears of being accepted by people. I am excited about my future, but I'm scared to leave the past. That's normal, I think.

Be yourself; look at your situation and how safe it is. Because, I don't think our society, the whole world, will ever be able to accept one thing; everybody is gonna have their own opinion. I guess I really don't think you can actually gain one hundred percent equality. Just as it is with blacks. Everybody has their opinion, and you have to be yourself and make it work for yourself. If you're yourself, and you portray a positive image, people aren't gonna look at your sexual identity. They're gonna look at this vibe you have. I've been able to do that. People look at me and don't look at, "Omigod, Eriq, you like guys *and* girls. . . ."

I definitely would say, don't lie. Don't lie to yourself especially. If you're attracted to something, that's natural and that's not a burden; it's not something that's a curse. I don't think it's abnormal. I think that you've got something special. It's what makes everybody individual. Go along your own karmic wheel and reach nirvana your own way. Be yourself, and that will get you what you want.

\* \* \*

## *JIM*

I'm seventeen and my birth date is September 27th. I live in Pleasanton, California. The bubble, that is. It's a little piece-of-shit town. It's pretty small; there's only 10,000 people there, I think. I have lived in Pleasanton all my life. I have one sister, Jamie, and my mom and dad.

I identify as bisexual and have since I was fifteen. I remember one day I was sitting at the dinner table. I was looking at food that I wanted to eat: "Do I want meat or potatoes?" I mean this speaking metaphorically. I just wanted both. It just clicked right then. Throughout the years, I'd look at men and I was physically attracted, and I'd look at women and I was physically attracted to them too. But with men, I don't have to like their attitude or anything; it's just a whole physical thing. With women, I have to make sure that they're intelligent. It's more mental with women; it's not mental with men. I've never been out with a guy but I have wanted to.

I try not to think about sexuality in general. It's just what I do. It's my life. To me, it's nothing big. It's no big deal to me. It's just another part of life. If I want to go do a gay parade one day, that's what I'll do–I'll go. I try not to plan much; I try not to plan out my life. If you have expectations and they don't turn out the way you want, you're disappointed in the end, and I don't want to be disappointed in my life.

Yeah, I think my parents know. They're the kind of people who wouldn't say anything to me if they knew. I haven't told them. I'm not really close with my family. When we go to family reunions, I'm usually the person who never talks or never says hi to anybody.

I just say, "Can we go? Can we go home now?"

It doesn't matter. I am gonna come out to my parents whenever I feel the need to. I wish they were a little bit more interested in what I do; they're like, "Oh, how was your day? Oh, great . . . I'm going to work and going somewhere else." They just don't pay attention to me. They don't seem to care. I tried to talk to them about it, but they just don't have time for me. It's sad. I'll probably wait until they are interested in what my life is about and in what I do. They don't even ask me who my friends are or anything.

I haven't really told anybody. If somebody wants to know what I'm about, they have to ask me. It's not like at an interview; they ask you, "Are you queer?" I'd say yes if they did, though. I'm not scared of it at all. If they can't handle it, too bad.

Whoever bothers to find out who I am . . . all my friends who I really care about end up knowing. It wasn't like a specific date that they knew, it would just build up to it, and then they would just ask me one day, and if they ask me, I would tell them the truth. They were curious about it, but they're a little bit skeptical about it; if they can't get used to it and if they don't feel comfortable around it, that's their problem, not mine. I've had to deal with a lot of losses with friends and stuff. But I don't let it get to me. That's their problem if they don't want to get to know me. I think I'm a pretty nice person.

My old girlfriend and I used to go out with this other couple, Summer and Candle, and they were both bisexual. Cathy hangs out with people who are gay and straight, just everybody. She thinks it's fun to have me walk along with her and say, "Oh, that guy's cute." She was just great. But we're not together now.

I still have feelings for girls, unfortunately. I had to go through a long period of time where I was just like, "Who cares if I want both?" You obviously can't have both at one time or at least that's not what I want. The next person I go out with will probably be a guy, though. I don't know. I haven't tested the waters there. But I know I'm attracted to guys, and I can be in love with anybody. I can be in love with a girl or a guy.

My school's really cliquey. When you walk down in the quad area, there's these groups of people gathering, and they're just gossiping, and there's a lot of whispering. I usually have my headphones on, listening to music. I don't really worry about it; I just go to class and go to my next class.

I only know one person who's gay and out. We've been friends since the fourth grade. He's cool. Pleasanton's this big bubble, and everybody's just heterosexual, Republican, and tight ass. I'm really sick of it. In a few years, I'm gonna go to San Francisco State. There's no diversity in Pleasanton at all, so it really just conforms. Sometimes I find myself conforming just to get by. It's pretty sad. I don't belong there; I just know I don't belong there.

My first encounter with the queer community was the Castro. Definitely. A friend took me down to the Castro, and I was just totally stupid to the whole thing. We went, and he bought some shirts like, "Nobody knows I'm a drag queen." And I got the "Recovering Catholic" shirt.

I think people in the Castro are a lot more open, and they really know how to have fun. If you're gay, bisexual, whatever, it's what you want to do. The whole point in life is to have fun and enjoy life. So if you're gonna enjoy life, I think that's just great.

I have a teacher at school who's gay, and he hasn't told anybody. He's really secretive about it, and I and my closest friend are the only ones who know at school. This teacher and I became friends. He's a really nice person. Everybody likes him. But I'm sure if people found out about it, they'd just totally back off from him. There's no sort of gay community at my school that would be supportive.

I've only gone out with one girl whom I totally fell in love with. Her name's Cathy. And at first, I was this immature little tenth grader, and I didn't know the first thing about love; she taught me what it was; girls have so many emotions. I think guys do too. But she was the only person I know who really understood me.

I've never been with a guy yet. I was tempted once. I was in this store–a clothes shop or something. Well, this guy was looking at me and my friend pointed it out. I was gonna go up and talk to the guy, but the guy was twenty-something. He was good-looking, too.

This was like a year and a half ago or something. I was really screwed up–not sure how I felt. I didn't say anything. I remembered going home and wishing that I had said something.

I want to do something helping people with AIDS, like counseling and stuff. I think it's really important. I want to do art–ceramics, sculptures; I like drawing with colored pencil a lot, for some reason. And I like drawing the human body a lot too. I don't know if I'll ever get married or have kids. I definitely won't have kids. I hate kids. I can't stand kids. If I loved somebody enough, I'd get married. But I don't think I'd have kids. If I was in love with the person I met, I would want to get legally married.

I think older people see being bisexual as a trend really. They call it a phase, and I think that's so dumb. Just because they weren't as open as we are now. I think it's so cool that most people have just accepted us and what we're about. In the past couple years, it's just gotten better, and I think it will just keep getting better. There's always going to be that small, hopefully small, percentage against us, but it's one of my dreams that it will just keep getting smaller.

I think that whatever makes whoever it is happy, they should pursue it, and I think they should do whatever they want as long as it makes them happy. You have to be selfish in life. You have to do what you want to do. I'm not really scared of just anybody finding out. I'm just scared of the rejection. I don't want anyone to reject me, but if they do, then that's something I have to deal with. Life goes on.

## NOTE

Excerpts compiled from *In Your Face: Stories from the Lives of Gay Youth*, 1999, The Haworth Press, Inc.

# The Road to Reality

*Larry Lawton*

doi:10.1300/J159v05n02_05

[Haworth co-indexing entry note]: "The Road to Reality." Lawton, Larry. Co-published simultaneously in *Journal of Bisexuality* (Harrington Park Press, an imprint of The Haworth Press, Inc.) Vol. 5, No. 2/3, 2005, pp. 39-46; and: *Bi Men: Coming Out Every Which Way* (ed: Ron Jackson Suresha, and Pete Chvany) Harrington Park Press, an imprint of The Haworth Press, Inc., 2005, pp. 39-46. Single or multiple copies of this article are available for a fee from The Haworth Document Delivery Service [1-800-HAWORTH, 9:00 a.m. - 5:00 p.m. (EST). E-mail address: docdelivery@haworthpress.com].

**SUMMARY.** A bi male convict serving time in a South Carolina federal prison recounts his early sexual attractions to both men and women and his brushes with the law over the course of two decades. He discusses his marriages to women who share his bisexual attractions, reveals the inner sexual politics of life behind bars, and outlines his slow growth into roles as both lover and mentor to other incarcerated bi men. *[Article copies available for a fee from The Haworth Document Delivery Service: 1-800-HAWORTH. E-mail address: <docdelivery@haworthpress.com> Website: <http://www. HaworthPress.com> © 2005 by The Haworth Press, Inc. All rights reserved.]*

**KEYWORDS.** Bisexuality, bisexual men, South Carolina, marriage, sexuality and bisexual activity in prison, coming out, military service, penal system

I'm a white male, forty-two, five foot ten inches tall, two hundred pounds, blue eyes, and light brown hair, usually kept shaved. I have numerous tattoos, and I'm solidly built. I grew up in a middle-class neighborhood in the Bronx, New York, the second youngest sibling of five in a typical Catholic family. My heritage is Italian, Irish, German, and Hungarian: a mutt. I did all the normal stuff a boy does growing up in the late '60s and early '70s in the Bronx: baseball, football, basketball, stickball, and handball.

I probably had ADD (attention deficit disorder). My teachers said I was a smart child, but I wouldn't sit still and didn't apply myself. I was thrown out of Catholic school at age eleven after numerous disruptions, such as the time I was caught passing a note asking the other boys to sign a paper saying they would fuck the teacher.

I transferred to public school and, being athletic and sociable, I got along. I rode the city bus to school with Bill, a guy from a big family in my neighborhood I had a hidden crush on. We used to hang out in the neighborhood and, when we went to the bathroom, I would sneak peeks at his penis while he was pissing. I always thought he might go that way, but nothing ever developed.

I knew at an early age that I liked both girls and boys. I used to work out with weights in my basement with my friend, Tom, and I would look at him in that special way. We hooked up occasionally throughout the years. Thirty years later, we still are very close and both bisexual. Tom will always be in my heart in the way only two people can who have walked the road we have traveled. He has been by my side my whole life and will be my friend until I die.

In the mid-to-late '70s, coming out as bisexual wasn't even thought of. Although I didn't know what the word meant, I had one foot in both worlds. I was sexually attracted to both guys and girls. I became very confused. I was a good-looking boy with blond curly hair, popular with the girls. I had two older sisters, and their friends and other girls were always hitting on me. I played spin the bottle, made out with girls, and was dubbed "Loverboy" by aunts and grandparents.

In 1979, some friends and I stole a car to go joyriding. We were caught and I was sent to Rikers' Island jail. As it was my first brush with the law, the judge gave me the option of going to state prison or signing up with one of the armed services.

I had six months to return with enlistment papers. I joined the U.S. Coast Guard two months before my eighteenth birthday. I truly enjoyed the Coast Guard and was retired almost six years later due to severe scoliosis, a back condition. Along the way, I had both male and female sex, enjoying both immensely. Of course, the male sex was very hush-hush, this being the early '80s, before the government devised the "Don't Ask, Don't Tell" policy.

I completed my GED and gained two years of college credits while in the Coast Guard. I would have stayed in the Coast Guard if not for my back problems. I would have completed twenty years and wouldn't be writing from prison now. Still, I am drawing a pension, so I have no regrets. Regret is a wasted emotion. It's the journey through life that makes us who we are. You might as well enjoy the journey, because this is what it's all about.

After departing the service in 1985, I fell back into trouble. I was a bookmaker, collector, and muscle for the Wiseguys mob in Brooklyn, New York. I was arrested on some charges I won't discuss here, found not guilty at trial, and went on with my life.

I met my first wife, Mary, and we moved to Ft. Lauderdale, Florida. Using my connections with the Wiseguys, I opened a pizza restaurant as a front, and quickly established myself in the area bookmaking and loan sharking. We had a son in 1989.

My bisexual feelings continued. My wife and I attended a swingers club. We discussed various sex encounters and I bought videos of bisexual situations. My wife also had bisexual feelings and she ended up going with females as well. We were both undercover, as our families are very old-fashioned. I still had urges for more man-on-man sex, but kept those feelings repressed. Our divorce in 1991 was not motivated by sexual conflicts, as we both got along real well in that regard.

I was the biggest jewel robber on the east coast. From 1990 until 1996, I made millions of dollars. Money was never a problem. In 1994, I married my second wife, Kate, in Las Vegas. Kate goes both ways also, and we were swingers from the get-go. Kate knew about my desires and we enjoyed threesomes with both men and women. We swapped partners, had two guys, two women, and pretty much anything went. I just wasn't ready to admit my true sexuality to close friends and family. I still wasn't totally out.

Kate and I have a nine-year-old daughter and are still technically married. We have a good understanding and will always be friends. We will never be a couple in the true sense of the word. We just grew apart–typical after doing a long stretch of time in prison. No hard feelings at all. I am very close with my two children and good friends with my wife and ex. That is the way it should and always will be.

In 1996, I did something that got me arrested and landed me here for twelve years. I could have walked on these charges if I gave up info on certain individuals, but betrayal is not in my character. I despise rats.

As a bisexual man of forty-two, I can now see how common bisexuality is in prison, whether one admits it or not. I knew I liked guys as well as women before coming to prison. I realized after coming to prison that I leaned more toward men. In prison, coming out as bisexual or gay, not easy in any situation, is compounded tenfold. I happen to be a very strong-minded type-A personality, a big help in coming out in any situation, and more so in the prison environment.

Everybody reaches a point in their lives when they say *Fuck it*. Being happy, truly happy, is what really matters. Of course, looking back I wish I had been more open at a younger age. I think we all do, but that's water under the bridge. "With age comes experience." Oh! So true.

I would say there is a fifty percent bisexuality rate in prison. Even the straightest-acting, toughest guys have some sort of man-on-man sex. It's usually behind closed doors and kept very low-key, whether it is watching each other masturbate, mutual masturbation, oral sex, or full-out anal sex. Romances do blossom but, even more so than casual sex, they're usually kept extremely private.

When someone new comes on the yard, you can see the pairing up, courting games, and typical relationship stuff such as jealousy and protection. It's plainly obvious if you have an open mind and look for it, say, when a good-looking younger guy comes on the yard.

I'm not into that courting game. For me, the situation has to be perfect. I'm very low-key. Although a lot of people know or think they know my sexual preference, I never actually come out and said, "Hi, I'm Larry, I'm bi." I'll tell someone if they ask, but like I said, that's not done too often. I believe in "Live and let live." I'm not sure it's justified either. Does a straight guy come out and say, "Hi, I'm So-and-So, I'm straight"? No! The circle of your friends, and your actions, speak louder then any words ever could.

Being outwardly gay or bi in prison can be very hard; it brings a whole set of extra baggage. Although extortion and rape are rare, the threat of violence creates a gnawing fear. Many people might know, or think they know, what you do, but it's really not mentioned, a kind of don't-ask, don't-tell thing. I think that's because of the survival mode prison instills in all people. Whether you're predator or prey, it's like the jungle: you hide your weaknesses and show your strengths. It's a shame our sexuality must be like that, but that's the way it is.

In another prison, I fell in love with a man. John was one of the guys in my unit who hung around with me and a few of the old-timers. John is twenty-six, six foot, three inches tall, 190 pounds, dark hair, and gorgeous brown eyes. He has a magnetism that attracted me immediately. Some people call it *gaydar*, I call it a mutual attraction. A kind of seeing into each other's souls.

One night, late in the TV room, John and I were alone, and the conversation turned to sex. To my surprise, John wanted to continue this topic. John turned out to be very open and eager to learn. I'm kind of intimidating, so for John to openly discuss sex with me was a shock. I do believe people of the same sexual preference can spot each other. Call it intuition or whatever.

I told John that I had sex with men when swinging with my wife. The man and I would have oral sex while my wife watched, or I would suck his cock with my wife, or vice versa. To my surprise, John was in a few threesomes himself and wasn't as shocked about my revelations as I thought he would be. In fact, clearly the man-on-man sex talk excited him.

We set up a time to meet a few days later. When you put up a sign to cover your door window, you are afforded some privacy. We met in my cell, talked about sex, what we would do, what we liked, and mostly calmed our nerves.

The air was full of sexual energy. We sat close together on the bed, and started touching each other. John has a perfect, very well defined cock and body. His cock is around six and a half thick inches. His balls are huge and hang perfectly. My cock is slightly bigger than John's in all ways, but his balls are bigger than mine.

I lay back on the bed and John took my cock in his hand and started stroking me. I was in heaven. It didn't take long before John had me shooting cum all over his hand and my stomach. I played with his cock, but he was nervous, so that's all we did.

A few days later, we again got together and John sucked me until I filled him up. I still distinctly remember that encounter. Isn't it funny how you always remember your first? Not my first male-on-male sexual encounter, of course: my first with John.

We decided to cell together and, with some maneuvering of cellmates, three days later we were living together. When living in a seven-by-eleven-foot cell with someone–sharing your toilet, beds, and lockers–you quickly find out how compatible you really are.

Our relationship blossomed from there, and we lived together for six months, which whizzed by real fast. I ended up getting in trouble and was eventually transferred in an incident unrelated to my relationship with John. John and I stay in touch and have plans for the future.

My relationship with John made me realize that I truly am bisexual. At first, a few good friends knew. Before long, most of the people we hung around with knew, or at the very least, strongly suspected we were a couple. I call it a kind of coming out. Even my blood brother, who was in the same unit as me, suspected, or knew. My brother and I are close and that wouldn't bother me in the least.

Being open about my sexuality legitimizes same-sex partners in some prisoners' eyes. Many men figure if that macho, tough guy can be bisexual, so can they. When you live in such a close environment, you learn to read people well. My estimate of fifty-percent bisexuality comes from using humor and joking to break the ice and then gaining people's trust so that they can, over time, approach me to ask questions about man-on-man sex, bi sex, and even straight sex. By hinting that they think I am bisexual, some of them are probably trying to come out, although the words *gay* or *bi* never actually are spoken openly.

Usually races stick to themselves in prison. Although race isn't an issue with me in having a relationship, having a fling outside your race can open up a real can of worms: protection, extortion, and that kind of stuff. You do see mixed pairings, but it's the exception, not the norm.

By far, Black men are the most bisexual. The Latino race is also very sexual. I'm not promiscuous, but I once had a fling with a Cuban. Although I speak enough Spanish to get by, the language barrier is usually the biggest problem for others. I have celled with a few Latinos and learned firsthand how fun and sexual they can be, under the right circumstances.

Understanding my bisexuality has been difficult, yet the older I get, the easier it becomes. When you understand that life is all about true happiness, it makes it all worthwhile. Coming out, at least to myself, has been the best thing I ever did. Inner peace is what it's all about, and I have that.

# The Big Switch

*Stephen James*

Available online at http://www.haworthpress.com/web/JB
© 2005 by The Haworth Press, Inc. All rights reserved.
doi:10.1300/J159v05n02_06

**SUMMARY.** A British male cross-dresser confronts the split in his personality between a male persona who desires women and a female persona who desires men. Intersections of gender identity, sexual orientation, and community politics complicate the author's self-understanding despite the clarity of his multiple desires. *[Article copies available for a fee from The Haworth Document Delivery Service: 1-800-HAWORTH. E-mail address: <docdelivery@haworthpress.com> Website: <http://www.HaworthPress.com> © 2005 by The Haworth Press, Inc. All rights reserved.]*

**KEYWORDS.** Bisexuality, bisexual men, England, transvestism, cross-dressing, body image, gender identity, masculinity, femininity

My given name is Stephen, but at weekends people call me Suzy. Every Saturday I put on a dress and a long, brunette wig and my world completely changes. Underneath the dress I wear nylon stockings, which I fix to the garters that run down my thighs. I hide my cock inside a special pair of panties and I put imitation boobs into a bra, which matches the special panties. On my feet I wear heels, very high ones, and I carry a handbag and wear makeup, too. At the weekends I'm a lady and I'm looking for a man.

It was during puberty that I first got the urge to make the big switch from man to woman. Back then, I just liked wearing the pretty outfits. I'd turn myself into the kind of girl that I wanted to fuck, then dance around in front of the mirror admiring the sexy reflected image. Maid? Cheerleader? Hooker? Nurse? Nun? Whatever kind of girl I was fantasizing about at the time, I was able to become. I was a totally straight guy pursuing a totally straight agenda. Although I dressed in drag, there was never any doubt in my mind that I was into women. Hell, the only reason that I dressed like a lady was that I wasn't getting laid. I was a scrawny teenager and the girls weren't interested, so I had to be my own girlfriend!

As the years progressed and puberty passed, I dated plenty of girls, always enjoying my heterosexual sex life. But at the same time, I was in the closet–I was in the closet at every given opportunity, dressing up to the nines in heels and hose, as soon as I was left alone in the house. It was like an itch that I had to scratch, a compulsive drive that I could not resist. And it intensified, too! Just like a junkie has to keep on taking higher doses of crack to get the same hit, so I had to go further each time

I dressed. It was no longer enough just to wear a nice skirt and panties. As well as that, I had to paint my nails, then to read women's magazines and even to shave off my body hair. By that stage, I wasn't just dressing up so that I could admire my sexy reflected image in the mirror, like I had done in my teens. Since I was getting laid a lot, who was I kidding by pretending that I wore a cheerleader's outfit in order to live out the sexual fantasies that I wasn't getting fulfilled elsewhere? I had plenty of girlfriends who I could have got to dress as a nurse or a nun for me, so why did I still want to dress up myself?

In an attempt to get an answer to that question, I went out dressed as Suzy. Before I'd only dressed at home, in private, but the junkie now needed a stronger fix and that meant revealing his feminine side to the world. I was nervous as hell walking out to my car, just in case the neighbors saw me tottering along in an outfit that most hookers would have dismissed as a little too much. I was totally dressed to kill that night, from my overstuffed bra to my black-seamed hose! My skirt was so short and my heels were so high that my legs seemed almost endless, probably visible from the moon.

It was a five-minute drive to the nightclub. I spent most of the time checking in the rearview mirror—not for other traffic, but to make sure that my makeup looked okay. I wanted everything to be perfect that night, wanted to be the prettiest girl in town. I liked the idea of having men salivating over me. A girl doesn't feel like a proper girl until she's capable of attracting some masculine attention.

When I arrived at the club, I saw a group of trannies climbing out of a taxi. Most of them seemed much older than me, but their clothes were no less revealing than mine. A neon sign was flashing on and off, reading "Tranny Night" in purple lettering. A burly security guard stood on the door. He welcomed the trannies inside with a courtly gesture, then repeated the gesture when I went in.

The interior of the nightclub was dark, except for the spotlit dance floor and the neon-lit bar. I had arrived quite early, so the place was virtually empty. It smelled of stale smoke and too much perfume, a common odor in tranny bars. I felt slightly self-conscious in my girlie attire, since there were several men seated at the bar and quite a few others dotted around at tables. Most of them glanced at me, checking out the new talent, and even though they were obviously tranny hunters, it still seemed weird to have them staring at me and to find myself being looked upon with lascivious intent. It was a compliment, though, and I couldn't hide my girlish delight when I heard a wolf-whistle directed at me from across the room. I looked over in the direction of the whistle and saw a pair of guys smiling back at me. The look in their eyes said they wanted to fuck me. A voice deep inside me said to let them do it.

Despite the inner voice, I didn't go over to the guys that night. Nervousness and self-consciousness got the upper hand, so instead I met up with the group of friends, who had told me all about the nightclub. Like a lot of people who have to wrestle with a sexual fetish, I had turned to the Internet to try and meet up with some fellow spirits. Thanks to those fellow spirits, I'd heard about the bar that held the monthly "Tranny Night." A group of us girls were meeting there that night to talk lipstick, lingerie and lace.

But not men! There were a group of five of us around the table that night and all except me were married. All of them dressed with the full knowledge and understanding of their wives and none of them were into men at all. When I mentioned the guys that had wolf-whistled at me, they just stared at me blankly, as if I'd committed some kind of social faux pas. Looking back, I realize now that the tranny that likes men is not always welcomed into the sisterhood. There are a lot of trannies out there that seem to take some kind of pride in the fact that they can wear a skirt one day and fuck their wives the next. "We're really just ordinary guys," they seem to be saying. But they're not speaking for Suzy.

As Stephen, I can understand their attitude. As Stephen, I'd much prefer it if Suzy was just a hobby, a dressing up game, that I played now and then. I'd put on the clothes and scratch the itch, then take them off again and resume normal life. That way my female quality time wouldn't impinge so much upon my man time. You see, Stephen wants to be a regular guy, but Suzy's extreme tranny desires won't let him. After all, how can a guy have a girlfriend when his female alter ego wants to go with men? If I still liked girls even when I was dressed up as Suzy, then I'd just have to find an understanding wife and incorporate Suzy into my sex life with her. Now that's not necessarily easy, but you can bet it's a whole lot easier than finding a wife who will let you slip out of the house once in a week in her nylons to go have your butt fucked by the construction workers mending the holes in the road.

Stephen is a man and Suzy is a woman. I can't state it any clearer than that. Making love to a woman as Suzy wouldn't satisfy my sexual urges, since Suzy longs to be touched and taken by a powerfully aggressive lover. I understand why she wants that, because as a man I like to play the role of the powerfully aggressive lover myself. When I date a girl as Stephen, I want to be a man for her. I like my scratchy stubble to cut her chin when I kiss her. I like to open doors and flex my muscles for her. Probably my exaggerated masculinity is my way of dealing with the fact that I know that I have this whole other side to my personality. It's a way of hiding the pretty girl that lurks beneath the man.

As Suzy, I flip completely the other way, from an extreme of masculinity to an extreme of femininity. I want the doors to be held open for *me* to walk through. I want my lover to flex his muscles for *me*. I want to hear my high heels clicking on the sidewalk and have my skirt swish all around my stocking-clad thighs. Suzy is the real deal, you see, not just some married man who wears frilly panties for kicks. Suzy's all woman and she wants everything that the average girl has, including the handsome lover.

Now I don't want this to sound as rude as it's probably going to, but I didn't really like my Internet friends. They were a letdown to me. They weren't prepared to go all the way. Sure, they'd dress up sweet and tease the guys, but they wouldn't put out, and I didn't understand that. At the next monthly "Tranny Night" I didn't sit with the cross-dressing married men. I stood at the bar and talked to lots of different guys, letting some of them grope me while they chatted me up. The DJ was playing old disco tracks and there was a whole bunch of trannies in tight dresses, padded out with fake boobs, gyrating on the dance floor. Someone had set up a pole in the center of the room and they took it in turns to entwine themselves around it. To me, they looked like men trying to be women, whereas I was sure I was the real thing.

My getting groped at the bar, while the other TVs goofed around playing at being pole dancers, seemed to confirm that opinion. The masculine hands on my feminine form felt so right, the fingertips causing a sensual frisson when applied to my nylon stockings or my phony bust. I was not at the club just to dance in drag: I was there to flirt and have fun with the guys. When I finally let a guy kiss my lips, it was the most natural feeling in the world. As he wrapped his arms around me and held me close, I felt warm and safe and one hundred percent woman. His thick moustache was tickling my face and I could feel his cock starting to bulge inside his pants. His body was sweaty and his muscles felt strong. I gripped my hands all over him to make sure that he was man enough to satisfy me.

That night, as Suzy, I took the man that had kissed me back to my apartment. We French-kissed and cuddled in my lounge for a while, his body resting on top of mine. I parted my thighs to let him climb between them, then I closed my eyes when he forced his tongue inside my mouth. His hands then pushed inside my dress and rubbed all over my shaven belly and my padded bra. I felt a real sense of vulnerability, like a girl must feel when she's about to surrender her virginity. It was a total switch from all my previous relationships, where I'd been the guy so eager to get his prick inside the sticky hole.

Fuck, that made me nervous! I'm talking about that moment when I finally took his cock inside my body. First time around, I chickened out on the whole anal penetration thing. Instead, once we got inside the bedroom, I just tugged down his pants and went down on his swollen cock. The guy was hung, but not so hung that I couldn't swallow his entire length. I sucked it, licked it, ate it up, until he squirted his juices inside my mouth. My head was totally Suzy that night. I was the prom queen sucking off the quarterback hottie.

As I swallowed down my lover's seed, I jerked myself off to a quick, triumphant orgasm. It was an immense sexual high for me, so common sense should have told me that it would be followed by a major low. The following day, now Stephen again, I felt dirty and confused, as if I was waking from some perverse wet dream. Suzy's clothes were strewn on the floor all around the bed and there was a note from the guy saying to call him the following weekend. I went into the bathroom and saw that my makeup was smudged all over my face. Here and there the makeup had got rubbed off altogether and I could see little glimpses of Stephen poking out from underneath his Suzy mask. Stephen was looking sad that day, like he didn't really know who he was or what he wanted anymore.

As I walked to work that morning, I saw hundreds of guys pass by me, not one of whom I felt attracted to in a sexual way. I would have been happy to have taken them to a bar to talk football and girls, but there was no way that I would have wanted one of them to stick his dick between my lips. I didn't even know what it was that made men attractive. What kind of face makes a man get called handsome? What kind of body does a so-called stud have? The guy I'd gone with the previous night could have been a matinee idol or a slob; I wouldn't have known. I wasn't into guys, but Suzy was. She wanted someone big and powerful, because his masculinity made her feel more feminine. If the guy was tall, then that made Suzy feel short and cute and girlie. If he had a moustache that tickled her chin, then she felt all the more delicate and fresh and shaven.

It seemed like an extra long walk to work that day, because I had so much going on in my mind. I was looking at guys and not finding them attractive and yet I knew that I'd given head the previous night and that I'd enjoyed being cradled in my lover's powerful arms. It didn't tally at all with what I normally felt when walking to work. It was usual for me to eye up the ladies, because I am a heterosexual guy! I'm not gay and

I'm not even bi. I just have to scratch this itch now and then. The itch is my urge to behave in a feminine manner, to become a lady for a certain length of time. It messes up my head so much because it makes me a split personality.

Take the average bi guy: he likes sex with men and women, but he remains the same person regardless of who he's sleeping with. Not so Stephen/Suzy. They are opposites, but they have to live in the same body. Stephen wants it to be hairy and muscular, Suzy wants it to be clean-shaven and petite. Stephen likes his own body odor, but Suzy insists on smelling of roses. Stephen likes blondes with impressive breasts, but Suzy needs a man to satisfy her cravings. One is masculine and one is feminine. If they were two individuals, they would have been made for each other–a hot date sure to end in honeymoon sex. As things are, though, they're constantly competing and neither seems to understand the other at all.

At the office where I broker investments, there are a lot of girls that the masculine me has always wanted to screw around with. The day after I first got laid as Suzy, I asked Debra out for a movie and an Italian meal. My itch had been scratched, perhaps a little too deeply, and I needed to redress the balance somehow. I wore a suit that night and I didn't bother shaving. Halfway through the movie, I placed a hand on Debra's thigh. I was back in the driving seat, once again the groper, no longer a vulnerable doll to be fondled.

Debra had made quite an effort for me that evening. Her skirt was split to mid-thigh and her sweater was shrink-wrapped around her pleasing breasts. I was genuinely attracted to her and, when we went to bed, I genuinely enjoyed it. As she parted her legs and I mounted her body, it felt good to be back on top. As my cock pierced her orifice and I slammed it hard inside her, I felt almost like I knew who I was again.

Our coupling that night was frantic and aggressive. I fucked her with incredible power, because I was so desperate to reassert my masculinity. From time to time I saw fragments of the night before, visual pictures filling my mind, stirred by some little action or taste or touch. When Debra clasped both her hands around my buttocks, I remembered Suzy grabbing her boyfriend's butt, as she pushed her mouth up and down his cock. When I kissed Debra's lips, I tasted her lipstick and thought was it hers or mine? When I lifted off her dress and saw her black lace bra, I recalled the way I'd had my falsies fondled. I had loved it when my jugs were squeezed, so I did to her what I'd had done to me!

Every image that I recalled of the previous night seemed to bring out a little more of the animal in me. I was so determined to put things right that Debra must have thought that I was some kind of sexual god. My every thrust was long and hard, delivered with a sweat-soaked power that had her yelling out loud with pleasure. If she'd only known the irony: that my masculine aggression was triggered in reaction to my feminine submissiveness. If only she'd known that we had no hope of a long-term relationship, because every so often I got this itch that would make me want to wear her underclothes and then find myself a sexual god of my own.

When eventually I came inside her pussy, I felt none of the immense sexual high that I had felt when climaxing as Suzy. It seemed to prove to me that the male orgasm is purely physical, whereas the female orgasm is all in the mind. Sure, I enjoyed the spasms in my crown and the blissful sense of release as the cum gushed out, but I didn't feel the overwhelming fulfillment that a woman feels when a man has understood her needs. When Debra came, just moments later, she wanted hugs and kisses, her body seemed alive. Me? I was ready to drift off to sleep. That's what a climax does to a man.

The following morning I woke up feeling even more confused than I had done after the night before. Debra was still in bed with me and she seemed like a good cure for my morning erection, until I spotted her tempting skirt and sweater upon the floor. That made me itchy, made me want to play dress up, made me want to explore the side of my personality that wanted Debra as a friend, but nothing more. While I waited for her to awaken, I imagined us drinking Starbucks' skinny lattés and discussing recent lays. She'd tell me how she found this guy called Stephen who was like some kind of wild animal in bed. I'd cross my stocking-clad thighs and tell her all about the time I gave head, then we'd hurry along to the nearest boutique and try on something revealing that the guys were sure to love . . .

And then Debra woke up and we walked to the office together passing guy after guy after guy after guy. None of them appealed to me in any way at all. I still don't know what's attractive about guys and something tells me that I never will. Now Suzy has an ideal man, I know that. He's a strong, masculine lover, who makes her feel like she's a genuine girl. But Stephen's straight, but then again, in a way, I guess you could also say Suzy's straight, 'cos she's a girl who likes guys, even though she really is a guy underneath all the makeup and the feminine attire. If this all sounds confounding to you, then you'll know how I feel each day. Part of me just wants to keep on dating Debra, but another part of me keeps on getting itchy. Am I straight or gay or bi or what? Am I Stephen or Suzy? Am I man or woman?

Three years on since I first sucked dick as Suzy, I still find it hard to answer those questions. Since then, I've been called all kinds of things: faggot, tranny, drag queen, queer, she-male, ladyboy, homo, slut. But all I know for sure is that my given name is Stephen, but at weekends people call me Suzy.

# Learning to Look at Bisexuality

*Randy McDonald*

Available online at http://www.haworthpress.com/web/JB
© 2005 by The Haworth Press, Inc. All rights reserved.
doi:10.1300/J159v05n02_07

[Haworth co-indexing entry note]: "Learning to Look at Bisexuality." McDonald, Randy. Co-published simultaneously in *Journal of Bisexuality* (Harrington Park Press, an imprint of The Haworth Press, Inc.) Vol. 5,
No. 2/3, 2005, pp. 57-64; and: *Bi Men: Coming Out Every Which Way* (ed: Ron Jackson Suresha, and Pete
Chvany) Harrington Park Press, an imprint of The Haworth Press, Inc., 2005, pp. 57-64. Single or multiple
copies of this article are available for a fee from The Haworth Document Delivery Service
[1-800-HAWORTH, 9:00 a.m. - 5:00 p.m. (EST). E-mail address: docdelivery@haworthpress.com].

**SUMMARY.** A Canadian graduate student scrutinizes his sexuality in terms of self-image issues and entering the erotic exchange of glances that affirms his sexual nature. The author asks: what is a bisexual self, or a sexual self of any kind, when one doesn't know how to approach men or women, and how does one learn to begin those approaches? *[Article copies available for a fee from The Haworth Document Delivery Service: 1-800-HAWORTH. E-mail address: <docdelivery@haworthpress.com> Website: <http://www.HaworthPress.com> © 2005 by The Haworth Press, Inc. All rights reserved.]*

**KEYWORDS.** Bisexuality, bisexual men, Canada, college students, bisexual identity, coming out, body image

In February 2002, I was surfing the Internet late at night, as usual. I knew that I had to finish my thesis in two months but I felt bored by my academic work and reading. I hadn't bothered developing a social life more sophisticated than the exchanges of pleasantries with casual acquaintances, so that kept me at home surfing online. I was browsing a USENET history newsgroup that I regularly participated in, looking for any unread discussion threads. In one thread, the discussion veered wildly from its original subject. As I paged down through the year-old comments, I came to one young man's posting, in which he casually mentioned that he was looking for a boyfriend.

My first reaction formed as a fleeting thought arising from the subconscious: *Oh, I'd like a boyfriend, that would be nice.* I absentmindedly paged down through a few more comments before I realized exactly what I had thought and what that meant. Three thoughts passed through my mind in the space of two or three seconds. First, *Oh, I'm bi.* Then, *Oh. I'm bi.* And finally, *Oh no, I'm bi.*

The shock of this realization kept me awake until 2:00 a.m.

I'd be wrong if I said that I had no idea that I had a sexual orientation. There were hints as far back as my early adolescence on Prince Edward Island in eastern Canada.

When I was 12, and attending a French-immersion summer camp on the Magdalen Islands, I asked a girl in eighth grade (an impossible two years older than me) if she wanted to dance with me at the camp's final dance. She turned me down, of course, since she was a camp supervisor. The whole instance passed with only mild regret during the dance as I sat scared on the sidelines, watching the others.

More significantly, when I was in twelfth grade, I attended a youth parliament, a mock assembly held in my province's legislative assembly, and there I met an attractive young woman, softly spoken and with a fine-featured face that reminded me of a fox, and short brown hair. I liked her as a friend; I thought that, perhaps, I could like her more. But then, before I could even imagine what to do, she found a boyfriend, a mutual friend also in attendance at that youth parliament. The rest of the winter was dominated by my slow emotional breakdown, as I gradually retreated from the world and tried to push this group of friends away from me.

I recognized only later that I felt oddly connected to her boyfriend. He was a young man quite similar physically to his girlfriend: tall, slim, fine-featured, intelligent, and witty. I considered him a friend, and enjoyed spending time with him. At the same time, though, I felt interested in something more. I didn't know what exactly "more" was; due to my unfamiliarity with close friendships, I assumed that I wanted to be a closer friend. Yet, the terminology of friendship didn't apply to how I felt. The whole question became moot when, by March of that year, I'd managed to completely alienate him and everyone else with a sudden, inexplicable outburst of rudeness.

I spent the season between high school and university in steadily deepening depression. At first, the depression seemed like something that would lift when the cold weather changed. But it didn't lift, it only got deeper. At university, I finally spoke to a psychiatrist and got a prescription for Zoloft, which with surprising quickness lifted the depression, and I promptly began being a perfect university student. A social life? A *romantic* life? I certainly needed neither. I hated being a teenager, and I saw no reason to do things I thought only teenagers did. A perfectly competent, perfectly distanced professionalism befitting a university student was all I wanted to adopt.

Of my six years at university, the first four passed sexless and loveless, with only one thing to remind me of possibilities. I didn't make friends during this period; I did, though, have plenty of acquaintances. I'd cultivated faultlessly polite and distant manners, as much to keep others distant while leaving a good impression as to treat these people well. One day in the university library, a smart, physically attractive student journalist whom I knew, and I were using adjacent photocopiers. Suddenly, during a friendly conversation as we copied articles, he asked me if I was gay. I was startled; without thinking, I replied that I wasn't. Afterward, though, I did wonder if I was gay, but didn't give it much thought as I rarely saw him around.

I masturbated frequently, almost entirely inspired by gay porn texts, but I never connected these fantasies to a sexual orientation. I fantasized about having heterosexual relationships, and I fantasized about having homosexual relationships; sometimes, even both at the same time. On the rare occasions that I considered the implication of these fantasies, I dismissed the idea that I could realize any sort of relationship as vastly implausible. My sexual orientation seemed of no practical relevance to me, Randy McDonald, university student *par excellence* and little else besides. If I treated all relationships as equally unlikely, after all, I needn't consider the question of my sexual orientation. Best to go back to my books and not to bother myself.

This changed after that night of browsing online discussion archives. In keeping with my enlightened university student attitude, I never minded people who weren't heterosexual. I approved of gay rights in general, and even agreed that same-sex marriage was acceptable. I didn't have to work through much of my own homophobia. The reactions of others, particularly my parents, worried me, and proved a major concern in the months ahead, but thankfully I found that I could easily manage others' reactions.

My biggest question, though, was *Who am I now?* In my first year of university, I took some introductory courses in philosophy, and Descartes' *Meditations on First Philosophy* influenced me profoundly. The whole idea that through careful self-examination I could discover everything of importance about myself–"I think, therefore I am"–fit my detached personal veneer perfectly, though it also demonstrated that the Cartesian model of self-analysis didn't work beyond the basic recognition of my own sentience. In order to learn more about myself, I had to explore the wider world. I just had no idea how I'd make these self-discoveries.

Before graduation, I accumulated a grasp of queer/bisexual theory. I read Bert Archer's *The End of Gay* (1999), Marjorie Garber's *Vice Versa* (1995), and discussion group archives and posted on newsgroups. I browsed articles in all of the relevant article databases and Web sites that I could find, I exchanged lengthy e-mails with a half-dozen people and chatted online with others. My claimed sexual orientation, though, stayed theoretical: I couldn't translate it from the realm of theory to action. I just couldn't understand how to look at *and* appreciate other people.

Just once after my realization, I met a guy through a mailing list and realized that I was interested in him. As Leonard Cohen put it in the song "First We Take Manhattan": *I'd really like to live beside you, baby / I love your body and your spirit and your clothes.* I found myself smitten. There were small but significant hints, I thought, that told me that he also saw the possibility for something more than friendship. We went together to a local GLBT dance a few months later, first having convinced myself that he did see this as a date. When we actually entered the ballroom, though, the whole affair was a nightmare thanks to the sheer foreignness of the environment. I felt paralyzed and didn't know how to look. I ended up leaving early. The guy said to me later that he understood where I was coming from, and told me that he still had a great time. Oh, a certain guy he'd had his eye on wasn't interested in his advances after I left, but that aside . . . At least we're still friends.

That episode didn't help me find out how to look, how to gaze, how to take an interest in people generally, how to get a simple idea. I kept trying to look, but I couldn't see anything. At most, I could get an aesthetic appreciation of others' bodies, but nothing really seemed to click, certainly nothing likely to lead to sex or romance, with anyone of either gender. Though I definitely leaned more toward men than women, I still identified myself as bisexual: that category, at least judging by one on-line newsgroup's definition, was elastic enough to include me. I experienced the same ineffectiveness, the same sense of missing something, with attractive men and women both.

By February 2003, I despaired that no relationship of any sort would ever happen to me. Perhaps I'd waited too late to try to develop that sort of sustainable, or repeatable, interest in others. Perhaps I was innately incapable of relating in an intimate way to others. Perhaps I thought too much; probably, it just would never work and I should just resign myself to this. I could still have something of a life.

They say that travel is a broadening experience, that the displacement of one's body can lead to changes in one's mind. This particular trip, made at the end of the summer of 2003, was taking me via the train from my home to my new graduate school in Ontario. I'd decided to spend two days in Montréal, which lay directly on my route. I told people who asked me why I was going there that I wanted to tour that beautiful city, practice my spoken French on the locals, enjoy myself generally before I embarked on my program. What I didn't tell them was that I was going to try to see if I could connect to anyone, to see if I could get my impotent gaze going one last time. If it didn't work out, well, I could throw myself into my graduate studies. If it did work out, though–it would be best not to bank on that, but it was nice.

My first night in Montréal, I went to the Gay Village. I walked up and down the street a couple of times, looking for what seemed like a congenial bar. I found one, bought a beer, and sat down. Two beers later, I almost ran out of there. That same sense of being out of place, and that same inability to focus my gaze on others, prevailed.

My second day in Montréal, I decided that I'd given it a legitimate try and tried to focus myself on touring. That day, I decided to focus on visiting Montréal's historic districts, and by the middle of that afternoon I ended up at an archeological museum. While waiting in line to get in, I noticed a slim, brown-haired young man standing a few meters away. He looked at me, and smiled. I was surprised. Slowly I caught on that he was looking at someone, and another few long seconds to realize he was looking at *me*. I didn't know why he was doing that. Throughout the museum tour, he stayed fairly close to me, but we didn't speak. I felt flattered, but I didn't know what to do, so I left alone.

It was raining heavily, and I ran into a nearby café to dry off. As I ordered my coffee, two younger girls came in, speaking Italian, or perhaps Portuguese. The shorter girl, with medium-length hair, a fine complexion, and lovely dark eyes, winked at me. I decided to be bold and respond; I smiled back. This began an exchange of glances and nods that went on for another half hour or so, until I left for the Gay Village again. I bought a book and, while leaving the store, I was surprised to see the young man from the museum at the checkout counter. We acknowledged each other again, but I didn't feel confident enough to do anything but exchange glances with him.

I walked to a Thai restaurant nearby, ordered dinner, and noticed a single slim, attractive man sitting to my right. He surprised me by starting a conversation, though I was definitely pleased that he showed interest in me. When he invited me to join him at a bar later that evening, I was stunned, but learned to adapt speedily to this unfamiliar situation.

Was I really bisexual, then? I wasn't at all certain if I had decided to call myself bisexual out of a panicked unconscious fear of what might happen if I were completely gay.

The question of my orientation hasn't been resolved by my pleasant recent experiences. I identify myself as bisexual whenever people ask. I find myself looking at attractive women and am still interested in pursuing a long-term opposite-sex relationship in the future. Although I'm content with my current boyfriend, I clearly want to keep my options open.

Regardless of the specific biological causes of same-sex attraction, a "true" bisexuality, a sexual orientation defined as *equal* attraction to the two sexes, may exist. Some people call themselves bisexual because they become more honest with themselves about their orientation over time. Many theories and much popular opinion argue that few people are innately bisexual, and others believe that we cross the great frontier of sexual orientation heavily influenced by our culture and environment. It goes against one's individual nature to violate the basic principle that a person's identity must be entirely self-contained and stable.

I prefer fluidity of sexual orientation and personality. These experiences have shown me that there are no insides or outsides, that there is no isolated individual who determines his or her own identity without referring to the outside world. How can you know if you're straight, gay, or bisexual, if you never see anyone who could be an object of desire, never learn what these words mean, never figure out how you can be categorized, or never extend your personal boundaries? I may never come to identify myself as either strictly heterosexual or homosexual, and may always feel confused about my true nature. After more than two years of trying to understand my sexual orientation, what's the point of trying to remove the uncertainty? Since categories always have ambivalent meanings, why not take full advantage of my ability to transcend such distinctions?

I like people, regardless of how they feel about me. Certainty my sexual orientation, whatever you want to call it, is focused more on men than women. I can conclude with equal certainty that my life is much more fluid than I could have imagined that first winter night. For now, it's enough for me to know that I can want others and be wanted by those same, no matter what their gender. What else do I need to know?

# Coming to Terms

*Ron Jackson Suresha*

Available online at http://www.haworthpress.com/web/JB
© 2005 by The Haworth Press, Inc. All rights reserved.
doi:10.1300/J159v05n02_08

[Haworth co-indexing entry note]: "Coming to Terms." Suresha, Ron Jackson. Co-published simultaneously
in *Journal of Bisexuality* (Harrington Park Press, an imprint of The Haworth Press, Inc.) Vol. 5, No. 2/3, 2005,
pp. 65-76; and: *Bi Men: Coming Out Every Which Way* (ed: Ron Jackson Suresha, and Pete Chvany) Harrington Park Press, an imprint of The Haworth Press, Inc., 2005, pp. 65-76. Single or multiple copies of this article
are available for a fee from The Haworth Document Delivery Service [1-800-HAWORTH, 9:00 a.m. - 5:00
p.m. (EST). E-mail address: docdelivery@haworthpress.com].

**SUMMARY.** A long-term gay-identified man recalls early negative sexual experiences with bi-identified men, only to reexamine decades later during a health crisis his latent desires for women. When he confesses his attraction to a childhood sweetheart, she reacts insightfully, "That opens up a whole new world of possibilities." He discusses his self-discovery as a late-blooming bisexual while entering a primary relationship with another man. *[Article copies available for a fee from The Haworth Document Delivery Service: 1-800-HAWORTH. E-mail address: <docdelivery@haworthpress.com> Website: <http://www.HaworthPress.com> © 2005 by The Haworth Press, Inc. All rights reserved.]*

**KEYWORDS.** Bisexuality, bisexual men, coming out, sexual misconduct, married bi-curious men, cancer, body image, Bear subculture, GLBTIQA journalism and advocacy, bisexual identity, sexual exploration, heterosexual women

My earliest exposure to the vocabulary of bisexuality came primarily from reading erotica. Both my parents had active intellectual curiosities about sex, sexualities, and sexual psychology, and our household served as a rich mine of books and periodicals that fueled my earliest sexual flames. By ninth grade, I had read *Portnoy's Complaint, Everything You Always Wanted to Know About Sex,* and *The Happy Hooker,* numerous issues of my dad's *Playboy* and, after my parents' prior divorce at age 13, my mom's *Playgirl.*

As progressive as my parents might have been, they hardly affirmed my being gay. Yet they must have known something was up: in junior high school, after my mom discovered me playing around with a fey neighbor boy three years older (he loved to lip-sync "Harper Valley PTA"), they sat me down and asked if I thought I were homosexual. I answered quite sincerely, No. They asked if I liked girls, and I said, "Sure."

My response to them was honest, essentially, as far as I knew. But I got caught up in the word *homosexual.* At the time, I thought homosexuality was about guys who liked to dress up in women's clothes and I knew, from having once tried on my sister's red silk dress once and seeing how ridiculous I looked in the thing with my already-sprouted facial hair, that I wasn't cut out for that sort of thing. Now, had my parents asked if I liked looking at men's bodies, I would have replied differently. But fear of my early same-sex attractions made me deny them, and my parents, probably eager to get nomimal affirmation of my heterosexuality, left the rest unspoken for the time being.

Although other events happened which undoubtedly informed my parents' assessment of my evolving sexuality, not until my junior year of high school in suburban Detroit, Michigan, did I cop to my attraction to men. I was active at the local community center that offered services for youth, including drug crisis intervention and peer "rap" groups that were adult-supervised. One evening, the group leader, a bearded, bearish social worker in his mid-twenties named John, on whom I had a crush, angrily provoked me to confess that I had had sex with men.

John immediately scuttled me into a private room with some slightly older guys for what can be best described as a heterosexual intervention. The door closed on six of us: John, divorced; two regular jockish guys from the hotline; a popular proto-metrosexual named Dane, who used to wear clear nail polish and his girlfriend's clogs; and Amory, one of the sharper, more serious teen volunteer senior leaders.

In short, during that conversation, each of the other men present in turn offered varying degrees of empathy for my admittance of homosexuality: Amory was the only one who clearly affirmed whatever form of sexuality or masculinity I might claim. Each made a point of affirming his heterosexuality, especially John, being the only one previously married with children.

How could I have articulated my fear of women, of straight relationships (my own parents were divorced the year before), or my masturbatory fantasies of John and Dane? As we filed out, they each offered me a firm handshake, except for Amory, who surprisingly pulled me into a quick hug, saying, "You can talk with me later about all this."

When next I encountered Amory in school, he took me aside and discreetly asked if I wanted to talk with him about "that subject." He told me he disliked how Dane and John handled the situation earlier and that he wanted to speak with me about some issues. I eagerly accepted an invitation to come to his house that evening, anxious to speak with a sympathetic, experienced peer.

In his room, Amory confessed that he considered himself bisexual, that he had sex with guys as well as his girlfriend. He stated that he enjoyed sex with men and women for different reasons and didn't care what most people thought about it but, because of his dislike of Dane, he refrained from coming out as bi in the group. Amory explained bisexuality in terms of the Kinsey factor, and suggested that I might consider myself a Kinsey 5, meaning that I was largely but not exclusively same-gender oriented.

I tried to absorb this information and apply it to my own situation but I couldn't even begin to sort out the complexity of the matter. Sensing my quiet desperation, with probably some genuine sympathy, Amory, a nice enough guy but not particularly attractive, drew me into a long hug. Then he asked if I wanted to have sex with him. As I had so little self-esteem those days–I thought myself particularly unattractive as a teenager and was amazed anyone would find me desirable–his proposition shocked me. Although not at all turned on, I was too polite to refuse. Though initially responsive to Amory's ministrations, winter chill and embarrassment strangled my erotic desire, and I returned home nauseated and confused.

Although Amory called to invite me several times to come over "to talk," I declined. Our initial sexual experience simply served to gather more shame and haze around whatever identity I might adopt.

I was attempting to define my sexuality and life clearly, but couldn't breathe through the black smoke of shame that had choked me since the evening of the intervention. Confusion overcame my daily life, leading to a serious suicide attempt several months later, which placed me out of senior high school year for six weeks and in what was then called a rehabilitation hospital. I returned home unable to address my sexuality with my therapists. Fighting my way out of depression, I managed to finish high school on time and land a scholastic achievement scholarship to the University of Michigan in Ann Arbor.

A far more troubling encounter with another bisexual man occurred the next summer, one month before I was to leave for my first year in college. While hitchhiking cross-country in Oregon, I was picked up by a fiftyish man who claimed to be married with kids. He offered a beer, which led to three, and I let my defenses down. As he got me drunk, he lecherously admitted to liking boys as well as women: "Ya know what a bisexual is?" I replied that of course I did, although I had very little clue as to what that meant other than what a straight man called himself right before he would ask another guy to have sex with him. The geezer then began touching my thigh, showed me straight and gay porn mags, and diddled my unavoidable raging hard-on as we drove along. He stopped at a rustic rest stop and took me inside the men's room. As we peed standing next to each other and he flopped around his semihard uncut dick, I realized my things were locked in his car and that we were miles away from the next rural town. He grabbed my shoulder and forced me to my knees, telling me to suck him off. After maybe ten minutes of fucking my face, uncaringly gagging me, and muttering nasty little nothings in his drunken drawl about fucking pussy, he shot his bitter seed down my throat and I shot in my pants.

My disgust with him and my own self-loathing exploded into a furious rage inside, expressible only through violence. I stood up from the filthy floor, coughed up and spat the cum in his face, and closed my hands around his neck. I wrestled him to the floor, blood spattering about, and almost succeeded strangling him when I was interrupted by the sound of a car pulling into the rest stop. In sheer panic, I grabbed the choking man's keys and drove away but, within a half hour, the cops caught up to me. I was arrested and jailed, unable to speak of the sexual component of the encounter with the driver who had picked me up hitchhiking. After three days in the Wasco County Jail, a court-appointed lawyer came to my cell. After some reluctance on my part to explain my actions, he gently explained that if the man had had sexual contact with me, at seventeen years old still technically a minor, his actions constituted statutory rape, whether or not he initiated it, not to mention a host of other crimes. If not, the prosecutor and court would doubtlessly try my case and convict me as an adult and send me to federal prison.

Bursting into tears, I admitted what happened. The court dropped the car-theft and battery charges against me and shipped me back home with the promise I would attend college and seek professional counseling. I saw a nice psychologist at a clinic for several months, with whom I could be honest about my sexuality, until he unexpectedly left the agency. I never heard if the married man in Oregon was prosecuted for molestation.

For the next twenty-five years, these two initial experiences with self-identified bisexual men created a highly negative prejudice against so-called bisexual men. I perceived bisexuality as secretive, duplicitous, and predatory. I often had sexual encounters with married men at rest stops and bars, but if the men I was sucking and fucking were in any way bisexual-identified, they either avoided revealing the fact or I refused to acknowledge it.

The year following the Oregon incident, my mom was killed unexpectedly in a car accident and, despite the protestations of my mentor and creative writing teacher, a bearish married man to whom I wrote unrequited love poems about entwining our beards together in passionate embrace, I quit college to settle her estate. I sold my childhood home and, at age 19, I moved back to Ann Arbor, where I continued to explore literature, arts, and gay culture. As a gay man, I continued to find acceptance and develop a vocabulary with which I could positively describe myself and my friends, but which did not include the term "bisexual." I learned and practiced yoga and meditation and began to straighten out my head.

However, another shift in my sexuality occurred beginning in 1977, during a period of voluntary, non-masturbatory celibacy while studying yoga in several Western yoga ashrams. Once the context of sex was removed from my daily life, I saw how powerfully my desire for sexual contact with others drove my interactions with them. When I stopped relating to persons based on their relative value to fulfilling my sexual desire, I developed a sense of humanity and equanimity that allowed me to see the essential dual female-male-androgynous divinity in everyone regardless of whatever gender or sexuality label they might assume. Although the power of my sexual desire proved too strong a force for me to ignore or resist, this spiritual worldview became my foundation for a new understanding of bisexuality and gender equality. Also, to the extent that I observed celibacy, this period of asexuality eliminated my risk of exposure to HIV during the early years of the disease's spread.

One night in 1983, I ventured out to an upstate New York bar, where I met a handsome, sweet bearded man named Stephen. I invited him back to my place and we spent hours of intensely passionate, versatile lovemaking that burned powerfully into the next afternoon. He asked to see me again and I agreed. Stephen returned every Sunday for several weeks, and as our affection for each other grew quickly, I unleashed the huge reservoir of pent-up sexual and emotional energy upon him, and believed that he also was falling in love.

Late one hot summer night, as I fucked Stephen in my bed to a spectacular mutual orgasm, he began weeping and crying out. I collapsed onto Stephen in a sweaty, hairy heap, kissing and holding him tight. At first I thought his tears came from the passionate sex but, rather than abate, his sobs increased in pitch until he seemed inconsolable. After fifteen minutes of this hysteria, Stephen calmed down enough to reveal that he was married with children and that I was the first man with whom he ever had sex.

The story of the following two months of the relationship is too involved to include here, but suffice it to say that my first affair with a married man was doomed. My next significant relationship with a bisexual man would not occur for another twenty years.

Five years ago, living in Boston, I turned forty. I began earnestly studying gender issues in general and queer masculinities in particular while preparing my first book, *Bears on Bears: Interviews & Discussions*. I also began questioning the solidity of my own sexual identity.

Although I broadened a working definition of "bear" to include bisexual men, I realized that I knew little about self-identified bi men.

Meanwhile, back in Detroit, I was caregiving for my father, who was dying of metastatic prostate cancer. Although in many ways more accomplished than my dad, I became keenly aware of the exchange of parenting roles between us as he became weaker in body and mind. In counseling, my therapist told me that the child assumes some of the roles and personality aspects of the last parent after his/her death. It wasn't until after my dad's death in April 2001 that I considered that part of the paternal mantle I was assuming might include his heterosexuality.

After my dad passed, I reconnected with Serina, a woman in Detroit who grew up about a block away from me, on whom I had a secret childhood crush. I considered asking her to the high school prom but was too shy and too poor to ask. Happily we reconnected during our twentieth high-school reunion and spent half the night amazed at being with each other, while my best high school pal Joel, already divorced, tried to put the make on her. In one of many long phone calls between Boston and Detroit, Serina told me about some same-sex experiences she tried.

Just after *Bears on Bears* was published, I met James at the Hibernation Run, a regional New England Bears club event during Presidents' Day weekend in Provincetown. James, a handsome redbear, was in the process of separating from his wife while coming out as bi, and attending a bi married men's support group. We hit it off and ended up spending the weekend together, and seeing each other afterward. Although I liked James greatly, I was anxious about getting emotionally involved again, having just ended a tumultuous three-year relationship, especially considering that my prior experiences with self-identified bi men were decidedly negative. But our friendship grew when I ended up moving from Boston to Providence into a house behind James's new apartment.

One day, I made an off-the-cuff assertion to Jim to the effect that we could do something a certain way because "we're gay." James had corrected me gently before about this misstatement but this time he turned to me and said sharply, "I'm *not* gay. I'm *bi*." I understood, having been his sexual partner as well as having listened to several stories of sex with women he shtupped, that James's erotic desire encompassed both men and women in equal, different, and positive ways. Suddenly I realized that my negative experiences with bi men had prejudiced me against bisexuality. In my ignorance, I believed that bisexuality wasn't as valid a self-identity as being gay or lesbian.

The following spring, while promoting *Bears on Bears* in New Orleans, my first visit in more than twenty years, I fell in love with the town and its motto of "Let the good times roll." Part of the city's attraction to me is how relaxed everyone seems about matters of sexuality. It was an atmosphere where I also felt relaxed about my contacts with men and women and, during successive visits at Southern Decadence and other events, I found myself noticing women more, in frequency and in intensity of erotic desire.

I returned in May 2003 to participate in the Saints & Sinners GLBTIQA litfest, invited by the organizer, Paul Willis, a good friend with whom I was co-editing a fiction anthology, *Kink*. Paul asked me to accompany a local bisexual author, Ellen, who was scheduled for the Saturday evening erotica reading, in her car to a private party honoring Patricia Nell Warren. At the reading held in Gennifer Flowers's nightclub in the French Quarter, Ellen, an attractive former stripper who had written a memoir called *Pretty Is Just a Face I Make*, had not yet read, so I listened to several male readers while waiting somewhat impatiently for her.

I was completely surprised when she read a sizzling section of her book, describing an evening when she and another woman had sex with a man, how turned on I became. I blushed almost continuously until she finished her juicy narrative, receiving the loudest ovation that evening, and she emerged from the crowd looking radiant and very, very sexy. As we drove to the party, we spoke animatedly and flirted sweetly, and I told her I had considered myself a Kinsey 5, although my sexual experiences had been exclusively with men. With a lump in my throat, I finally said the word—"I think I might be bisexual, too." Ellen encouraged me to keep my mind and options open and, although throughout the evening at the party we chatted now and again, we left separately.

As I went to sleep that night, I noticed how disappointed I felt at not having the opportunity to spend more time with Ellen. Back home, when I told James about this encounter, he teased me, saying, "Watch out—you might be becoming bisexual yourself." To my surprise, I agreed.

In April 2003, a lump appeared in my left salivary gland that, over several months, swelled painfully. Although all the initial tests looked benign, the doctor recommended that the mass be removed surgically as soon as we could schedule it. The operation required a two-day stay in the hospital. I had friends checking in on me the first few days after I returned home but, when finally home by myself, I became quietly desperate, feeling very alone and in the dark. We still had no clue as to what the tumor was; knowing many long-term survivors of AIDS, I feared cancer far more than HIV infection. In either case, I had to do some hard thinking about my life–not the easiest task when drugged up on painkillers.

I hadn't spoken with my childhood friend Serina for many months, so I called to tell her about my surgery. After I explained my medical situation, she showed me so much care and support during that hour-long phone call that I came close to tears several times, feeling her love in a way I never thought possible with a woman. I told her about other recent events, and that I thought I was actually bisexual. Her response was ebullient: "That opens up a whole world of possibilities!"

We discussed the idea of my coming to Detroit for a visit, although it would depend on my health. Unspoken was the thought that if I were to visit, we would consummate the affection we had had all these years.

After the call, I burst into tears. My heart churned with tumultuous emotion–the power of a woman's complete love for me. I pictured her holding and comforting me, assuring me that everything would be fine. I realized that I had become aroused and began playing with my cock. The more I cried, the harder I became; the stiffer I got, the harder I wept. I allowed myself to fantasize about making love with Serina: her soft breasts, her reassuring kisses, her sexy voice, her sweet smell, the weight of my body atop hers, gently slipping my erection inside her, holding each other tightly, fucking slowly at first, then increasing the pace until . . . I came hard, crying, shouting, and shooting a spectacular shower of jism. As I recovered my breath and my senses, I realized that my life had dramatically changed.

Several weeks later, the results from the final biopsy of the golfball-sized mass removed surgically detected an unusual, moderately aggressive, but quite treatable cancer. The doctors recommended, in case any rogue cancer cells jumped ship from the lump already removed, radiation treatment for six weeks, every legal working day, as a safeguard. They would treat a triangular patch from the top of my left ear, down above the jaw line to the side of my chin, back to about the spot near, say, Frankenstein's bolt, and up along the bottom and front of the ear.

Two weeks into treatment, moments before a photographer was to arrive at my home, I was washing my face when a clump of hair from the middle of my beloved beard fell in the bathroom sink. The situation at first seemed catastrophic, but the photographer encouraged me to go through with the session. Having to literally put on a brave face kept the shock and fear away. Eventually I lost all the hair on that patch, and I joked that even my radiation treatment, which looked like a pink triangle, was queer.

Cancer dramatically evolved my relationship with my body and sexuality. I detached from my body and became aware of its neutrality of desire: it wasn't necessarily my body that preferred men to women, it was my mental state–a kind of misogyny or gynophobia. Regardless of the reasons in my past for my previously exclusive homosexual preference, I no longer felt I had the luxury of time to exclude any possibilities in the future.

Twelve days after my surgery, two weeks before I started treatment, in October 2003, I made the two-hours-plus car trip to Provincetown, Massachusetts. That weekend, I attended the Lambda Literary Conference, where I met a man, Rocco, a family physician who writes poetry. Rocco made an immediate impression on me and we spent part of the weekend together. Long story short, we fell in love. Rocco walked into my life at a time of crisis and offered his devoted care and unselfish support, his love.

I was skeptical of his reaction when I eventually told him about my newly discovered bisexuality, but quickly I saw how he completely affirmed, embraced, and supported my process. Although various folks have had curious and dubious reactions when I've mentioned my bisexuality (it's hard to avoid the topic when one is editing two anthologies of bisexual men's writings), every person in my life who matters has validated my coming out as bisexual. What ultimately matters, though, is how I perceive and bless my own process.

My second coming-out experience corresponded to an entirely new vision of my body while I experienced my father's death, sold my house and moved twice in ten months, underwent cancer surgery and radiation treatment (entirely effective, I'm happy to add), and met and fell in love with my partner. The pain of coming out again has proven more positive than my first arduous process of self-discovery as a homo, but just as intense, if not more so.

Coming out–whether gay, lesbian, bi, or trans–is a complex metaphor for self-discovery and life actualization. To declare one's non-heterosexuality in any manner queers one's world in a truthful, positive way–though admittedly not the sole means of attaining a queer sensibility. Coming out from gay to bi is part of my life's journey, just as a straight man would feel that coming out as bi or gay is part of his. For some gay men coming out a second time as bisexual, such as myself, we are simply expanding the way in which we queer the world.

It saddens me so many gay, lesbian, and straight folks have marginalized bisexuals, transpeople, intersexed, and other queer non-monosexual folks. I am shamed by my own prejudice, believe me. How dare I expect acceptance from others if I can't affirm everyone's sexuality? If I disparage others' sexual and gender expression, and reinforce old stereotypes and prejudices–especially if I already know the difficulty of coming out–I need to take a good, long, hard look at myself. What difference does it make from where we come if we agree that we're all heading in the same direction?

Evolving consciously to transform a central aspect of one's personality requires incredible inner strength, compassion, and self-reflection. Bisexual and transgendered folks understand what it means to grow a sexual vocabulary that can describe worlds of acceptance and transcendence, of which many non-monosexuals might only dream.

Coming to terms with an evolving sense of masculinity and sexual identity has taken its own good time to unfold, and coincides with a period of positive transformation of the GLBTIQA civil rights landscape. The future looks as bright as a sunflower. It's a joy, and still somewhat scary, to think that after thirty years of gay male sex, that I have a whole new sexual universe to explore. Accepting myself as bisexual allows me to broaden a vocabulary with which I can meaningfully describe my body and my world, and to interact with the whole of humanity with equanimity. The winding road which I have been paving seemingly by myself, one yellow brick at a time, has joined up to a path where many other men who, in whatever manner they think of themselves as bisexual or otherwise behave bisexually, walk toward a profound goal.

# Part Two: Extending Bonds of Marriage and Family

## Coming Out Bi and Large

*Jim Fenter*

[Haworth co-indexing entry note]: "Coming Out Bi and Large." Fenter, Jim. Co-published simultaneously in *Journal of Bisexuality* (Harrington Park Press, an imprint of The Haworth Press, Inc.) Vol. 5, No. 2/3, 2005, pp. 77-86; and: *Bi Men: Coming Out Every Which Way* (ed: Ron Jackson Suresha, and Pete Chvany) Harrington Park Press, an imprint of The Haworth Press, Inc., 2005, pp. 77-86. Single or multiple copies of this article are available for a fee from The Haworth Document Delivery Service [1-800-HAWORTH, 9:00 a.m. - 5:00 p.m. (EST). E-mail address: docdelivery@haworthpress.com].

**SUMMARY.** A married man recounts the difficult process of coming out as bisexual to himself, his wife and children, and colleagues and friends. The author's self-image as traditionally masculine and his attraction to men and women who fit traditional gender images initially complicate his ability to understand himself as non-heterosexual. *[Article copies available for a fee from The Haworth Document Delivery Service: 1-800-HAWORTH. E-mail address: <docdelivery@haworthpress.com> Website: <http://www.HaworthPress.com> © 2005 by The Haworth Press, Inc. All rights reserved.]*

**KEYWORDS.** Bisexuality, bisexual men, marriage, children of bisexual men, Bear subculture, coming out, body image

My coming out as bi occurred in a series of stages: coming out to myself as bi, coming out to myself as a Bear, coming out to my wife, coming out to family and friends, and finally, coming out publicly to strangers.

Girls and women attract me. Hyperfeminine characteristics like large breasts and curves in "all the right places" turn me on: a nice, heart-shaped ass, soft shoulders, and just a subtle cinching of the waist. One characteristic that people of both genders to whom I am attracted share is size. I like big men who look like men and not like boys, and I like big women who look like women and not like little girls.

It was physically dizzying the first time I said to myself, "I am bisexual," after having repressed it for so long. I had always felt attracted to men, particularly to hairy men with facial hair or a heavy five o'clock shadow. Muscularity and chest hair also turn me on. Even at age fourteen, I found men who had all the hypermasculine secondary sexual characteristics just breathtaking. In other words, I was attracted to Bears, though I didn't then know that term as a description of the male body type that stimulated me, nor was it even known in gay parlance at that time, from what I understand.

As it turned out, I have a very bearish body type. I worked out fanatically in my youth to lose weight, which also helped build the frame that continued to develop into the large guy I am today. I'm not actually obese, just big and fairly muscular, with a bit of a gut. I'm also a fairly hairy individual, but my red body hair is difficult to see unless one is close up or I'm wet. Of all the males in my family, I'm the only one who developed chest hair and it seems I got everybody else's quota. When my brothers would comment on this, I'd tell them they simply didn't want it bad enough.

I rationalized that I admired these male bodies because that's what I wanted to look like. This bit of self-deception was easy to absorb because it was true. I wanted to look like Tom Selleck, Steve Reeves, and especially Lee Majors in the episodes of the Bionic Man where he would grow a beard and show his chest hair. Even the Smirnoff ad with the illustration of a Tsarist Russian nobleman with a perfect beard was a turn-on.

In the seventies, I read several "Ask Beth" teen-advice newspaper columns and, whenever there was a question from a teen confused about being attracted to their same-sex best friend in a romantic or sexual way, Beth would explain it as a "phase everyone goes through."

When you're raised Catholic, the second oldest of seven kids, and grow up with the unwavering rule that we don't air our dirty laundry outside the family, talking about emotions or sexuality is not easy. That wouldn't be so bad except that the other unwavering rule is that if we talk about emotions, they had better be positive ones, as defined by my parents. Emotions perceived as negative were to be overcome and not discussed at any length. So, I grew up being unable to talk about certain things to my family or to anyone else, either.

Not that I blame my parents for any of this; their generation grew up through the Great Depression, and they dealt with these issues the only way they knew how. But the degree to which this uncommunicative tradition is taken is still striking to me. About a week after I had come out to my parents, my mom told me that she had gone to the M – –'s for their weekly night of cards. I asked if she had told Mrs. M – – about me. Her reply: "Oh no! I don't think we need to tell everything about our family to everybody!"

Perhaps this wouldn't be so surprising, except that this woman and my mother have been friends since before they met their husbands. And my parents have been playing cards almost every week with this couple, since long before I was born. And yet, my mom is hesitant to talk to one of her best friends about something personally unpleasant or embarrassing, or to reach out for help or support for herself, which is a trait that I have inherited–I simply didn't know how to ask for help. I know she and Dad love me, but it was disconcerting in a way, to find that I was now "dirty laundry."

Add in the fact that I had never heard of "bisexual," only "gay" and "straight." I attended a suburban high school in the '70s without any sex education classes at all. Any kind of perceived weakness was pounced on and the offender labeled a "faggot," "queer," or "homo"–no matter that the behavior that prompted the bullying may have had *nothing* to do with sexuality.

It was clear to me then that being gay was not a pleasant life. I lacked any information that would have helped me to figure out that I am bisexual. Since I knew I wasn't gay, the only option left to me at the time was that I was straight, so that's what I decided I was. Reinforcement for this decision came a few short years later when AIDS hit the headlines in my early twenties and gay men were dying horribly all around the world. We know now that it wasn't just a gay plague, but that was how the media played it up in the early '80s. I knew I didn't want any part of a disease that would ostracize me from all the people I loved, before it killed me none too pleasantly.

So I spent a lot of time waiting to pass through the "phase" of being attracted to men as well as to women. When I was a teen, I thought, "Well, when I'm in my twenties I will outgrow this." When I was in my twenties, I thought, "Once I start dating, I will outgrow this." When I was dating, I thought, "Once I get married, this will go away," and on and on, through having children, getting the house with the picket fence, and hitting my thirties.

Not that I didn't make at least some attempts to resolve the internal struggle that I was going through. In my early twenties, I went to Provincetown, Massachusetts, on several occasions, with the idea that I would see if anyone would hit on me. Nobody did.

I told myself then that I was not effeminate at all, and all I knew of gay life at the time was that gay men were effeminate. To me, that meant that gay men could sense that I was not gay. And if they weren't sensing that I was gay, then I must not be gay, because they would know if I were. It sounds stupid, but it was easier to project my judgments of myself onto others than to sort it out in my own confused state. There was also internalized homophobia to deal with: being anything but straight made me less than a "real man," in my mind.

I dealt with the same-sex attractions by masturbating to fantasies of sex with men. In my marriage, I still did this and my wife would sometimes catch me and wonder aloud if I could "ever get enough." But this was the only way I knew to release the tension and frustration over not being able to accept this part of myself, and it worked, at least to some degree.

I am a bisexual who "cycles" (that's my word for it, anyway). I will be predominantly attracted to one gender for a varying period of time and then it will "flip." There is always some level of attraction to both, but the "cycling" phenomenon really messed with my head and still does, though to a lesser extent, now that I have more information to help me understand what's going on.

So I was constantly living my life for tomorrow, always expecting things to get better when various life milestones were attained. Except that things never did get better and the feelings never did go away. Every few years beginning in my early twenties, I would run down my emotional batteries and head into depressions that grew increasingly longer and deeper, and included suicidal thoughts. I simply could not reconcile my attraction to men with the man that I thought I was.

I think the catalyst for accepting my own bisexuality and for much of what I have experienced since then has been access to the Internet. In 1998, I had access for the first time in my life and discovered a whole world that I hadn't even suspected existed. I quickly discovered that I wasn't the only married man going through this struggle. I was not a freak, after all. I was not alone.

A wealth of information was now available to me for research into bisexuality and what it meant to be bisexual and married. I found the Boston Bi and Gay Married Men's Group (BMMG), which proved to be a lifeline. I also found the first online chat room I ever participated in at <www.bisexual.org>.

Coming out at the age of forty, I went through hell for eight months. I experienced long periods of insomnia, including several weeks when I didn't sleep at all except for short naps when I got home from work and retreated to my room. Then I would stay up all night and try to stop the tornado in my head–thoughts that whirled around with no two ever dovetailing. I lived in constant fear of what would happen next. When you're that vulnerable and three a.m. rolls around and you still can't sleep, it's not too great a stretch to start imagining different ways to commit suicide. I felt that the pain that coming out would inflict on my wife and children, whom I love more than my life, would be so bad that they would be better off if I were dead, and then they'd never know. I felt sure that I had, and would continue to, disappoint everyone in my life, so why not just get it over with? One more letdown, and then no more from me.

I decided with absolute certainty that I had to either tell my wife and best friend in the whole world that I was bisexual, and put my entire world at risk, or kill myself before anybody ever found out.

I got myself into therapy, which saved me from myself and helped me to come out to my wife. I had been telling her for a couple of months that I had discovered something in therapy that I had to tell her, but that I just wasn't ready to do it yet. Looking back on it, I can see that it was probably torture for her, but I was trying to balance assuaging her fears with my own fear of what would happen when I did tell her.

My wife could not help but try to "guess" what it was I had to tell her, as if it were some kind of surprise present about which I could give her hints. When I finally came out to her that August night, it was during one of her guessing games. She asked, "Is it that you're gay?"

I must have given something away when I said no, maybe a hesitation. Whatever it was, it prompted her to ask: "Are you bisexual, then?"

I was terrified that the person I loved most in the world would reject me. I would have to leave home in disgrace and shame. Worst of all, I was almost insane with worry that she would prevent me from seeing my children.

I just broke down and started crying. I asked her if she hated me. I told her of standing on an overpass over the Turnpike, waiting for a truck big enough to do the job right. I asked her if she wanted me to move out. I asked about all the fearful things that I had imagined happening at this point, including my fears about not being able to see my children.

I should have given her more credit. It was so difficult for me to have this conversation, but I needed to know what she was feeling about me right away.

To my surprise and relief, she was very understanding. She held me and told me it would all be OK, and that we would get through it somehow. Little did we both know then how true those words would turn out to be, though not in the way she intended. Later that month, I got a tattoo of a satyr on my right shoulder to symbolize my acceptance of my nature. She thought it was just my midlife crisis. Maybe it was but, on the whole, I think she would have been happier if I just bought a Corvette like all the other midlife crisis guys.

After seven months of trying to "get through it" constantly, during which she had several angry episodes and said some hurtful things, I understood that she was entitled to her anger. She didn't sign up for this. During this time, her emotional outbursts increased in frequency and intensity. I didn't like where our relationship was headed.

In my BMMG support group meetings, I considered whether some of the stuff that I was so afraid of happening *should* be happening. I decided to move out for a month for a trial separation. My wife thought that I would get it out of my system by having sex with men, discover that I didn't like it, and return to her.

Before I moved out, though, I had to tell my parents, so they could come find me if they missed me. While I was on the subject, I decided to inform them why I was moving out. This wasn't an easy decision, but I had already done the hardest thing, which was to come out to my wife.

I have to give credit that coming out to my parents went well to my gay brother, Michael, who came out to them a few years earlier. They probably thought they had dealt with all *that* business.

At one point while we were still trying to work around the issue of my bisexuality, my wife commented that two gay children out of seven were the odds my mother could have expected. When I replied that I wasn't *gay*, I was *bi*, she retorted, "Fine–one-and-a-half gay children, then!"

When I came out to my parents, they were stunned for a little bit, then Dad asked me if I felt sure about this. I replied that I was. He said that when he was in the army, a guy might like the look of another guy and like him in a platonic way, so that you wanted to hang around with him, but there were other guys who were just trouble . . . then he kind of trailed off, not sure what to say. For a moment, I wondered if another big revelation was forthcoming, but Dad was just rambling, seeking entry into a topic that made him extremely uncomfortable. I told him that my attraction to men was sexual, and he became silent again.

Then Mom picked up the conversation: "You have to help me here. You say you're bisexual–but what about your wife and kids?" I replied that I was pretty sure that they were *not* bisexual, but only time would tell. That earned me a smack from Mom.

With the same twisted sense of humor, Dad asked if I would be one of those guys who hung out at rest areas. The Attorney General of Massachusetts had just directed State Police to stop harassing gay men at rest areas, so his was a topical question. I assured him that I had no desire to hang out at rest stops. He quipped, "Because you *can* now, you know." Great. Cruising tips from my dad. That, of course, earned Dad a smack from Mom.

As it turns out, I didn't have sex with anybody during that trial separation. And when I returned after the month was up, I told her that I thought that we should probably talk about a divorce. What she wanted was to acknowledge that I was bisexual, but to still have a monogamous relationship, so I couldn't have sex with men or anyone else but her. Which was not surprising, given that we had always been monogamous. But I felt I needed to explore this side of me, and I really couldn't do it via a fantasy life. I had tried that for twenty-five years and it didn't work. I had just grown wings and she was telling me that they were very nice wings, but please refrain from flying. As time went on, it also became clear that she would never truly look at me with the same respect that she once had. I told her that, at best, I felt merely tolerated and she agreed with that assessment of her feelings toward me.

We decided that I would stay in the house another year and a half until she finished school and got her teaching certificate. I fixed up our third floor bedroom and bathroom. I stayed up on the third floor for about nine months, working through the tears and feelings of worthlessness and self-hate because I was hurting the last person in the world that I want to hurt. And yet, I had to become the man I knew I am meant to be.

Dwelling on the negative feelings I experienced then brings back memories dangerous and insidious. It's so easy to find the negative in all that transpired, yet I struggle daily to find the positives. And as time goes on, seeing the rightness of my decision gets easier for us both.

Today, she and I discuss our divorce proceedings civilly (well, mostly so). We really do get along well, and not just for the sake of the kids. We were best friends for eighteen years and we couldn't just drop that overnight. It's been a long, tough road that we've gone down together and apart. We've always watched out for each other. I can't see that changing anytime soon.

I moved out almost two years to the day after I first came out to her. During that time, I came out to a gay friend at work, who reacted a bit stunned and overjoyed, and to my gay brother and his partner, while they were in town from San Francisco. My brother received the news soberly, as he liked my wife and was worried about her. His partner decided I needed a "coming-out" dinner and night of gay-bar hopping around Boston, so that's what we did.

It took me the rest of the year to come out to my other five siblings. I came out to them in the order that I felt comfortable with, and every single one of them was supportive, if somewhat confused. They expressed sorrow over the fact that my marriage was ending, as they all love her. I assured them that nothing had to change and that I wanted them to have a good relationship with her. That has happened. Just recently, she went on vacation to San Francisco with friends, she stayed with my brother and his partner, and they all had a wonderful time.

I came out as bisexual to my oldest son a few months ago. I asked him if he was hurt, or if he had questions. He said, "No, we covered that in health class last period." Now, I *know* that there will be a lot more that we will have to explore, but I can't make him tell me what he's feeling. I just have to wait for him to come to me. As for the two youngest, I feel that they are too young yet to understand what it all means.

I am still not out at work, though some people probably suspect. They are certainly confused, as I have dated women since I've been separated. But occasionally, I talk about some aspect of my life that leaves them wondering. I look at it like this: I didn't talk about my sex life when I was with my wife, why would I start now? It's none of their business.

With this contribution, I come out to a wider world. I was out to the members of my online divorce support board as to the reason for our impending divorce. I got some feedback that was negative, but overall I have made some friends who are keepers.

I don't know what will happen next or where I go from here. But I am not living afraid every day of my life anymore, either. I have only vague notions of where I'd like my life to go, but somehow, I know that my family and I will all be OK. I still love my kids and they still love me. My wife and I will always have some kind of relationship and, for my part, I will probably always love her. The rest is a big adventure that will unfold before me. And I kinda like it that way.

# A Candle Burning at Both Ends

*Alfred Corn*

Available online at http://www.haworthpress.com/web/JB
© 2005 by The Haworth Press, Inc. All rights reserved.
doi:10.1300/J159v05n02_10

[Haworth co-indexing entry note]: "A Candle Burning at Both Ends." Corn. Alfred. Co-published simultaneously in *Journal of Bisexuality* (Harrington Park Press, an imprint of The Haworth Press, Inc.) Vol. 5, No.
2/3, 2005, pp. 87-93; and: *Bi Men: Coming Out Every Which Way* (ed: Ron Jackson Suresha, and Pete
Chvany) Harrington Park Press, an imprint of The Haworth Press, Inc., 2005, pp. 87-93. Single or multiple
copies of this article are available for a fee from The Haworth Document Delivery Service
[1-800-HAWORTH, 9:00 a.m. - 5:00 p.m. (EST). E-mail address: docdelivery@haworthpress.com].

**SUMMARY.** A formerly married gay man speaks up for the feminine in both women and men and examines gay men's feelings about bisexual men from the standpoint of gender roles and concerns about male identity. Although eschewing dichotomous existence, he reflects on earlier married life and his love and respect for women, and concludes that the road not taken is still visible from another road and still has its attractions and value. *[Article copies available for a fee from The Haworth Document Delivery Service: 1-800-HAWORTH. E-mail address: <docdelivery@haworthpress.com> Website: <http://www.HaworthPress.com>* © *2005 by The Haworth Press, Inc. All rights reserved.]*

**KEYWORDS.** Bisexuality, bisexual men, gay men, coming out, marriage, poetry, heterosexual women, masculinity

I discover in myself a certain bias against words with the prefix *bi-* and wonder if others do, too. Bipartisan, binational, bilingual, binomial, bipolar, bisexual: I suppose it taps into an ancient taboo against things that are double, cloven, ambivalent. Lives, hooves, feelings should be unitary: anything else is duplicity and dysfunction.

When I was a kid, I soon learned to fear being called a "sissy." Resembling a girl is just about the worst thing a little boy can do. It leads to being ostracized by both sexes. That is exactly what happened to me. I had two older sisters, whom I sometimes tried to imitate, no matter that they didn't enjoy the company of a tag-along little brother when they played with their dolls or staged a Thumbelina tea party using miniature porcelain cups and saucers adorned with pink roses. Meanwhile, any boy noticing me looking with interest at a doll immediately felt it was his duty to beat me up. When he discovered that I didn't know how and didn't *want* to fight back, he wrote me off forever as a "sissy," someone he would never roughhouse with again or even talk to.

Disdain for the so-called feminine male is one of Western civilization's deepest themes, affecting custom, law, and art. In fact, the gay subculture itself for the most part considers its "nelly" members as either figures of fun or contemptible caricatures. Looked at objectively, though, the set of behaviors, speech, and gestural language of the nelly male isn't really feminine, it's something else altogether. Women (except those who for performative reasons or simply in order to be funny strive to adopt the camp pose) don't speak or act the way a nelly gay man does.

Gay men more often than not regard the bisexual male as some sort of threat. He betrays the cause of Gay Liberation by sleeping with women, just as the prejudiced part of society says all men can and should do, exclusively. His existence suggests or proves that the homosexual orientation is a *choice*, and therefore one that could be reversed as soon as the importance of having sex by the book is impressed–by force, if necessary–on the gay person. On the other hand, the bisexual male is, by one method of reckoning, more masculine than the exclusively gay male. And since a gay male wants a male as his partner, the more masculine that partner is, the better. In gay personal ads I have seen hundreds of demands that the applicant be "straight-acting." I have never seen one that said, "I prefer effeminate men." The bisexual male, the married man, and the dad are all erotic fantasy types in contemporary gay life. Actually, many gay men disdain other gay men as partners and feel desire only for heterosexual men, whose straight "purity" apparently remains untainted by the fact of this one encounter. (If it is the first and only, which isn't likely.) But everyone knows that vast numbers of males who consider themselves 100 per cent heterosexual will have sex with a gay man so long their involvement goes no further than insertion, never allowing themselves to be penetrated in turn. Which would in any case spoil the whole thing for the gay man who only desires heterosexuals.

Are these men bisexual? Are men in prison who are penetrated against their will bisexual? I say not. Was Frank O'Hara bisexual the night he and Patsy Southgate got so drunk they climbed into bed and made love? I say not. In my view bisexuality is an identity that is partly innate and partly chosen. A true bisexual person says he is that, and I would like to think that the statement is made with pride instead of embarrassment.

It is possible for a bisexual to choose to be either straight or gay, and the latter choice is the one I've made. Like many gay men I was once married to a woman. Like few gay men, I told the person I married *in advance* I was gay. Gay sex was all I'd known until then and all I thought I wanted. This particular free spirit was so accepting of my being gay, I was deeply touched. The story began in the mid-1960s, before Stonewall, before gay civil rights, and certainly before gay marriage. New York, where I lived, still had anti-sodomy laws and bars were still being raided. I knew few gay men and not one gay couple. I dreaded the life I was apparently going to be forced to lead: secrecy and imposed guilt aren't my thing. There was also the fact that, although casual sex was readily available, I had no luck getting so much as an affair off the ground. I would sit in Village bars listening to tunes with words like "Please send me someone to love," and feel despairingly certain that nobody was ever going to be sent.

Ann, my wife-to-be, told me it was nifty that I was gay, and that her only regret was, well, she'd always thought I was attractive and now she would have to give up the fantasy of sleeping with me.

"Do you necessarily have to give it up?" I asked.

"I don't know, do I?"

"We could try the experiment," I said. We could. We did. We were happy. In a matter of days we were using the L-word. After a period of living together, we went a step further and had a civil wedding ceremony. All told, we shared domicile for five years. During that time, we had sex every week several times. Although I went out by myself to gay bars at least once a month, during those sixty months, I probably had sex with men only about fifteen times. Predominance was all on the side of heterosexuality, not gayness. I enjoyed lovemaking with Ann, and so did she, in the beginning. But at some point it stopped working for her, as I slowly came to perceive. We've never discussed this, so I don't know why. I can theorize that she may have believed I'd eventually become exclusively heterosexual and, when she saw that I would not, began to withdraw psychologically. But she certainly never said so. We were pulled apart by other forces, too, divergent career interests among them.

Meanwhile, Gay Liberation was finally making some headway. I began to feel I'd placed a premature and pointlessly narrow set of restrictions on myself. One of the casual encounters of that time suddenly changed into real passion and with that came the desire to establish a long-term relationship. When I told her about this, Ann and I agreed, after several discussions, to separate. It took a long time for me to get over the divorce. But after a year or so, we found we could be friends and that's what we continue to be. She is happily married and has been a supportive observer of the four long-term relationships I've had with men.

Since that marriage ended, I've never had a relationship or even a one-night stand with a woman. There are many bisexual men who choose to be exclusively straight so as to continue their roles as husbands, fathers, or career professionals. Bisexual men who choose to be exclusively gay are, I'm pretty sure, few. Why did I make that choice? It seemed to me, after the breakup, that my desires for men were stronger. Certainly the desire to love a man and be loved by him was overwhelming, an experience that had until then been out of reach to me. I also concluded that it was better to keep yourself only unto one person. My excursions outside the marriage had undermined what Ann and I had. So I ruled out the possibility of having sex with anyone but the man I loved; which also meant ruling out bisexuality. Besides, at that moment, with the Stonewall battle cry still ringing in our ears, bisexuality was regularly mocked as dishonesty or cowardice. I wanted to be a correct Gay Liberationist, just as I wanted the gay movement to achieve the civil rights we were entitled to. So I never described myself as a bisexual in those years, knowing it would only alienate my gay friends. I wanted to be a good, upstanding member of my community; I had a reputation to maintain. And so my life was exclusively gay.

So what happened to my desire for women? It never went away, but it was sublimated, transformed. I became just as ardent for the Women's Movement and feminism as I was for Gay Liberation. I formed strong and sustaining friendships with women. I listened to them and learned from them. I read their books and studied the art they made. I praised their work in private and in public. It is quite clear to me that our society will remain damaged and incomplete until women achieve full equality of opportunity with men. I know that much of the spiritual wealth of my life traces its origin to women, and I do what I can to justify the time and energy that women have devoted to me.

I find many women heart-stoppingly beautiful to look at. They have lovely, musical voices, delicate gestures, a ready access to emotion, and more often than not a subversive sense of humor. Most women (in my experience) are kind and attentive, especially where the weak and vulnerable are concerned. They have a valuable sense of outrage when injustices are done to the defenseless, a political anger that has been channeled into important changes in law and public policy. Some of my favorite art is about and/or by women. For these reasons, I always feel a lift in spirits when I encounter them.

But I don't ever plan to have a sexual or romantic relationship with a woman again. Even if she were herself bisexual, it wouldn't feel right to make that commitment. I was once the cause of pain to a woman and I do not want to be that again. And I know it would cause me pain, too, if the woman I loved sometimes slept with another woman. I would understand her decision perfectly but still be left with the peculiar anguish of feeling helpless–no matter what efforts I made to provide her with the feminine physical attributes that she desired.

I know that there are bisexuals, men and women, who are perfectly comfortable having simultaneous love relationships with both sexes. If I had begun leading a bisexual life earlier, among other bisexuals, I might feel just as comfortable as they seem to do. But my experience is what it is, I'm conditioned as I am, and I don't find a motive strong enough to drive me through the long process of reconditioning it would require. I admire the proud bisexual, and I plan to remain a gay man exclusively, glad that so many women have wanted to be my friend.

Meanwhile, being gay is a blast, and no gay man ever needs to justify to *me* why he only wants to sleep with men and not women. Women are not a sexual requirement or a badge of social honor; they deserve to have only those who deeply desire them. I didn't regard myself as superior to straight or to gay people when I was bisexual, and nothing about my category strikes me as inferior to anyone else's now that I am exclusively gay.

I have never written about these things and never even spoken about most of this in private. It was time I did, and I'm glad I have.

# Minus the Sexual

*Moss Stern*

Available online at http://www.haworthpress.com/web/JB
© 2005 by The Haworth Press, Inc. All rights reserved.
doi:10.1300/J159v05n02_11

[Haworth co-indexing entry note]: "Minus the Sexual." Stern, Moss. Co-published simultaneously in *Journal of Bisexuality* (Harrington Park Press, an imprint of The Haworth Press, Inc.) Vol. 5, No. 2/3, 2005, pp. 95-99; and: *Bi Men: Coming Out Every Which Way* (ed: Ron Jackson Suresha, and Pete Chvany) Harrington Park Press, an imprint of The Haworth Press, Inc., 2005, pp. 95-99. Single or multiple copies of this article are available for a fee from The Haworth Document Delivery Service [1-800-HAWORTH, 9:00 a.m. - 5:00 p.m. (EST). E-mail address: docdelivery@haworthpress.com].

**SUMMARY.** A busy, prominent Philadelphia polyamorous married male activist, musician, and father challenges misconceptions and stereotypes of bisexual male promiscuity. Who has time for it? *[Article copies available for a fee from The Haworth Document Delivery Service: 1-800-HAWORTH. E-mail address: <docdelivery@haworthpress.com> Website: <http://www. HaworthPress.com> © 2005 by The Haworth Press, Inc. All rights reserved.]*

**KEYWORDS.** Bisexuality, bisexual men, coming out, marriage, children of bisexual men, monogamy, polyamory, open relationships, GLBTIQA political advocacy

Bi men are sluts, right? We're promiscuous, insatiable hedonists. We're notorious for sneaking out on our wives to have anonymous sex in the bushes. We'll do it anywhere, anytime, with anyone.

Oh, yeah! That just describes me to a tee!

Meet Moss Stern, one of the most visible bi men in Philadelphia. I've been a highly active volunteer in our local bi group, BiUnity, for more than twelve years. I've been interviewed about bisexuality on TV, on the radio, and in straight and queer newspapers, and I've spoken to a variety of student groups about bi issues. I'm also a singer/songwriter who has recorded and performed a lot of tunes with explicit bi content.

That, however, doesn't mean my sex life is the stuff of fable and song. As a matter of fact, these days sex is usually one of the last things on my mind.

I'm the forty-two-year-old father of a terrible-two-year-old. My wife and I are both polyamorous as well as bi, but between the pressures of work and the responsibilities of parenthood, I not only hardly have time to *have* sex . . . I don't even *think* about sex much lately. My thoughts are more focused on work, finances, politics, music, and my family.

So, as Carrie Bradshaw might say on *Sex and the City*, what does it mean to be bi–when you're minus the sexual?

For one thing, I still live outside the Land of the Straight–where men are men, women are women, people of the opposite sex are desired but despised, everyone is presumed heterosexual, and monogamous marriage and parenthood are considered each individual's manifest destiny.

I also live outside the Home of the Gay–where men are men, women are women, people of the opposite sex are considered unappealing, and relationships between men and women are strictly friendly, political, or professional, but never sexual.

In both monosexual camps, men and women are understood to be worlds apart. But they're not—not to me. Certainly, there are some differences, but I believe we're much more alike than we are different. Maybe that's why I can love, and lust after, men and women alike.

I don't even really believe in masculinity or femininity as our culture defines them. I may like to drive aggressively, but I also enjoy reading *Cosmopolitan*. I may love action movies, but I can also express my feelings. I may usually wear pants, but I also own more dresses than my wife does. (Someday I ought to buy her a purse so she can stop borrowing mine!) To me, gender attributes are like a restaurant menu: I'll take some from this column and some from that one, as the mood strikes me. I find it sad that most people in the world are so imprisoned by gender . . . and very often victimized because of it, particularly if they are women.

As a middle-class white guy, I lead a relatively privileged and comfortable existence. Compared to most minorities I have nothing to complain about. Just the same, I have definitely experienced my share of heckling and harassment for being bi. I've been called names and threatened. I've been dissed by straight people for being a fag (true) and a probable AIDS carrier (untrue). I've also been sneered at by gay men and lesbians for claiming a sexual identity that they regarded as a fraud and a copout.

These experiences have affected me, ironically, in an important and quite positive way: I believe I'm more conscious of prejudice and social injustice. At least, I can remember the fairly callous person I was in my teens, before I came out; I used to laugh at my classmates' homophobic, racist, or sexist jokes with hardly a twinge of conscience. Coming to recognize that I myself belonged to a despised minority, and discovering firsthand what it feels like to be harassed on those grounds, helped me begin to challenge both my own and others' prejudice.

Becoming active in the queer community led to various forms of activism, participating in protests, speaking to the media, and volunteering with local organizations. Over time, my opposition to intolerance and oppression has progressively grown, and my bisexuality has played an important role in this process.

However, before I misrepresent myself as a relentless, indefatigable freedom fighter, I have to admit that I sometimes censor my self-expression with regard to my bisexuality and polyamory to avoid confrontation, just as most other people do. Not every battle feels worth fighting. Not every conversational opening seems safe.

That's why it's so wonderful to be around other people whose perspectives on gender and sexuality are like my own. Among bi folks, I can say what I think and feel without worrying whether they'll get it. And, I find it wonderfully refreshing and stimulating to hear other people express similar sentiments. I've been involved with BiUnity for so many years because it's a little corner of the world where people actually make sense to me. I want to preserve that corner so that I, and others like me, can visit and relax in it now and then.

I get a similar experience of "family" at the annual BiCamp weekend organized by Biversity Boston. Scores of bisexuals descend on a campground in western Massachusetts—socializing, skinny dipping, spending the night in tents (not necessarily their own), and otherwise enjoying each other's company. Camping and being outdoors is nice, but the feeling of community is what really inspires my wife and me to make the eight-hour trip every summer—and, for the past two years, to bring our son along.

I admit that I sometimes wish there were a little more sex in my life. Maybe, on some level, I've even internalized the stereotype that a bi man ought to be a super slut, and therefore I feel like a failure as a bisexual. Or maybe it's just my libido issuing little complaints from whatever corner of my psyche it's hiding in. Either way, I hope that one day, I will actually find the time, energy, and inspiration to be more sexual again.

But fundamentally, it doesn't really matter. I'm still bi, with or without the sexual. Wherever I go, whatever (or whomever) I'm doing (or not doing), my bisexual nature and perspectives will always be a big part of who I am.

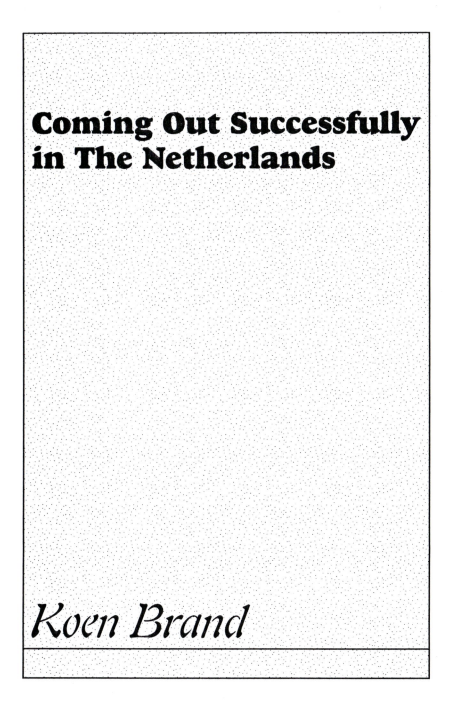

# Coming Out Successfully in The Netherlands

*Koen Brand*

Available online at http://www.haworthpress.com/web/JB
doi:10.1300/J159v05n02_12

[Haworth co-indexing entry note]: "Coming Out Successfully in The Netherlands." Brand, Koen. Co-published simultaneously in *Journal of Bisexuality* (Harrington Park Press, an imprint of The Haworth Press, Inc.) Vol. 5, No. 2/3, 2005, pp. 101-109; and: *Bi Men: Coming Out Every Which Way* (ed: Ron Jackson Suresha, and Pete Chvany) Harrington Park Press, an imprint of The Haworth Press, Inc., 2005, pp. 101-109. Single or multiple copies of this article are available for a fee from The Haworth Document Delivery Service [1-800-HAWORTH, 9:00 a.m. - 5:00 p.m. (EST). E-mail address: docdelivery@haworthpress.com].

**SUMMARY.** A Dutch married man and father of two recounts coming out with his wife's encouragement and support, and his exploration of sexuality with another openly bi married man. Reprint from *Journal of Bisexuality,* vol. 1, 2/3, 2001, Haworth Press. *[Article copies available for a fee from The Haworth Document Delivery Service: 1-800-HAWORTH. E-mail address: <docdelivery@haworthpress.com> Website: <http://www.HaworthPress.com> © 2001 by The Haworth Press, Inc. All rights reserved.]*

**KEYWORDS.** Bisexuality, bisexual men, The Netherlands, marriage, children of bisexual men, heterosexual women, Internet discussion groups, coming out

My name is Koen Brand, and I live in The Netherlands, a country that you might know of in various ways: a country of polders and dikes, tulips and windmills, or as the country of Amsterdam with its red-light district, or even the country where soft drugs can be legally bought for one's own use.

In February 1999, I acknowledged to myself that I am bisexual.

I wish to offer in this article a glimpse of the way I handled my coming out, a coming out that till now seems to have gone quite smoothly as compared to other people's stories that I have heard and read about. First, I want to relate something about the country I live in and then describe my family and myself. Lastly, I will describe something about the process my family and I have gone through since February 1999.

The Netherlands, or Holland as it is quite often incorrectly called abroad, is a small country. The longest distance from North to South is about two hundred miles and from East to West some 120 miles. The lowest point of the country is seven meters below sea level, and the highest point is only 322 meters above it. It is densely populated, as we have over sixteen million inhabitants in this small area.

We are known for our windmills, some of which are still in existence. A lot of them were used in the past for our struggle against the water. They pumped the water out from the low parts of our country. When you fly to The Netherlands and land at Schiphol Airport, you actually land several meters below sea level and our famous dikes keep the water out.

The Dutch people have a way of dealing with drugs that is frowned upon in quite a number of other countries. The main feature of that drug policy is that we do not look upon drug use as a criminal problem but rather as a health problem. From that it follows that soft drugs like can-nabis are quasi legal. However, we do deal harshly with hard drug deal-ers–but with the hard drug addicts themselves, we treat them from a medical perspective.

The Netherlands is a constitutional monarchy: a democratic country that, since 1898, has been reigned over by queens. It is also a country that has a lot of openness about sex. I already mentioned Amsterdam's red-light district, but that's not what I mean here. Our children are usu-ally well informed on the facts of life. Condoms are easily found. In ad-dition to a low level of abortions, it seems we have the lowest number of teenage pregnancies in the world. We are also very liberal with respect to people of diverse sexual orientations.

I was born in Amsterdam in July 1953. Right now I am forty-seven years old. I am the oldest of four children. Both sisters divorced this past year. My brother is still in his first marriage. My mother died in 1998 at the age of seventy, and my father is seventy-five years old. His hair has just grown back after chemotherapy. Because my father changed careers a number of times, I lived in several parts of the coun-try. But for over thirty years now, I have lived in the southeastern part near Helmond.

My wife Annette is one month younger than I am. Fortunately, I am the older one because she had said she would not have married someone younger than herself. We were married young, at the age of twenty-one. In November 1999, we celebrated our twenty-fifth anniversary.

I have been working in Information Technology since 1974. I entered that field in the traditional way: learning your profession as an appren-tice while you work. But some years ago I decided that I also wanted a formal degree, so I started studying again and successfully completed it in July 1999.

In 1998, my wife decided that she also wanted to go back to school. She started a four-year program to be a sign language interpreter.

We have two sons, Roel, twenty-three years old, and Jaap, twenty-two. They are both studying in universities (Information Technology and Mechanical Engineering). Roel has been together with his girl-friend, Inge, since April 1998. Jaap has had a girlfriend since May 1999. We live in a small community with less than six thousand people. The nearest larger town is called Helmond and has seventy thousand inhabitants.

My attraction to other men surfaced in my late twenties. I had one ex-perience seventeen years ago where my wife and I had a sexual relation-ship with another couple. In this experience, I found out how it feels to sexually touch another man. When I was singing in a choir over ten years ago, there was a gay man with whom I flirted. This continued for some months until I left the choir (not because of the gay man but because of a new director whose style of music I didn't like). From time to time, these feelings of attraction to men surfaced, but I never acted on them. However, my wife and I openly discussed these feelings.

In February 1999, I stayed home from work because I thought I had caught the flu. When I didn't get better, I went to my doctor for some tests. These turned out negative. Nothing was wrong with me physically. My wife raised the possibility that my illness might be psychological in nature and specifically caused by my struggles with my bisexuality. She is a doctor's assistant and some weeks before had told me a story about a patient of hers who had come there for a medical check-up. During the tests, he started talking to her about the fact that he had been severely ill for a long time until he accepted his own gayness. After that time, his health had remarkably improved.

After a lot of talking with my wonderful wife, I came to terms with my own bisexuality and decided that I had to integrate that side of myself into our lives. Another reason that I love my wife dearly is for her bringing up this subject, a subject that has brought a lot of uncertainty about the future into her own life. But from the start, I was absolutely certain that our bond was and is strong enough to integrate this change into our lives.

In retrospect, it seems that the main difficulty regarding my bisexuality was the fact that I did not want to acknowledge it to myself. One reason may have been out of fear of not being accepted. I think that is also why I was always better able to communicate with women than with men. I subconsciously held my distance from men because I was afraid that I might be attracted to them and that it might develop into something I did not want: a sexual liaison.

From the time I acknowledged to myself that I am bisexual, many developments have occurred. The first thing I did was to begin getting information on bisexuality. Initially, the Internet was my main source of information. When you type in bisexuality on one of the search engines, you end up with many Websites. Of course, part of it is X-rated, but you also find a number of serious sites on the subject, such as www.bisexual. org and www.binetusa.org from the USA and www.bi.org from the UK. I also joined the Straight Spouse Mailing List, which I discovered on the Straight Spouse Network pages. On this mailing list, you can find posts from both straight spouses and their gay, lesbian, or bisexual partners. Every day one can read posts from a number of compassionate men and women. Their posts really helped me develop my own way of dealing with my bisexuality.

You learn about people who are still fresh from the shock of their spouses' coming out. There are those people that have dealt successfully with their spouse's gay or bi side either by integrating it into their lives or separating in a positive way. The comparison between the process after revealing this to the spouse and a roller coaster comes up regularly. I even began to contribute my two cents' worth to the discussions. The sharing of ideas and experiences on this list has really helped me, and I gleaned many things to think about–thoughts and ideas that entered into the talks with my wife about the way our relationship was developing. One thing became very clear from the mailing list: each of us has to find his/her own way of dealing with his/her bi side.

Besides the Internet, I also tried other ways of becoming informed about bisexuality. One evening I visited a gay group in Helmond that was discussing the subject of bisexuality. Because it is difficult to find other bisexuals, I visited two different bisexual support groups and joined one of them. The first group, called GoBi, meets in Nijmegen. The one I joined has a name that is untranslatable into English (Bi-kring De Samenkomst, which means Bi-circle The Gathering) and is situated in Tilburg. Both support groups are situated about 40 miles from where I live. The support group meets once a month. It is a mixed group of bisexual men and women that talk about subjects related to bisexuality. We also meet socially once a month in a gay disco. In addition, I also became a member of the Dutch National Network for Bisexuality.

The relationship with my wife has essentially not changed. We are still a loving, caring couple that can and do show affection to each other. Sometimes when we walk together, we talk about what people might think when they see us. Do they see us as a couple married for almost twenty-six years? Or do they think that we are newlyweds? What has changed is the fact that I am consciously expanding my bi side. This also means that we are dealing with integrating my bisexuality into our life together. We keep working on our relationship and communicate more in order to be able to absorb these changes.

One major change has been that I have developed my bisexual side to the point that, with the consent of our respective wives, I have begun dating another bisexual married man. I met Henk at the bisexual support group that I talked about earlier. The four of us met and talked several evenings before my friend and I spent our first evening together. At the request of his wife, we both were tested for HIV before we had our first date.

The relationship with Henk is not just a sexual one. We also share time being intimate without being sexual. In talking together, we get to know our present feelings as well as our past history. We enjoy just spending time together, whether it is going on a hike, visiting a bar, or sometimes we share an evening eating, drinking, and talking about the road we are traveling together with our wives.

In the past year, I have also made a number of new friends in the bisexual community. I volunteered to be on the committee that will organize the first European Bisexual Conference in June 2001.

After I admitted to myself that I am bisexual and at the same time came out to my wife, we then decided to tell our family and friends. I must admit that the first few times I told the story it was quite stressful to me. This was especially true when I told my sons and their girlfriends. Some of the people we told voiced their concern about our marriage. However, since we both showed that we love each other and intended to go on together, none of them reacted in a negative way. The last ones we told were my parents-in-law. We both feared they would worry unnecessarily about our marriage and us. We decided to tell them at last, because we did not feel easy with the lack of openness about situations when I was not home because of activities for the bisexual organizations. My parents-in-law still accept me for who I am, but my father-in-law remarked, "I could have expected this from anybody but you." It seems my pedestal has been lowered a bit.

I did not get negative reactions when I came out at work. I told a female colleague in the early stage of my coming-out, and she was very understanding and supportive. Over the past year, I have also told my story to my direct superior as well as a number of other colleagues: all reacted in a most positive way. In my opinion, the reactions I got are characteristic for the country I live in, a country where the majority of the people are tolerant of sexual and ethnic minorities. I realize that in other countries I could have met with very different and probably negative reactions.

Essentially, the major aspects of my sex life have not changed. My wife and I still enjoy each other very much sexually. It is true that we have had our periods where one or the other did not need sex as often as the other. However, on the whole, we feel that over the years, as we got to know each other better and better, our sex life has become deeper, more varied, and more enjoyable. Probably, those periods of less interest will reoccur in future, but we have learned that they will also alternate with honeymoon-like periods of intense interest and satisfaction.

Besides the sex life I have with my wife, I have now developed a sexual relationship with another man. This is new to Henk as well as to me. I have found it very different to be with a man: how we touch each other, how it feels to be touched, and having sexual intercourse with another man. It is exciting to travel into unknown territory (pun intended). I have learned to make love to my wife over the past twenty-five years. With my boyfriend, we are just starting to get to know each other's likes and dislikes and the way we react to each other. But it satisfies something in me that I have never been able to satisfy before. It is different from sex with my wife, and it feels complementary.

One of the fantasies I have had for a long time is that the three of us are in bed at the same time and both my wife and my boyfriend pamper me. I do not think this will happen in the near future. I think my wife might want to try it, but his wife has a lot more difficulties with integrating his bisexuality.

It is always difficult to predict what the future has in store for you. When you look around in nature, you find diversity wherever you look. Every niche in ecology is taken. Personally, I feel that every man, woman, and couple has to find out for him/her/themselves the best way to live. What element of the diversity they fit in: whether it is single, married, living together with a partner of either sex, living together with a partner of both sexes, monogamous, polyamorous, etc. Of course, when you are in a committed relationship, you have to take other(s) into consideration. An open relationship might be the superior alternative to serial monogamy. In heterosexual relationships, monogamy is likely not as common as some people want to believe. The specter of diversity also exists there. As long as we can integrate that diversity into our lives, I would say, "So what?" An evolutionary rule over the millions of years of our past has been "Adapt or become extinct." That's about adaptation on a macro level, but on my own personal micro level, adaptation has also been essential to me. Adapting to moving to another town, to a new working environment, to being married, to being a father, to bisexuality.

My wife and I realize this rule of nature and are indeed able to adapt. From the time I admitted to myself that I am indeed a bisexual man, I have been able to draw from an enormous reservoir of energy from which we draw while working on our relationship and I am working on discovering myself.

We confidently look to the future where we continue with our ability to adapt and expect still to be together in another twenty-five years.

## NOTE

Excerpt taken from the *Journal of Bisexuality*, 1(4), 2001, The Haworth Press, Inc.

# Miniature Golf

*Marc Anders*

Available online at http://www.haworthpress.com/web/JB
© 2005 by The Haworth Press, Inc. All rights reserved.
doi:10.1300/J159v05n02_13

[Haworth co-indexing entry note]: "Miniature Golf." Anders, Marc. Co-published simultaneously in *Journal of Bisexuality* (Harrington Park Press, an imprint of The Haworth Press, Inc.) Vol. 5, No. 2/3, 2005, pp. 111-117; and: *Bi Men: Coming Out Every Which Way* (ed: Ron Jackson Suresha, and Pete Chvany) Harrington Park Press, an imprint of The Haworth Press, Inc., 2005, pp. 111-117. Single or multiple copies of this article are available for a fee from The Haworth Document Delivery Service [1-800-HAWORTH, 9:00 a.m. - 5:00 p.m. (EST). E-mail address: docdelivery@haworthpress.com].

**SUMMARY.** Married father of teenage boy reveals the complex and ambivalent process of coming out to his son, and the boy's genial acceptance, during an evening of miniature golf. After an admission from the boy's mom about her husband's male lover, an awkward effort to explain his sexuality becomes a significant turning point for the father and son. *[Article copies available for a fee from The Haworth Document Delivery Service: 1-800-HAWORTH. E-mail address: <docdelivery@haworthpress. com> Website: <http://www.HaworthPress.com>* © 2005 by The Haworth Press, Inc. All rights reserved.]

**KEYWORDS.** Bisexuality, bisexual men, Palm Springs, coming out, marriage, children of bisexual men, recreational activity, parenting

It's dusk, that phase of a desert day when shadows fall across the San Jacinto Mountains hovering over Palm Springs like a protective mother. The day's heat is fading with the sun, bringing people outside again.

Megan and I have come from Santa Barbara for the weekend with Sean. Unlike my recent visits alone, this is a "family" trip; relaxed time for bonding and play without the pressures of home.

Sean and I are at the second hole of Camelot Park, the miniature golf course he loves. At twelve, he's already proficient at golf on real courses and I know he wants me to learn to play. So periodically I try to overcome my own disinterest in golf–a particularly boring non-sport, if you ask me–by playing miniature golf with him.

"I'm ahead by three strokes already, Dad." As always, Sean keeps score. I can trust him not to cheat, because he can easily beat me. I don't even have to *try* to lose, as I do when we play chess. He is as natural an athlete as I am not.

"Well, don't count your horses yet, Sean." I run my hand through his hair as he tries to duck. "I'll come into my own around the sixth hole."

"Yeah, right." He gives me the wink he's been practicing. If he were older, I imagine he'd be rolling his eyes as well. His eyelashes are unusually long, one of the physical traits I know he gets from me. I've been telling him recently how a wink–at the right time–is magic to women, and I've been giving him winking lessons every few days. Teaching Sean to flirt is easier for me than playing catch with him. It's a small gift he'll value when he's older.

We pass the Dutch windmill with the unrealistic rock bottom and the wood fringe of tulip cutouts. Jeezus, who thinks these things up?

The fourth hole is better, a fake haunted house that overlooks a large lake with empty bumper boats. This ominous structure, full of potential secrets, reminds me of the talk I need to have with my son.

"All right, Dad," he says. "I'm seven strokes ahead now. You'd better get serious."

He's grinning ear to ear, revealing the metal bands the orthodontist fitted him with three weeks ago; there goes another five grand, I'd thought at the time, but Sean's worth it. A cooling breeze lifts his brown hair slightly and I'm aware that he–still cherubic in many ways–is one of life's undeserved gifts. And I know I've put this talk off long enough.

"Sean, I notice there aren't many people around"–I'm still trying to think of a reason to postpone this talk, but I can't seem to–"and I need to talk to you about something."

"What's that, Dad?" He picks up the ball, turns toward me, flashing braces again. "You're up, ace."

"Well, ah"–fuck, I'm really stalling. I have to just get it out–"do you ever wonder about my sexuality, Sean? I mean . . . what it really is?"

He looks pensive, not taken aback so much as questioning the randomness of what I just asked. I take my next swing; the ball goes completely outside the low concrete barriers. Sean laughs, shrugging his shoulders as if to show he's not surprised by my poor performance. Or, perhaps it's his body-language response to my unexpected inquiry.

Megan's been wanting me to have this talk with him for two months–ever since that early Sunday morning call from Eric about changing my training appointment. We were reading the paper in bed and Sean came in and plopped himself in between us, as he often does. The phone rang and I answered it.

"Who was that?" Sean asked.

"It was Eric."

"Ah . . . Eric," Sean said, pausing. "Your lover?"

Megan and I glanced at each other, astonished. What did this mean?

Later, when we talked about it, we both realized that our house was more open than most. We could be watching television together and if there was some particularly hunky guy on the screen, I might point it out to Megan–without regard to Sean's presence. I think I probably did it on purpose, but without premeditation.

"He knows you're bisexual, Marc," Megan said. "He's seen the signs his whole life. You're very open around people you're close to–and now he's probably asking for verification; that's what the question about Eric meant."

We didn't want to be the kind of parents who teach secrecy and denial as the basis for family life; we wanted something healthier.

"You remember what Jackie Kennedy said?" I asked.

"No," Megan replied. "I don't. What did your idol say?"

"Well, seriously–you *know* she was a sensible person."

"Okay, sure. What did she say?"

"She said 'If you bungle raising your children, I don't think whatever else you do well matters very much.' I agree with that."

So, both of us having come from bungled childhoods, we agreed I should have this talk with Sean–especially since he was nearing puberty. I knew this would be more difficult than the "birds and bees" talk we had two years ago while hiking a Santa Barbara mountain trail.

"Dad, why don't you take that shot over? We won't count it."

"Okay," I say, retrieving the ball. I set up for another swing. Can this generous boy tell how nervous I am?

"You're a good sport," I say. "Now, what about my question?"

"I think you're probably bisexual, Daddy."

Sean has lapsed back to "Daddy" as he makes this emotional hole-in-one. Now what do I say?

"Yeah, son, you're right. I'm bisexual. I have been for a while."

I take my second-chance swing, wondering how this revelation may affect our close relationship. Surely, I reassure myself, this is better than hiding from my son such an important part of myself. I need to be authentic. How would Sean react if he found out years from now? I try to convince myself that he would feel utterly betrayed.

This time, the ball stops inches from its hole. One more stroke brings it home.

"Good job, Dad. You're getting better. But I'm still eight strokes ahead." He seems unfazed by what I've told him, but I'm not sure.

We move on to the eighth hole, a Russian St. Basil's with blue, gold, and pink turrets. The sun's gone now, and the overhead lights have blinked on, along with multicolored neon throughout the park. A gurgling fountain helps mute the laughter from four players following us too closely.

"Sean, don't you want to ask me any questions?"

"No, Dad."

"I thought you might have questions."

"Not really."

He walks ahead of me, toward the ornate Japanese pagoda at the tenth hole. I'm remembering how, when Megan was pregnant, we'd both thought she was carrying a girl and I knew, with certainty, how much easier that would be on me. Conditioned by our Puritan culture, a son would ignore the bisexual aspect and go right to the gay–homo, queer, fag–stereotype. A daughter would not find the revelation as threatening as a son; a daughter would love you just as much.

Of course, my married fuck-buddy Tim doesn't feel this way. He will keep his secret from his family no matter what; he'd be appalled at my disclosure and my lack of discretion.

I wait for Sean's turn. He approaches this pretend course as seriously as if he were playing Pebble Beach. The pagoda, three tiers high, looks like a wedding cake trimmed in black icing. Just behind Camelot Park is the Desert Palms Inn, a neighboring gay hotel. Its background, with multiple rainbow flags flying high, appears to merge with the red and teal walls of the pagoda.

I haven't been to the Desert Palms in years, not since before Sean was conceived. One night when Megan and I were in Palm Springs, I had fallen asleep watching a late movie, then suddenly was jarred awake by a commercial. I was groggy, ready to climb into bed with Megan. And yet, there was that powerful hormonal urge that comes infrequently, most often when I know sex-hunting men are nearby. The maxim, "Always yield to temptation because it may not pass your way again," was a rule I lived by.

I dressed quickly in blue jeans, tank top, and boots. Then, while walking across the hallway of our condo, the noise of my boots scuffing the tile floor awakened our dog, Topper. One bark was enough. I returned to the bedroom, leaned over the bed, and petted Topper's head, reassuring her. I let her lick my face. Topper contentedly curled up against Megan, who turned over drowsily.

"Is everything all right, darling?"

"Yes," I said. "I'm just going out for a while."

"Okay, darling," she replied. "Please be careful." Megan understood I was going out to play and all that mattered to her was my safety.

As I pushed the button to open the garage door, I realized that the danger itself that Megan warned me against was the force that drove this nascent desire. Nevertheless, in a moment I was on my way to seek a satisfaction that my wife could not provide: the thrill of getting off in the bushes behind the motel with other anonymous men.

I'd never been to the Desert Palms as a guest. Rather, I understood that I and other married men like me had become one of the extra attractions that kept this infamous place fully booked.

I'm not going to share *this* information with my son.

Sean and I cross a bridge toward the last hole, stopping at its crest to look at a waterfall with water so deeply blue it reminds me of Ty-D-Bowl toilet cleaner water.

"Son, surely you want to ask me something about what I've told you."

Still, he refrains from asking questions that I'm sure he must have. While taking four separate putts to get the ball into the last hole, I offer him the heterosexual pedigrees of his two grandfathers, attempting to preclude any self-doubt that could arise because of his father's deviance.

But he has no questions; he's tallying the score, perhaps more comfortable with his priorities than mine.

"Sorry Dad," he says. "You lost again. Eleven strokes."

Have I lost, I wonder? I want to pat Sean's head, comforting him as I do the dog, letting him lick my face so I know he's really okay.

"Really, son. You know you can ask me anything."

Sean comes close and takes the little putter from me. He looks up.

"Relax, Dad. It's cool."

# Long Journey Ahead

*Jason Large*

[Haworth co-indexing entry note]: "Long Journey Ahead." Large, Jason. Co-published simultaneously in *Journal of Bisexuality* (Harrington Park Press, an imprint of The Haworth Press, Inc.) Vol. 5, No. 2/3, 2005, pp. 119-126; and: *Bi Men: Coming Out Every Which Way* (ed: Ron Jackson Suresha, and Pete Chvany) Harrington Park Press, an imprint of The Haworth Press, Inc., 2005, pp. 119-126. Single or multiple copies of this article are available for a fee from The Haworth Document Delivery Service [1-800-HAWORTH, 9:00 a.m. - 5:00 p.m. (EST). E-mail address: docdelivery@haworthpress.com].

**SUMMARY.** A closeted married dad of two reveals his confusion over tentative early sexual explorations with men, describes his recent contact online and in person with local gay and bisexual male community, and anticipates liberation from the self-imposed limitations of married life. *[Article copies available for a fee from The Haworth Document Delivery Service: 1-800-HAWORTH. E-mail address: <docdelivery@haworthpress.com> Website: <http://www.HaworthPress.com> © 2005 by The Haworth Press, Inc. All rights reserved.]*

**KEYWORDS.** Bisexuality, bisexual men, coming out, marriage, children of bisexual men, sexual exploration, Bear subculture, heterosexual women, parenting

I grew up in semi-rural Rhode Island on the only farm in my school district. After attending grade school there, I did some college coursework nearby in Providence. I met my wife-to-be in ninth grade, graduated, and married her at age twenty-two. My daughter is eighteen and my son is sixteen. I really used to enjoy family life, especially when my grandparents were here. We always had a big family get-together. I loved it.

During puberty, I used to play around with the neighbor kids and other guys. I remember one boy and his brother clearly. While playing around outside, we would pee together, then compare to see who had the biggest tool, then touch and stroke each other, getting hard and shooting together. I remember how much fun it was playing around sexually with them.

Deep down, I have always been attracted to the same sex, but deathly afraid to show it. Even before my more recent explorations, I'd jack off fantasizing about men. Masturbated a lot. Growing up I used to sneak into my father's room to swipe his porno mags showing guys fucking girls. Looking at their cocks, I thought about how nice their big cocks were. Oddly, once I found a newspaper article my father had that talked about father-and-son sex, which got me incredibly hot. My father never did anything to me, but I sure was attracted to the idea.

I was definitely attracted to girls then, too. I met my girlfriend and back then loved to explore with her as well. I stopped playing with guys after I started high school. I looked damned good back then: 130 pounds, thirty-inch waist, hairy all over, clean cut.

Back then, if you weren't married or seeing someone, you were considered queer—you were strange, a freak. Still, I never thought gay or bi men were bad people. I have always had an open mind; even now, if my wife makes a negative comment about a gay guy, I just roll my eyes like she is clueless.

It's funny that, after we finished school, my girlfriend almost left me because I didn't want to ask her to marry me. I didn't want to make a commitment and buy a house. My sister asked me who else I would see. Since I couldn't come up with a reason not to, I asked my girlfriend to marry me. What a dumb reason, I think now.

While my wife was pregnant with our first child, I worked in inventory. I counted merchandise throughout the store and in the storerooms. It was at work that I had my first grown-up male-to-male sex.

The boss's son, who helped during the summer, came down one day while I was checking stock as usual. I was bent over some boxes, counting, and he rubbed his crotch right up against my ass. I took it as funny haha the first time, but then another day he did it with his pants down, rubbing his cock against me. I was shocked but I found the experience exciting. I saw that his cock was thick like mine, but angled slightly right.

He asked if I had ever wanted to suck cock and I lied, "No, not really." He said that if we went upstairs to the warehouse, he would suck me. Well, with my wife nine months pregnant and me horny as hell, what do you think I did? If he was willing, I had no problem letting him suck me. I loved that he found me sexually appealing and loved sucking my hard cock. I stroked his cock until he blew his huge load all over the floor. He sucked me again and soon took my sperm and loved it. It happened only once more before he left to return to school.

It was nice to find someone that was interested in me, but I was too scared to come on to anyone like that. Then my first child was born. After we brought my daughter home from the hospital, she fell asleep on my chest at home. I have loved my kids every moment since. From then until a few years ago, I concentrated on my wife and family life.

For years, I viewed my life to be that of a family man with a wife and kids. At first, my wife and I did have an attraction. I honestly loved her and thought she was sweet and sexy. At work, the men would talk about women who came in the store and stuff, but I was married and had what I needed—although she never gave me head.

I started feeling dissatisfied with our sexual relations three years ago. I've always been the one to try a new position or do something different. Neither my wife nor I seemed particularly interested in satisfying the other person. We were always night-sex people, very seldom having sex in the morning, and never during the day.

I feared my attraction to men and managed to put it mostly out of mind. Well, not fully. There were times, for instance, I would watch the lawn man from my second-story bathroom window and jack off, thinking about how big his cock might be. Eventually I realized that I was always thinking of guys when I jacked off; fantasizing about men gave me so much pleasure.

Five years ago, I bought a mail-order dildo and stashed it in the attic at a place I manage, where I also kept some male porno. When I wasn't busy with other things, I would go over there to look at the magazine pictures of hard cocks. I wanted to know what it felt like, having one of those men put his big cock in my hole and fuck me hard. I enjoyed playing with my ass with a dildo several times. I would get naked and stroke my cock and use the dildo and cum. I was amazed at the pleasure I gave myself this way.

One morning on my day off, I was lying in the sun nude, tanning. I was horny as fuck and started to wave my cock around, getting all sweaty and hot and now hard as a rock. I got out my dildo–a red flexi rubber six inches long and three-quarters-inch diameter, with no balls. I hadn't played like this with the dildo in about a year. The dildo went in real easy. Too easy. The red dong slipped deeper inside me and I couldn't get it out.

I was dying. I had my fingers up there fishing for it and could feel it but couldn't get it out. The last thing I wanted was to go to the hospital emergency room and have them remove this thing from my ass. I would have just as well left it up there indefinitely. I drove home with the dildo up my ass in a crazed panic. Luckily for me, no one was home. I crammed some Vaseline up my ass, sat on the toilet, and pushed and pushed until it popped out. I wanted to never play with my ass any more, and never again did I use that thing.

I didn't do much for a while after that incident. I just beat off to mail-order gay porn. I never had another sexual encounter with a guy until recently. I've thought about it plenty, but I'm too chicken to cruise, and I don't go to bars. Besides, I have no time: I manage a property and work sometimes fifty hours a week.

About four years ago, I started cruising the Internet. Having access to the Internet helped me find some fun gay porn. I printed some hot male pics from the Net and stashed them in my briefcase.

Shortly after, my father died and a bad situation at work arose, both of which together dramatically blew my world apart. My father's death hit me especially hard. I never felt close to my dad, although otherwise it was a close Italian family. Maybe my job as a "paper pusher" didn't interest him at all. I guess it's a guy thing: my two brothers work on trucks. A few years ago, while in therapy, I told my mother that I couldn't remember my father ever saying directly to me, "I love you." How sad I felt, knowing that I would never hear those words from him.

Then a hellish situation at work developed: my boss, who was married to my best friend, a woman I had known for years, left the company to start his own business. When I examined the accounting books later, I found out that he had been stealing from the company.

I felt my wife wasn't emotionally supportive enough during those difficult times. She considered the situation at work to be my own private, personal problem. I asked her to help, to come to a therapist with me just once, and she refused. I ended up seeing a shrink by myself. Therapy helped me deal with my father's death, and I got through the thing with my friend and boss, but I never discussed my sexuality issues with the therapist. I didn't like that he mistakenly thought I was having sexual feelings for my boss's wife, but in reality she was just a close platonic friend, whom I felt I had betrayed by telling her that I discovered her husband's crookedness.

My family no longer felt like a home. I felt like a broken man.

Not long after that, I was cruising the Net and found a regional e-list for gay and bisexual fathers. I joined, hoping to make friends, although it seemed that most of them lived too far away from my home. Right after I joined, the list moderator added "& Bi" to the official group name. I later joked to him that he did that just for me.

At first, I was just curious about who was on the list. I started e-mailing and chatting with other closeted married bi men. Six months later, I decided to meet a married guy with three kids from an online men's sex site. All he wanted to do was to suck me off. He liked my cock, and I enjoyed getting a good blowjob from him.

I talked online to a man named Gary about his situation and mine. Gary lives with his wife and she knows that he fools around with guys. Gary offered support and information. He assured me that there are many guys in my situation, and invited me to an informal dinner with the dads and the local "bear club," whatever that was.

Also though the e-list, I contacted Dwayne, a massage therapist, and asked if he would see me professionally. I was looking not only for relaxation but also for support. Knowing Dwayne was bi or gay attracted me. I talked to him twice before making an appointment for a massage. I had gone to a masseur years before and remembered that the physical contact would give me a hard-on, and wondered if the same thing would happen with Dwayne.

The second time I went to Dwayne, I couldn't help myself. Dwayne's a male-partnered, formerly married dad. He's a warm, strong, sexy, confident, masculine older guy and I was incredibly turned on. He just touched my inner left thigh and I got completely hard. My dong just flopped all around like a fat antenna. I laughed in embarrassment but my erection stood full and proud, betraying my hormones. "Just a normal reaction from the massage," Dwayne chuckled while remaining professional, but I could tell he enjoyed the look of my thick manhood.

Until that moment, lying there with a man's hands on me, it had been hard to admit that I might be gay or bisexual. Now it was literally hard, if not impossible, for me to ignore.

Dwayne hosted me at my first gay and bi dads and bears dinner. Not knowing what to say or do, I was shy and mostly hovered around Dwayne as if I were his younger brother. I totally loved the dinner conversation and felt really at home with the group. Meeting other men who were just like me was definitely affirming. I felt I was making gay and bi friends in the same position of being married with kids, now finding themselves looking for a same-sex partner or friend. These guys seemed like normal men–some looked just totally hot! I have a soft heart and a hard cock for dark-haired masculine guys.

One bi guy, Ryan, eyed me from down the table that evening. Ryan took interest in my coming-out process as a bi dad, and I enjoyed his attention, advice, and willingness to introduce me around. One night, I arranged to meet him at his place. I wasn't sure if he wanted sex, and I was scared but curious. I hoped I would enjoy bottoming. Turns out, I sure did! Afterward we even enjoyed a shower together–getting clean after was way cool. But Ryan has a partner of his own and is as busy with work as I am.

The last time my wife and I had sex, nearly a month ago, she started on top but I ended up doing her cunt from the back like a dog because I can fuck her good enough from the back. I didn't want to look at her, just to have sex with her. I don't have any desire to have sex with my wife, but I know she will want to fuck again soon. She talks me into sex most of the time nowadays. When I make this important step in my life and leave my wife, I'm almost sure that women will not be a part of my sex life again. Whatever that makes me, I am fine with that.

If my wife found out that I have been having sex with men, she would immediately tell me to leave. I know it will be very hard but I am letting go of the fear of what divorce may bring. I hope that eventually she will support my choice.

My social and sexual contacts with some bi and gay men who are very safe assures me that it is possible to explore what I want in a bi or gay life, which is enjoying sex and love with a man. But right now, I'm too scared to show my feelings.

So here I remain, completely closeted at home and work, out to nobody except for a few bi and gay men. I know deep down how I want to live the rest of my life. I have a positive image of the future with my family, but finding a partner seems much less certain. If I could find Mr. Wonderful, I would marry him.

I've lived twenty years of my life as straight. I'm just a normal, hard-working guy, knowing deep down that I want something very different now. I must make a real *change* that will make me happy but, knowing that I will hurt three people so close to me, I want to do myself in.

So many things run through your head when you have a difficult situation. I know that the inevitable truth will hurt. I have also contemplated suddenly moving to another state. Then I could really start on my wish list: lose twenty pounds, get a tattoo or two, and get my nipples pierced (ouch!). So much fun is totally appealing.

But I know that neither suicide nor running away is the solution to my problems. I hope that I can get enough support for what I am trying to accomplish. One year from now, I see myself continuing to work my ass off. I would hope by then I have my own place someplace, with close friends. Working close with my wife to keep the kids' heads on straight. That will never change.

Five years from now, I can see myself in a house of my own, enjoying life with some special man, but also sharing fun times with friends and enjoying the company of men who are in the same type of relationship. And having my kids visit me any time of day.

My daughter will adapt to the coming changes, I'm sure. She is older and we seem to have a good relationship. My son, on the other hand, is at a tender age with a somewhat serious girlfriend. I'm not at all sure how he will react. I want to be their father figure and I hope that never changes, no matter the marital status of my wife and me. I'm sure they know the terms gay and bisexual and know the difference between them. I'm not sure if they actually know bisexual or gay kids, or other kids with a bi or gay parent.

I know it will be the greatest challenge of my life. I have been digging deep in my heart to discover where I want my life to go but, no matter what happens, no matter how my family and others accept me, no doubt it's going to be a long journey ahead.

# Why Not Stay Married?

J. "Mac" McRee Elrod

[Haworth co-indexing entry note]: "Why Not Stay Married?" Elrod, J. "Mac" McRee. Co-published simultaneously in *Journal of Bisexuality* (Harrington Park Press, an imprint of The Haworth Press, Inc.) Vol. 5, No. 2/3,
2005, pp. 127-130; and: *Bi Men: Coming Out Every Which Way* (ed: Ron Jackson Suresha, and Pete Chvany)
Harrington Park Press, an imprint of The Haworth Press, Inc., 2005, pp. 127-130. Single or multiple copies of
this article are available for a fee from The Haworth Document Delivery Service [1-800-HAWORTH, 9:00
a.m. - 5:00 p.m. (EST). E-mail address: docdelivery@haworthpress.com].

**SUMMARY.** A Canadian gay dad, married 51 years, answers the question: Why would a man not stay married simply because he chooses to take a male lover? The author examines the shared values (social justice, family, art, mutual respect and love) that enable "mixed" relationships to thrive and prosper. *[Article copies available for a fee from The Haworth Document Delivery Service: 1-800-HAWORTH. E-mail address: <docdelivery@ haworthpress.com> Website: <http://www.HaworthPress.com> © 2005 by The Haworth Press, Inc. All rights reserved.]*

**KEYWORDS.** Bisexuality, bisexual men, gay men, Canada, marriage, children of bisexual men, heterosexual women, open relationships, coming out

Conventional wisdom holds that once a man discovers his sexual interest in other men, whether exclusively or in addition to interest in women, his heterosexual marriage must end. Some men, however, find enough to value in their marriage to wish to continue that relationship, while also having male-to-male relations, whether with or without the knowledge of their wife.

A sexual relationship with their spouse may not be the thing they most value in their marriage. If that relationship is to continue as a sexual one, it is vital that great care be taken not to introduce a sexually transmitted disease to one's wife.

The first thing to be understood, I think, is that regardless of the importance of the sexual urge, the personal relationship of any two persons, whether same or opposite sex, should consist of much more than sexual attraction. Sexual orientation is often as much an affectional and intellectual preference as one of lust. The relationship with another person is affected by that person's gender in ways other than just its sexual expression. Many men, even the most exclusively heterosexual, find rewards in male bonding through sports and other exclusively male activities, as do women with women.

Why would a married gay man continue his married life and a relationship with a male lover, it is sometimes asked. Having celebrated my fifty-first wedding anniversary recently, and having had male lovers for thirty-two years, and for the past five years with a currently twenty-six-year-old man, I'll try to answer.

Perhaps part of the answer for me is that I married not so much out of romantic love (a Hollywood fiction, we both assumed at the time), but deep admiration of the wit and wisdom of a woman whom I met at a student conference. As a Southern boy, I had never met a woman my own age who looked me in the eye and challenged me in political and theological discussion. It was also at that conference that I met the first Black person of whom this was true. The realization of the basic equality of genders and races was a major turning point in my life.

After five days together I proposed, and was accepted a few weeks later. Marriage followed in nine months, both having moved to the same city from our respective states for university and graduate school.

Five years living together in another culture (Korea), political and social values evolving in tandem (civil rights and peace movements), and above all shared parenthood helped cement our bond. That bond held even when we both discovered (she first with a person of another race, and I later with a person of the same gender) that romantic love was not a fiction. It perhaps helped that her experience was with a close friend of mine, and mine was with a close friend of hers. In fact, we each introduced the person who was to become our first romantic love to the other.

The marriage continues because initially there was the shared parenting (in our case five and later six pre- and early school age children at the time we each fell in love for the first time); shared social, political, and religious interests and experiences (in our case work in another culture, the Southern civil rights and peace movements, and migration to another country and denomination); shared cultural interests (in our case reading and discussing the same books, and attending the same performances); and the selection, building, and decoration of homes (currently a three-floor log house on a mountain overlooking the ocean).

Above all, there is now a half century of companionship.

Why then the lover? The joy provided by a same gender lover, for some of us, is quite different and fulfilling in a way nothing else can be. Most of my ex-partners remain my closest friends. My first lover of more than thirty years ago visits monthly, recently for three days. Often I have dinner with a former lover here, in Vancouver, or San Francisco.

I do not resent that my former lovers in time wish to move on to a partner who can be totally their own (in two cases a woman). The time with each was a delight.

It is good to see my reality occasionally reflected in motion pictures and writing. The motion picture *His Secret Life*, and the biographical compilation *The Other Side of the Closet*, can help the heterosexual partner feel less alone in their experience.

In the best of all possible worlds, one should be completely honest with both partners. It is best when each can know and respect the other.

# When the Head Is Separated from the Body

[Haworth co-indexing entry note]: "When the Head Is Separated from the Body." Gallardo, Michael. Co-published simultaneously in *Journal of Bisexuality* (Harrington Park Press, an imprint of The Haworth Press, Inc.)
Vol. 5, No. 2/3, 2005, pp. 131-138; and: *Bi Men: Coming Out Every Which Way* (ed: Ron Jackson Suresha,
and Pete Chvany) Harrington Park Press, an imprint of The Haworth Press, Inc., 2005, pp. 131-138. Single or
multiple copies of this article are available for a fee from The Haworth Document Delivery Service
[1-800-HAWORTH, 9:00 a.m. - 5:00 p.m. (EST). E-mail address: docdelivery@haworthpress.com].

**SUMMARY.** A married Latino bi man living in the Southwest U.S. discusses the importance of family in Latino culture, the ongoing process of negotiating life with his wife, and the fulfillment of his personal sexuality and family and community roles. *[Article copies available for a fee from The Haworth Document Delivery Service: 1-800-HAWORTH. E-mail address: <docdelivery@haworthpress.com> Website: <http://www.HaworthPress.com> © 2005 by The Haworth Press, Inc. All rights reserved.]*

**KEYWORDS.** Bisexuality, bisexual men, Southwestern U.S., marriage, children of bisexual men, Latino/Hispanic macho culture, multiculturalism, coming out, heterosexual women, open relationships

"What's it like to be married and bisexual?" asked Paul, a young, good-looking Latino broker in his thirties, who said he was also bisexual, as he sat next to me at a gay bar one recent February night. "Are you really married? How does it work? What does your wife think about it?" Many questions: some have answers, others are works-in-progress. As a married, bisexual Latino man in my forties, my life is focused on finding the right balance. Not just any balance but the balance that works for me in *my* life: balancing the straight with the gay; being true to myself and being real to the gay and straight communities, the Latino community, my family, my friends, my sexual partners. Not everyone accepts me or understands, or wants to understand.

How can a man married to a woman desire to be with other men? Why would a wife allow it? Many would agree that marriage is a union between two people. Others have asked me, "Why don't you just get a divorce?" I feel it is possible for two people to get to a place in their lives where each will let the other be who, and what, they are. Space is provided, space is taken, and then it becomes an ongoing effort to find a balance, delineated by the two people in the relationship and other people as they enter and exit in relationships with me.

It is not like I married my wife and later came out to her. I came out to her before we were married. Maybe she did not know the depth of my M2M (man-to-man) love, but she knew that there had been others before her and that they had been men. People have often asked me why I married her if I had experienced M2M love. Was I satisfied with men alone? I wasn't. I came of age during the 1970s in a conservative Catholic city. I was involved socially in the gay scene that centered in bars and parties but I never really felt totally comfortable in this environment. I was never really successful in long term and supportive relationships with men. Maybe it was my internalized homophobia? Maybe it was low self-esteem? Maybe I could not figure out how to live as a gay man in a predominantly straight society in a conservative city? Whatever it was, I feel differently now. I'm older and I now live in a place that I feel is more supportive of GLBT people.

In 1985, I met my wife. We fell in love and got married. I desired to build a life with her. My motivation for getting married was the same as any human being, whether straight or gay. I desired safety, acceptance, comfort, company, and to love and be loved. Now, as we enter our seventeenth year of marriage, it is difficult to imagine a life without her. I value her companionship, our history together, our common interests, and our efforts to make a difference with our lives and in our occupations. We come from similar family backgrounds from the same area. We are both professionals–no children. We live with the hope that the other will be there for us in the future.

How does she feel about my bisexuality? She doesn't like it but she knows bisexuality is a part of me. She has mixed emotions about it. Sometimes it gets crazy, and the drama surrounds me. I meet someone new and the pasture looks greener on the other side, and we come to the verge of breaking up and going our separate ways, but something always happens and keeps us together. She says it's God. I say it is fate. We both know what each would be losing if we threw it all away. And yes, there are many difficult trials, moments of fear and uncertainty about our future together, and periods of separation, but our love for each other endures.

Bisexuality is more common in our society than commonly believed. Only you don't hear about us, much less read about this aspect of male culture. In Latino culture, this aspect of men's lives is not talked about: *no se habla, no existe* ("if it's not mentioned, it doesn't exist"). Latino cultures in the States are still very homophobic. It is difficult to break through the traditional wall of silence in Latino cultures because our *familias* and *cultura* shun anything queer, let alone bisexuality or, worst of all, being openly married and bisexual. Although our sexual lives are private, some Latinas, especially lesbians, have spoken out and continue to break boundaries in sharing personal stories. It is time for Latino bisexual men, especially bi married men, to follow suit.

When Latino bisexual men are judged by their promiscuity, the culture applies the term of *el mañoso*: a sexually voracious person, a player who cannot satisfy his libido with just one woman or just one man, but must have sex with as many people as possible to satisfy his desires. Although most married bisexual men are not *mañosos*, our wives may initially think so. We simply seek a balance missing in our lives.

Exacerbating the problem is evidence that Latino MSMs (Men who have Sex with Men, who do not identify as gay or bisexual) comprise one of the fastest-growing segments of people living with HIV and AIDS. In Latino communities, there is still much homophobia, oppression, and denial.

As a tail-end member of the Baby Boomer generation, I'm also sandwiched between varying levels of acceptance of my bisexuality. Younger liberals in their twenties don't blink an eye. Liberals in their thirties are sometimes more accepting and have more friends who run the spectrum from gay to straight. Straight liberals in their forties are often uncomfortable with it. People fifty and older may not even know how to talk about this lifestyle. They themselves came of age when bisexuality and homosexuality were not discussed in public.

In our birth families, sometimes coming out takes one's whole life. One decides who needs to know what, and discloses information when the time is right. In my life, I try to walk the talk. I've talked to my family about myself. Some of my siblings don't accept me, some of them don't understand it but, perhaps because we are now older, we can start to talk about it. On a recent visit back home, I sat having a few tallboys with my younger brother in his truck in the driveway of my mother's house and we talked about my "duality." He didn't put me down or joke about it, as machos often do, but accepted me for who I am–his brother.

In traditional Mexican-American families, *la familia* is the sacred foundation of living; anything less is seen as profane. Add the notion of *pecado* (sin) to the mix. The final ingredient for men is shame. If you sleep with men, you're weak and sinful, you're not your parents' son, you are not even a man. If you're straight, even if you have an operation to castrate yourself, you will still be a man inside to them. In Chicano families, when you are not straight, you are other–relegated to live in between the shadows of your straight brothers and sisters. Pray that no one finds out what you are because your *familia* will suffer because of your weakness. What will people say? So one must do the obvious–move away, start a new life elsewhere, take up with people like yourself, and attempt to tear off your head from your body. Mesoamerican goddesses not only affected women, like the dismembered *Coyolxauhqui*, the moon–we, as bisexual men, have also become Coyolxauhqui's children.

Your body can roam the ends of the earth but the head stays at home, in the memories of your family, who see you occasionally and sometimes only on holidays. Sometimes once a year; sometimes never, until someone close to you dies and your body is called back to fill the emptiness of your absence. But by then, you are so different that you cannot imagine what it would be like to return home or how to fill that emptiness. Emotionally, as a bisexual married man, I sometimes feel a deep sadness because I cannot find true bliss. Maybe as bisexuals, we are in a constant state of searching for an inner peace that we may not have.

"But the head must never be separated from the body!" a therapist once told me. "Some men have a horizontal split, the head from the heart and the gut from the organs. Your head tells you to do one thing and your heart and gut agree or oppose what you think, but the head must never be separated. Some men think with their organs, don't listen to their head, and override their hearts. Others are all gut. Others never get out of their heads."

Purists in the gay and lesbian community take issue with bisexuals, including married men. We are asked to make up our minds as if we could decide to be either straight or gay, but we are both. The gay and lesbian community is not monolithic; there is a wide spectrum of individuals in the gay community. How people enter into relationships with other people, whether same-gender or not, varies greatly depending on values, background, upbringing, needs, and gender roles. Both gay men and lesbians have open relationships: if it's consensual and both parties agree, fine. The spectrum of relationships in the gay and straight communities is wide, although sometimes folks forget the people who live in the middle.

Communication with other bisexual married men is important, if you are lucky enough to find them. In an effort to dialogue with other men in the same circumstance, I joined several bisexual married men's electronic mailings lists, notably Closed Loop, which is promoted as a bisexual alternative to marital monogamy. One site states, "A closed-loop relationship consists of two married men who are involved in a relationship, not just a sexual encounter. The two men are committed to their marriages and have an exclusive relationship with each other. Their relationship is separate from the married relationship they have with their wives." The goal is to provide marital stability and for both men to bond with each other.

A closed-loop relationship usually consists of two married men who live close to each other, who don't cheat on their wives with other women, and who don't fool around with other guys. It is promoted as an actual friendship between the guys, not just a sexual liaison. The bond between the guys is separate from the married relationship they have with their wives. The goal is to provide marital stability and to bond with another man. The idea is that there are *only* two guys. It is important to note that there are also electronic lists out there for wives who are living with bisexual husbands and who need support for their situations. I have personally never had a Closed Loop relationship.

Men join the Closed Loop list to locate prospective male partners like themselves. These lists are important because these men deal with tremendous pain and the inner conflict of being married yet desiring male partners. Some live with the constant fear of being discovered. If they come out, they meet with so much disdain that it dramatically changes their lives.

Communicating with bisexual married men is one thing, meeting them or meeting gay men who accept the fact that you're married is another. Initially in my relationships with men, I was met with mixed feelings because I was married, so now when I meet a man that I am interested in, I tell him that I'm married–upfront. Some men have told me that they don't want to be second best or the third wheel in a relationship. Others are intrigued. Others say that they, too, are bisexual, but are only dating men at the moment. For as many men who have rejected me for being married to a woman and desiring men, many more have embraced me for my honesty about who I am. I have communicated with several bisexual married men online and have met only one other Latino married bisexual man in person. One world where I have found other married bisexual men is in the Bear culture.

I work in an environment that accepts and supports gay and lesbian persons, although bisexual married persons are clearly in the minority. I know of one other man in my workplace who is married and bisexual, but we haven't formed a club. I think others in my workplace struggle with the idea that someone can be married and bisexual. I, too, struggle to balance my identities because society is predominantly straight. I've worked on various projects and have been a member of efforts that promote the contributions and lives of GLBT persons, yet I feel I often have to walk the fine line between heterosexuality, homosexuality and bisexuality. There are sometimes questions about my personal life that I don't answer. I do not talk about my duality in public for fear of being labeled, judged, or becoming a target of a morality lesson. In our families, the topic is often silenced but it is always there. Our gay families sometimes may not understand it or accept it. In some of our communities, it is difficult to even speak about it.

It is time to break the silence, to explore and articulate the complexity of being married and bisexual while desiring same-sex relationships, a conflict far more prevalent than people think or discuss. Thousands of men nationwide, whether living in urban or rural areas or somewhere in between, whether or not their wives or families know, share my experience and my feelings toward other men. And if the thousands of wives of these men knew about the uncertainty and suspicions that my wife has experienced, perhaps some would choose to make it work. Although the Internet has played a large part in demonstrating to bisexual married men that they are not alone, still countless others are isolated and living lives with inner turmoil.

Life is short. I think positive bisexual self-acceptance is part of the process of maturity. Central to the process of making peace with the reality of being married and bisexual is maintaining a healthy, self-nurturing internal dialogue that maintains self-love and care, yet another part involves coming out to those you love and care for. It is not about being careless and taking risks but being responsible: to yourself and your needs, to your spouse's needs, and to the needs of the other people in your life. Our pursuit of finding the right balance to sustain a complex life works as long as everyone involved is willing to make it to work. Paramount for bisexual married men is for us to be true to ourselves, in the hope of finding partners who will let us become the men we are destined to be.

# Part Three: Interacting in Evolving GLBTQ Communities

## Life Among the Monosexuals

Available online at http://www.haworthpress.com/web/JB
© 2005 by The Haworth Press, Inc. All rights reserved.
doi:10.1300/J159v05n02_17

[Haworth co-indexing entry note]: "Life Among the Monosexuals." Califia, Patrick. Co-published simultaneously in *Journal of Bisexuality* (Harrington Park Press, an imprint of The Haworth Press, Inc.) Vol. 5, No. 2/3, 2005, pp. 139-148; and: *Bi Men: Coming Out Every Which Way* (ed: Ron Jackson Suresha, and Pete Chvany) Harrington Park Press, an imprint of The Haworth Press, Inc., 2005, pp. 139-148. Single or multiple copies of this article are available for a fee from The Haworth Document Delivery Service [1-800-HAWORTH, 9:00 a.m. - 5:00 p.m. (EST). E-mail address: docdelivery@haworthpress.com].

**SUMMARY.** A bisexual kinky ex-Mormon transman (female-to-male transgender) challenges biphobia in lesbian and gay communities, and examines his own quest for a gender and sexual identity true to his nature. *[Article copies available for a fee from The Haworth Document Delivery Service: 1-800-HAWORTH. E-mail address: <docdelivery@haworthpress.com> Website: <http://www.HaworthPress.com>* © *2005 by The Haworth Press, Inc. All rights reserved.]*

**KEYWORDS.** Bisexuality, bisexual men, transgendered men, lesbians, biphobia, Mormons, leather and fetish sex, GLBTIQA community advocacy

The first time I publicly identified myself as a bisexual, I was sweet seventeen and speaking to a drunken crowd of college boys and girls (including many of my dorm mates) they hoped to fondle or fuck. I was already controversial for my heavy use of pot and acid and my regular attendance at the University of Utah's feminist consciousness-raising group. Having been indoctrinated as a Mormon missionary, I was a stiff little prude with a martinet's attitude about telling the truth, no matter how unwelcome. I was also probably high on grass.

Everybody laughed, and one of the boys said, "I don't think you know what you're talking about." Then the subject turned to what record to play next. The guy who got up to change the album also turned the lights down, and after that I can only remember sitting alone, with everyone else paired up on the floor, cradled by large bright pillows, while I wondered how to find my way home in the dark and on foot. It was clear that the girl who had given me a ride was not leaving this apartment until early next morning.

I did know what I was talking about. Theoretically. I'd lost my virginity a few months ago by riding up and down State Street with my cousin until we found a car with two cute guys in it. We followed them, they pulled over, we went to their apartment, and I went into the bedroom to ball with the tall muscular handsome one while my cousin fended off his ugly duckling friend. It was brief and unpleasant, that first intercourse, but I tolerated it like a little soldier. I wanted it out of the way ("it" being virginity). When the man above me pulled out, he said with some alarm, "Are you okay?" I was pale from pain and, though it took me years to figure this one out, shock at being so nakedly confronted with my female genitals.

I explained this was my first time, and he was dumbfounded. "Geez, if I'd known, I would have . . . uh, I think your friend is calling you." I sympathized with his lack of alternative scenarios. I was five-foot two and weighed 135 pounds, I was 36-26-36, and had long, honey-brown hair, but I thought I was fat and ugly. I knew I was not the kind of person anybody would fall in love with, and nobody would ever linger sensuously over my body in bed. It was my mission in life to fall in love with people who were perfect and immortalize them in poetry, every line of which would make me hate myself more and more.

I'd fallen in love with a woman on my dormitory floor who was on the swimming team. She was butch, muscular, and extroverted. But she'd been sent to school out of state by her parents, who wanted to get her away from a small-town scandal about her affair with her female gym teacher. Malta (not her real name) said she wanted to marry a rancher and have seven sons. She fucked a lot of guys, and she was flattered but bewildered about what to do about a shy intellectual with a dirty mouth who was trying to get her stoned and slipping poems under her door every night.

Eventually I had a nervous breakdown about my unrequited love for a woman and ungratifying sex with men. I dropped out of school. I moved into Salt Lake City's brand new women's center (a two-bedroom apartment rented by a dyke couple who had founded the campus C-R group) and tried to figure out what kind of social life somebody like me was going to have. It rapidly became clear that if you said you were bisexual, straight people thought that meant you were a slut who would try anything, including the occasional adventure with girls. Whereas lesbians thought it meant you were a closet case who needed to face facts and come out as gay. And nobody would talk to you or sleep with you because it was 1971 and who knew from bisexual? Gay rights barely existed, let alone any notion of pansexuality or polyamory or sex and romance that was not based on gender essentialism.

I got swept up into lesbian separatism, which thankfully didn't last more than a few years. I still regret some of the unfeeling things I did during that time to men who wanted to be my friends and to straight women who wanted to sleep with me. (Okay, some of them just wanted to be my friends, too.) It was the sexual freedom movement that changed my life and got my bedroom humming, if only with the oscillations of a vibrator. A volunteer stint at San Francisco Sex Information's hotline cleared enough weeds and sludge out of my psyche to allow a more friendly policy toward my sadomasochistic fantasies. A few years later, I had founded the first lesbian-feminist S/M support group, Samois.

During the years that followed, the Feminist Sex Wars raged in terms that were so bitter, it is hard to convey the damage that was done to younger sex radicals. Those of us who opposed censorship and supported sexual diversity were maligned, excluded, demonized, and kicked out of women's bars and bookstores and events. We were harassed when we did speaking engagements and trashed when we published articles. We were blacklisted–outed at our jobs and in academia. If a feminist bookstore was gutsy enough to carry some of my books, they might be taken off the shelves and literally burned. Keeping my sanity in the midst of so much chaos took every particle of my energy.

Having sex with gay men was a wonderful respite, my only "down time" in a life that was stressful whether I was debating Women Against Pornography or trying to handle the antagonism and drama that kept flaming up in Samois. A bisexual lover, Cynthia Slater, had introduced me to her kinky men friends who were into bondage, whipping, and fisting. I was mesmerized the first time I fisted a six-foot tall, butch, bearded leather fag. This was not the kind of sex I'd had with men before. I was not being penetrated. I was the stud, and he was the slut. I felt safe and very tender toward him. It was his own safety I feared for, and I resolved to train myself to provide a good long ride without any abrasion. I met a bisexual older guy at work who was straight-appearing but fag-identified. He thought my shaved head and smart mouth were fetching. We became fuck buddies, a relationship that lasted, on and off, for nearly twenty years.

But I was still calling myself a lesbian. A lesbian who did S/M with gay men. The term "queer" was not yet in vogue, but I was essentially trying to explain to people that this was queer sex. The leatherdykes didn't like it. But my bottom women lovers weren't fucking me, and my steady male trick was. And perhaps because he was 98% gay, and I switched off and fucked him 50/50, it didn't bother me. I loved it. For the first time in my life, I could relax and enjoy the sensuality of a night of lovemaking that might or might not turn kinky. My vagina was a musky gateway to a good time, not a leaky inconvenience lurking behind a dildo harness and bitching about not getting off.

The shitstorm about my failure to be a 100% woman-born-woman-fucking-women-born-women-only erupted when I published an article in the *Advocate* about lesbian S/M and said that if I had a choice between being marooned on a desert island with a vanilla lesbian or a leatherman, I'd pick the boy. The day after this article appeared, I got a phone call from Barbara Grier, who was preparing my lesbian sex manual, *Sapphistry*, for publication. "We do not publish books by bisexual women," she said. "*They* have their own resources." Actually, there was no place I knew of where bi women could publish their books, but the scorn in her voice made it clear that she didn't give a damn.

So I caved. Once again I told Barbara Grier the old lie. I was not bisexual. I was a dyke who sometimes did S/M sex with men. Gay men. She let my book see print, but forever after our relationship was poisoned. I never again had a conversation with her that was free of antagonism.

I don't know if a younger generation that grew up with terms like *genderqueer* and hates identity politics can understand how painful it was for lesbians then. There were no antidiscrimination laws. Harassment on the street was an everyday occurrence, and so was bashing. We worked shit jobs if we could get any job at all. Just by being who we were, loving who we wanted, and looking the way we felt most comfortable and attractive, we made ourselves hated. And so the lesbian community was defensive. The obvious enemy was men. Men were the ones who shouted names at us, beat us up, fired us, and sometimes stole our girlfriends. We somehow ignored all the hostility we got from homophobic straight women. With the rise of First Wave Feminism, we weren't sex perverts anymore, we were revolutionaries. And women who slept with men as well as women were traitors. Double agents. Not to be trusted.

This happened about the same time that I experienced a peak in my gender dysphoria. There were too many times when sexual fantasy, cross-dressing, and role-playing left me angry at the reality of my anatomy. It was hard to put my putative maleness away once the scene was over. It seemed to me that most of my lovers wanted a partner who would do all of the things that men did, without actually getting the credit for being one. I was unhappy with the way my genitals looked and functioned. No amount of consciousness-raising about eradicating misogyny was going to fix this. I was cunt-friendly as long as the pussy in question belonged to somebody else.

One of my earliest memories is telling my highly amused parents and grandparents that I should have gotten an electric train for my birthday because I was a boy. "If you're a boy, where's your penis?" my grandmother asked. Always quick on my feet, I retorted, "My father took it off with a clothespin." Saying I was a boy got old fast, and I learned to keep this conviction to myself. But once I saw a pair of leather shorts that also allowed me to strap on a dildo, I was intent on constructing all kinds of male personae and enacting sexual fantasies about them. I was torn up about who I really was–a blonde in a black dress who wore really high heels and wielded a merciless cane? A butch dyke in motorcycle leather with a perpetually greasy fist? Or a gay man cheated by biology and circumstance?

When I checked out "having a sex change" in the late 1970s, the process seemed cumbersome and isolating. I didn't want some doctors at a Stanford medical clinic having the right to decide if I could become a man or not. The photos of surgery that I saw made me cringe. I knew only one female-to-male transsexual (he had given a talk at a health conference) but he was far away and I had been way too freaked out to ask him any personal questions. I couldn't handle what was going on in the lesbian-feminist community and start taking hormones as well. I knew that everything I'd ever done or said politically would be swept away if I identified publicly as a guy.

So I put my gender heartbreak aside for two more decades, and kept pursuing the strategy of living as a different kind of woman who did everything that men could do. At age forty-five, I faced the fact that it wasn't enough. I still felt like I should be a man. I should have a beard and balls and a dick. I should have a deep voice and muscles. Being a woman was fabulous. I was grateful for my years of experience in Women's Country. But I didn't want to die without finding out if testosterone would ease my daily struggle to stay in my own body. Lesbian sex had become onerous for me. I disassociated nearly every time a female partner tried to give me pleasure. And I kept hearing that my sexual style was too male–I was too promiscuous, too intent on fucking, too focused on orgasms, too good at playing the fantasy bad cop, incestuous daddy, pedophile priest, or horny teenage football player.

I made the decision to come out as bisexual at almost the same time. If I was going to discredit myself as a spokeswoman for polymorphously perverse dykedom, why not go all the way and use the term that had fit me best when I was seventeen? Right now I'm at a point where I ask myself, as a guy with a beard, a flat chest, and a pussy, who can I have sex with and *not* be bisexual in someone's eyes?

Usually when I come out there's a certain amount of exhilaration. But this didn't happen for me when I started asking interviewers and friends to use the label "bisexual." In fact, it was almost depressing or anticlimactic. How come? Perhaps because I missed the first, exciting phase of bisexual activism. I hadn't been part of founding the bisexual groups or publications that claimed a portion of the queer agenda for their own. It was hard to give up the elitism and exclusivity of being a leatherdyke. I had internalized the scorn that radical lesbians felt for bisexual women when I first came out. Poor things, they hadn't connected all the dots yet and become freedom fighters on behalf of women. They were trapped in the patriarchy by their love of cock. And what an odious thing to be attached to! (Now hand me my purple, rotating dolphin dildo.)

I was saturated with hatred of men and anybody who loved or wanted them. A part of me still wanted to divide up the world into the good people who might be able to lead my species into an egalitarian utopia (women) and the bad people who hung on to their privilege and did everything they could to prevent social change that would make women's lives better. It's deflating to have to think about the ways that women conspire to keep themselves oppressed, and uncomfortable to accommodate the seriousness of male feminists. It's this mindset that made it difficult for me to connect with bisexual community or politics, and that continues to be difficult for me.

A few years ago, I was asked to give a keynote address at a conference for Affirmation, a support group for gay Mormons. I was shocked to see how many of the men had brought their wives. I wasn't sure how many of them were still sleeping with their wives, or what these women thought about taking their husbands to an event where guys were obviously hooking up with one another. Some of these guys were keeping their marriages intact for religious or sentimental reasons. Yet there was no dialogue at the conference about bisexuality.

Then one of them asked if "the lady" I had brought to Las Vegas was my wife. He was puzzled and disapproving when I told him that she was my girlfriend, and I'd brought my boyfriend as well. The woman I was currently having sex with had come along with my ex-boyfriend and our son. But I hadn't kept her around as a cover for secret gay activity. I knew that some of the Mormon men in Affirmation would allow themselves to drink or party with one another, but not have sex. That wasn't my policy at all. Paradigms were clashing all over the place. I suppose the primary difference between me and them was that once I acknowledged my same-sex desires, I no longer wanted any affiliation with the religion that had been forced on me in my childhood. Mormonism will always be part of my personal history, but it's an unwelcome presence. I don't see any chance for reform within that church. You can't muster the strength to update a religion that you no longer believe. If an angel came down from heaven and gave Joseph Smith some golden plates to translate, I'm a three-legged emu.

The attempt to force a B into the LGBT acronym often seems as awkward to me as the presence of all those Mormon wives at the Affirmation banquet. The gay community has budged barely enough to acknowledge half of bisexual people's lives–the half that involves same-sex love or eroticism. I hear awful stories all the time about bisexual people's thwarted efforts to get recognition or services from gay institutions. One good example is a bisexual male/female couple who tried to get relationship counseling at a supposedly LGBT agency in San Francisco. They were told they were not eligible for services because they were straight. How many times have you seen HIV education programs that claim to be for "gay/bisexual" men? If you attend these events, you'll discover that they never include any information relevant to bisexual men's female partners. This is wrong, and it has to stop. This is not inclusion, it is censorship, and biphobia.

Bisexual people may come to a place where we realize we need to recreate all of these things for ourselves rather than piggyback onto a movement or culture that doesn't really want us. Or perhaps I still have a bias toward purity and separatism that is out of step with political reality in the Twenty-First Century of Coalition.

Whether we're relating to gay or straight people, bisexuals come up against very strong prejudices that seem to be an inherent part of monosexuality. For example, a gay male lifestyle is based on a strong attraction to other men. However, a disconcerting portion of it is drawn from an aversion to or hatred and fear of women. I've often been confused about whether lesbianism has more to do with loving women or hating men. Heterosexual men may have sexual fantasies about girl-on-girl action, but it usually does not involve women who look like and believe and feel and behave like real lesbians. The same thing goes for straight girls who may have a smidgen of the fag hag in their makeup. The vehemence a straight man will express in his repugnance toward one guy fucking another guy will equal if not surpass his fervency when searching for a lovely lady with loose knees and a cocksucker's pout.

It's unhealthy to hate anyone. The strongest response we should have to a sexual preference we don't share is indifference. All forms of monosexuality are warped by subconscious hostility toward The Other. Bisexuality is incomprehensible to such people. Where is the fear and loathing? I feel happier and more grounded as a bisexual because it brings me closer to having compassion for all human beings and bodies. I can feel the frailty and bliss of all flesh. It's so much easier to deal with other people on an individual basis. I can see people more clearly if I have not first lined them up in one gender category or the other.

Sex with people who strongly believe they are always and only men or women is pretty strange. I have no idea what it feels like to grow up your whole life content with your genetic sex and happy with your genitalia. I cannot imagine a life that is not full of stress and secrecy about conflict with my body, hormones, and secondary sex characteristics. Perhaps I'm bisexual because my own body is both male and female, just as my life has been that of a woman and a man. Other transpeople are the only ones who can empathize with my consternation, and so they are more likely to be my romantic or erotic refuge than a gender-congruent, genetic male or female.

Do I still believe a gendered class system exists in which men wrongly hold most of the power? Yes, I do. But keeping men out of my life and my orifices will not make me a more powerful person or a better feminist. Truth to tell, my most recent male lovers have been gentler, more patient and accepting, and more honest with me than the women I've loved. When I take another man in my arms, I feel as if I have come home. But I can remember days when it felt that way to embrace a woman. And those days may come again.

So it seems I must take my pleasure and spiritual refreshment where it is offered, and allow my Creator to decide where those gifts will be bestowed. The vessel is less important than what it contains. People are not commodities. Unlike canned goods, they should not be labeled before they can be tasted.

# Half-and-Half?

*Victor J. Raymond*

[Haworth co-indexing entry note]: "Half-and-Half?" Raymond, Victor J. Co-published simultaneously in *Journal of Bisexuality* (Harrington Park Press, an imprint of The Haworth Press, Inc.) Vol. 5, No. 2/3, 2005, pp. 149-154; and: *Bi Men: Coming Out Every Which Way* (ed: Ron Jackson Suresha, and Pete Chvany) Harrington Park Press, an imprint of The Haworth Press, Inc., 2005, pp. 149-154. Single or multiple copies of this article are available for a fee from The Haworth Document Delivery Service [1-800-HAWORTH, 9:00 a.m. - 5:00 p.m. (EST). E-mail address: docdelivery@haworthpress.com].

**SUMMARY.** A bisexual Sioux/Scottish man explores the commonalities between growing up as a member of two races and having a sexuality that crosses ordinary social boundaries. He confronts the misconception that people with complex identities must feel divided or not whole. *[Article copies available for a fee from The Haworth Document Delivery Service: 1-800-HAWORTH. E-mail address: <docdelivery@haworthpress. com> Website: <http://www.HaworthPress.com> © 2005 by The Haworth Press, Inc. All rights reserved.]*

**KEYWORDS.** Bisexuality, bisexual men, multiculturalism, racial and ethnic identity, GLBTIQA community advocacy, coming out

I always knew I was different from the other kids. From a very early age, I was aware that I saw things differently from most folks, and I knew that I was taking risks by showing who I really was. But I'm not talking about my bisexuality. I'm talking about my racial background. I'm a member of the Rosebud Sioux tribe, and also have English and Scottish heritage: it's what happens when your parents are from different racial and ethnic groups.

Growing up as a child in an academic household, I had all the books I could read, and my family participated in pow-wows and other Native American activities. Even so, I was always aware that there were kids who had lighter skin and kids who had darker skin than me. Growing up, I tried to navigate the tricky waters of acknowledging my heritage; it made playing "Cowboys and Indians" particularly fraught with unexpected hazards. And I looked for answers to the questions I asked myself about who I *really* was, looked for them in religion and fiction and life.

Religion was interesting. I recall helping out in an Episcopalian memorial service for the chapel on our family's land in South Dakota, and watching the Sun Dance at Crow Dog's Paradise. Like some kids, I learned about magic and paganism, and read Tarot cards for my friends. And I wondered what God looked like, what He (or She) thought about people, when there were such deep divides between Indians and white people.

History was instructive. There were no family records from more than 150 years ago on my father's side of the family, and this served as a reminder of how much things had changed in a very short period of time. My mother reminded me recently of how much time I spent growing up reading about the past: "I could never refuse you when you wanted to go to get more books." (I racked up considerable amounts of library fines as a kid, to the dismay of both my father and mother. However, they kept taking me to the library.) I quickly learned that often there was more than one perspective on events in the past, and that made me wary of blind faith in what I was taught in the present.

Fiction was fun–particularly science fiction. The best stuff I read as a kid showed me that the future was an incredible and unknown place, where possibilities existed far beyond than those dreamed of in the philosophies of my teachers. But most of the heroes were strong-jawed white guys, and I looked almost in vain for Native American protagonists. I wasn't particularly bothered, just puzzled by it all.

And somewhere in there, I also read about sex and sexuality.

There's a dim memory from when I was a kid, of my keeping pictures I had cut out from magazines of bodybuilders, and then stripping them out of my notebook, because I was afraid of my friends finding out. I had posters of beautiful female models up on my wall (along with the map of Middle-Earth); I knew *those* were okay. But I learned to clam up about wanting to see handsome guys.

But I read about it. I walked along the backside of the stacks, and skulked into the "adult sexuality" shelf area–the *HQ76* section for you Library of Congress fans. It was the '70s and there were lots of books appearing, not all of them agreeing with each other. I looked for words to describe myself and, when I ran across *bisexual*, I realized I already had a pattern for understanding it in my racial background. It didn't hurt that reading all that science fiction provided a pretty good picture of societies where *being* bisexual was considered normal. As my friend Margo told me not that long ago, "When you've read about humans having sex with beings from entirely different planets, sex between two humans of *whatever* gender seems completely normal."

So by the time I was a teenager, I was quite aware that I had my feet firmly planted in several worlds, and just *maybe* this was an advantage. But it often didn't seem like one. I dated girls, but had crushes on guys. I had lots of white friends, but got annoyed when they talked about "Injuns" as if they didn't exist or were somewhere far, far away. Or worse yet, made jokes about the Indian housing project on the south side of the city. For a while, I tried to act like I wasn't anything at all–refusing to label myself. But that felt like I was running away, and it didn't sit right. It left me with a very important question, one I keep answering even now.

What am I?

Here's what I learned from that time, and from the work I've done since then: I'll be damned if I'm "half and half" of *anything*. Our society pushes hard for divisions and percentages, whether it's the Bureau of Indian Affairs, or the AKC, or the dairy lobby. My race and sexuality are not numbers–I'm not a "2 percent" dairy product, they are part of me as a whole person. Accept me as I am. Don't try to stuff me into a wax-paper box formed and folded by preconceived notions of how the world works.

Sound familiar? It should. Bisexuals have spent a considerable amount of time working for acceptance by the gay and lesbian communities, and have faced considerable opposition. "But we don't get half-bashed!" we reply to gays and lesbians suspicious of our supposed ability to retreat into heterosexual privilege. This game of "one-downsmanship" is unproductive, and puts bisexuals in a position of always having to "prove" the worth of their queer credentials. So long as we keep talking about the "purity" of races or sexual orientations, people like me will get relegated to the fringes of acceptability. And I'm not willing to accept that.

There's a considerable amount of work being done on biracial and multiracial identity, and one of the fascinating things I've read about comes from the self-descriptions of *Hapas*–a word used to describe people of part-Asian and/or Pacific Islander heritage. One of the things many *hapas* have mentioned is that they don't feel like they are "half-" this or that. They feel like they are "doubles." They have an awareness of *both* of their cultures of origin (or even more than two), and often a sense of the hazards involved in claiming these heritages for themselves, when those who have "pure" racial pedigrees might not want to acknowledge them. And there is little doubt that there are embedded power dynamics that *must* be brought to the surface and examined if we want to really understand what's going on with *hapas*, with *mestizos*, with the growing number of people who aren't "whole milk" *anything*.

In the midst of all of this, you'd think this makes people like me great "bridge-builders" between different communities, able to explain one to the other. This isn't necessarily true–there is more *opportunity* for this to happen, but it depends on everyone being willing to listen. When it comes to race and sexuality, lots of people are not very good at listening. And I'm suspicious of the idea that having a category of "in-between" communicators somehow relieves everyone else of the responsibility of learning, listening, talking, and understanding.

Robert Terry once wrote about inequality that people are always moving between positions of privilege and disadvantage, and often don't even notice when it happens. It's when it gets institutionalized that people start paying attention: "that's why a meeting of three 'ups' is a board meeting–and a meeting of three 'downs' is pre-revolutionary activity." When you come from a background of *both* "up-ness" and "down-ness," you can't help getting jarred by the pressure to pick sides.

Perhaps the most important thing I've learned from being bisexual and multiracial is that "group membership"–getting your ticket punched–doesn't accomplish much of anything, aside from a warm glow of fellowship. This "warm glow" is not inconsequential–there's a lot of pressure from all sides to own it.

Was Eleanor Roosevelt a lesbian–or bisexual? Is Tiger Woods "black"? So long as we think that this sense of group membership is where our struggle stops, we will never accomplish the real work of overcoming inequality and oppression. If anything, all we're doing is reinforcing our positions of "up-ness" and "down-ness." It is how we deal with one another across lines of difference that matters–are we acting with integrity? With honesty? With awareness of all of the things that bring us together *and* all of the things that hold us apart?

The answers to these questions are the measure of our ability to resist oversimplifying the world and complexities of human existence.

# Thirty Years Out

*Woody Glenn*

[Haworth co-indexing entry note]: "Thirty Years Out." Glenn, Woody. Co-published simultaneously in *Journal of Bisexuality* (Harrington Park Press, an imprint of The Haworth Press, Inc.) Vol. 5, No. 2/3, 2005, pp. 155-162; and: *Bi Men: Coming Out Every Which Way* (ed: Ron Jackson Suresha, and Pete Chvany) Harrington Park Press, an imprint of The Haworth Press, Inc., 2005, pp. 155-162. Single or multiple copies of this article are available for a fee from The Haworth Document Delivery Service [1-800-HAWORTH, 9:00 a.m. - 5:00 p.m. (EST). E-mail address: docdelivery@haworthpress.com].

**SUMMARY.** Longtime bi male activist recounts his coming-out process and thirty years of activism and change in the gay, lesbian, and bisexual communities in Boston. Over time, communities of and for bisexual men have grown and strengthened, despite setbacks and challenges. *[Article copies available for a fee from The Haworth Document Delivery Service: 1-800-HAWORTH. E-mail address: <docdelivery@haworthpress.com> Website: <http://www.HaworthPress.com> © 2005 by The Haworth Press, Inc. All rights reserved.]*

**KEYWORDS.** Bisexuality, bisexual men, gay men, Boston, Bisexual Resource Center, GLBTIQA community advocacy, polyamory, open relationships, coming out

My coming-out process began in the early 1970s when I was in art school. I had a girlfriend and was living with someone I was going to school with. He and I became attracted to each other and started having sex. I thought, "This is interesting. I seem to like this, but I also seem to like having sex with my girlfriend." I didn't have language to describe what I was, so I thought, "maybe I'm becoming gay." This was even before the term "lesbian" was widely recognized; it was just beginning to come into play at that point, and bisexuality was hardly discussed in the mainstream. So I said, "I guess I'm going to stop being attracted to women, and just be attracted to men." But then it didn't happen.

One of the radio stations in New York City, WBAI, had queer programming in the early '70s, which I listened to all the time. They started talking about bisexuality, and I thought, "Oh my God, that's who I am!"

So I introduced my girlfriend and my boyfriend to each other, and it was an unmitigated disaster! This was before I completely understood polyamory or other ways of negotiating open relationships. My girlfriend was horrified and went screaming into the night, never to be seen again.

My boyfriend and I weren't calling ourselves boyfriends. We were both in the closet and out of touch, and we didn't frame our behavior in any way other than: this is something we're doing so we're not bored while we don't have girlfriends. Except I did. When he discovered that I did, he was perplexed: "Why would you want to have sex with me if you have a girlfriend–why bother?" I said, "Well, because I really like you." He got that. So we had a somewhat neurotic relationship for a few years, and then it came to an end.

But that relationship got me to face the coming-out process. The first time I'd been confronted about my attractions was in high school. I was in a boarding school, had been away at a ski weekend, and tried to seduce a friend, who told his therapist, who happened to also be mine. That was before I was ready to admit my feelings to myself. Now I was ready to deal better. So I decided that I needed to come out to my Mom and Dad and my family, and I did. This was 1971.

My family was very supportive, and they dealt with it, albeit with some bumps. One of my sisters, attending college in Boston, convinced me that I should move here. She knew there were many queer people in Boston, and signs of an emerging gay community: Boston had its first Gay Pride Rally in 1971. So I moved to Boston, and in 1973 I marched in my first Gay Pride parade.

My sister also knew somebody who did a radio program in Connecticut, the type of public service program the FCC requires broadcasters to provide space for. On the program, someone from the National Organization for Women interviewed me on the subject of bisexuality. Amazingly enough, nothing bad happened as a result of coming out so publicly.

Within a month or two of that interview, I became friends with a woman involved in the early formation of the bi community. She was studying with a speech therapy instructor by the name of Elaine Noble, who became the first openly lesbian or gay person elected to the Massachusetts House of Representatives, in 1974. She was elected out of my neighborhood in Boston, and I worked on her campaign.

The community back then definitely wasn't "GLBT." This was only a few short years after Stonewall, and there was very little consciousness about bisexual people. My friend who worked with Elaine Noble had debates about bisexuality with Elaine, and they got into some very heated arguments. Trans people weren't ever discussed, at least in my slice of life. So it was really "the gay community," it wasn't even "the gay and lesbian community."

And there were no community services. The Daughters of Bilitis held community meetings, and I went sometimes to slide shows or other presentations they sponsored at the Community Church of Boston, in Copley Square. That's my earliest memory of anything involving community activism that didn't happen in a gay bar.

I had to be creative to have relationships with other queer folk, because I hated loud music, I didn't drink a huge amount, and I couldn't stand cigarette smoke, so gay bars were not really "happening" for me. I did volunteer work to build relationships with people, which led me to becoming an activist. I had to be; there wasn't a choice. Today we do have a choice. It was a cold and very lonely time, not a good experience.

But there were other bi people. I'd meet other men and discovered they liked girls too, but they liked me! We talked, we had nookie. But few of them were public about it, they were hard to find, nothing like today. So I was more readily able to have relationships with women than men at that time, because there were more of them available. Eventually, during the late 1970s and the first half of the 1980s, I was in a marriage-like relationship with a woman. It worked well in many ways and lasted eight years. We lived together, were domestic partners for a good part of that, and were monogamous, which I had never tried and thought would be good to try. She knew I was bi; I wasn't hiding anything from her.

Bisexuals, at the time, were viewed very badly by gay men and lesbians in general. There was a lot of fear. Not just from gay men: there was tremendous anxiety in the lesbian community, particularly around women who were bi; it was a terrifying idea for some people. As late as 1989, I remember bisexuality being a major, major rumpus in the community.

But gay men in particular gradually became less scared, and by the late '80s, I was pretty comfortable having relationships with gay men who knew I was bi. If there was any kind of relationship, if it wasn't just a quickie, we'd talk about it.

I was also working at the queer community center of that time, and I would talk to people about the subject, because the Bisexual Resource Center (BRC) was just getting incorporated, and we had an office in the center. Many of the people there felt comfortable about that, although there were plenty that didn't.

And occasionally somebody would sneak into my office when nobody was around and close the door, clearly terrified. They were gay and they would say things such as, "Oh my God, I've noticed I'm attracted to women, oh crap, what am I gonna do?"

It didn't take a rocket scientist to see what happened to bi people. In that day and time, if you came out as bisexual, especially if you had previously identified as gay or lesbian, things were going to be rough for you. So I did a lot of counseling around that. Working at the community center, unfortunately, I endured a tremendous number of personal attacks from leadership in the community, just for being there. At one point I was literally thrown out of the Gay Pride director's office for suggesting that there should be a bi contingent in the parade. Bisexual women had it even worse, if they came out. So the price to me, emotionally, was tremendous, it was very hard work.

Still, it was important that I be there. I was involved with the founding of the community center and keeping it running, and this one in particular was the last GLBT community center we've ever had in the Boston area. It lasted for three years, and most of them had a record of no more than that or shorter. We accomplished some very good work while it existed. I can think of people whose lives we saved who still mention how important it was to them.

In the meantime, by the mid-1980s the Boston Bisexual Women's Network (BBWN) had formed, and then the Boston Bisexual Men's Network (BBMN). BBMN was holding meetings in the Old Cambridge Baptist Church in Harvard Square. The meetings were monthly, and they also published a monthly newsletter. The group was social at first, but as time went by they became more organized, and we started looking at whether BBMN and BBWN ought to merge into something larger, or create an umbrella organization, which is what we have today in the form of the BRC. I got heavily involved, and in 1987 and 1988 I had first the BBMN office, and then the BRC office, in my home.

By 1989 there was a committee of people up and down the Eastern seaboard who were providing stewardship of a small pot of money for hosting bisexual conferences in different locations. We had several such conferences: in Hartford, in Portland, Maine, in New York City, a couple at Harvard University. They were regional conferences in name, but in reality people came from all over the country. So they became national by default. The one I remember most fondly was the first one I went to, as an attendee rather than as an organizer. I was getting into being bisexual as a political thing rather than just as a personal thing, and the concept of being in a community and being organized excited me. The conferences were a good way to start getting involved in the community; there were workshops on all kinds of subjects and plenty of opportunity to meet other bisexuals. Up to two hundred people attended each of these conferences, and each conference made a little money, so the pot of money kept getting bigger and bigger. It struck many of us that we should do something with it beyond simply planning the next conference.

By this time Alan Hamilton and I had become partnered. His partner Pepper knew he was bi, he'd been out to her all along, and Pepper was active as a straight ally of BBMN and BBWN. She introduced us to each other; in fact, she set us up on our first date. So Alan and I were doing a lot of political activist work together. And he was working in high tech and making good money. At the time, the community as a whole was not convinced that the financial risk of opening an office for the bi community, getting a commercial phone line, and having office hours would be worth it. So Alan and I leveraged it with our money. We told people that we would open an office, and I would do fund-raising to pay the bills, but if we ever came up short and the funds began to drop, we'd underwrite it. We had to agree to underwrite it for three years, until it became self-sufficient, so I spent a goodly amount of my time begging for money, to make sure I could pay the rent and the phone bill and keep the lights on. I left the antiques importing business I was working for and I took the center seat for several years, until 1993, and then other people took it from there.

And people came in vast numbers. We were overwhelmed. In fact, the initial experiment we made with the Bisexual Resource Center has never been repeated. We originally intended it to be a local organization for people who could drop in and use the services or talk by telephone. We opened the door and hung out the shingle. But in some ways the structure just wasn't there, either in terms of people power or financially, and still isn't. Because the demand was very intense. I would have several counseling meetings booked per day. I could spend six to eight hours on the phone continuously, segueing from one call to the next by call waiting. In essence, I was a dumb social worker who had just enough business administration background to get himself into really serious trouble.

Within a year it became evident that we were serving an international audience. I would frequently get calls from overseas, usually from people in the military. I would get a lot of calls from other parts of the United States, from very isolated places where there was not yet an identified queer community, let alone a bi community. These were people for whom I could do little more than listen to them cry on the phone. Some of them would call up in a drunken stupor: that was the only way they could place the telephone call.

So this stimulated the need for development of other organizations around the United States and Europe. Now there's a national organization that's gone through many different incarnations, BiNetUSA, and the Bisexual Resource Center has evolved into an activist and educational organization rather than the counseling service I had envisioned. Meanwhile Robyn Ochs, another of the co-incorporators of the BRC, started a directory of organizations that identified themselves as serving or including bisexual people, the International Bisexual Resource Guide, and over the years it has gotten quite thick. The success of the directory ushered in the concept of having "product," where we actually had educational materials, public brochures on various issues related to bisexuality, or safer sex, and any number of similar things.

Then, enter the Age of the Internet. By the conference in 1998 at Harvard, the Fifth International Bi Conference, which Wayne Bryant chaired, we organized primarily using the Internet. We had an organizing committee from around the globe, and a core group here in Boston, which I was involved in. We had people pouring in from over twenty countries, as far away as Japan, India, and Africa.

Over the last few years, I've been only marginally involved in the bi community. I became involved in an organization called The Alternatives To Marriage Project, which promotes alternatives to traditional marriage as well as advocating for greater access to marriage rights for people who want them. But I also ran a drop-in support group at Fenway Community Health, a gay, lesbian, bisexual, and transgender health clinic in Boston, under the auspices of their research department and with state funding, for men who were curious about bisexuality or questioning their sexuality or identity in general.

Over the years the bi community has grown tremendously. There *is* a community now. Boston is one of the few cities in North America where bisexuals have a large, recognizable community.

Also, labeling is less loaded than it used to be. There are people now who feel comfortable using any number of labels. That goes well beyond the bi community; I know heterosexual men whom you'd be hard pressed to guess are heterosexual without knowing them. They're men that hug and kiss each other and they're very "queer," except for the fact that they happen to be heterosexual. I have a new boyfriend who doesn't label himself anything. But people still do label themselves bi, and there isn't nearly the rumpus there was in the early '90s or the late '80s about that.

All I ever really cared about was that people, however they identified, could be comfortable and open about who they were. Over time, that's become more and more possible.

# Coming Out Swinging

*Gregg Lind*

[Haworth co-indexing entry note]: "Coming Out Swinging." Lind, Gregg. Co-published simultaneously in
*Journal of Bisexuality* (Harrington Park Press, an imprint of The Haworth Press, Inc.) Vol. 5, No. 2/3, 2005,
pp. 163-170; and: *Bi Men: Coming Out Every Which Way* (ed: Ron Jackson Suresha, and Pete Chvany) Harrington Park Press, an imprint of The Haworth Press, Inc., 2005, pp. 163-170. Single or multiple copies of this
article are available for a fee from The Haworth Document Delivery Service [1-800-HAWORTH, 9:00 a.m. -
5:00 p.m. (EST). E-mail address: docdelivery@haworthpress.com].

**SUMMARY.** A statistician and sexual adventurer in Minneapolis-St. Paul, Minnesota, explores the process of coming out to himself and his female partner. He criticizes the limitations placed on male-on-male expressions of desire, even in communities where an open attitude of sexual liberation is presumed the norm. *[Article copies available for a fee from The Haworth Document Delivery Service: 1-800-HAWORTH. E-mail address: <docdelivery@haworthpress.com> Website: <http://www.HaworthPress.com> © 2005 by The Haworth Press, Inc. All rights reserved.]*

**KEYWORDS.** Bisexuality, bisexual men, GLBTIQA community, Internet support groups, heterosexual women, fetish sexuality, coming out

## *THE BOTTOMLESS BOWL*

Whether you call it "Swinging," "The Lifestyle," or "Sportfucking," there's a lot of wild sex going on in suburban bedrooms all around the Twin Cities (Minneapolis-St. Paul, Minnesota). Yes, seriously. Hot gangbang action, daisy chains, and cumbaths that would make some porn stars blush. Needless to say, we wanted in.

Let's start at the beginning:

My female partner, Charlie Copper, and I are very open sexually: we're consensual non-monogamists who met in college. We are a rare example of the intensely physical five-night stand that developed into true enduring love. We had far more desire than experience, and together explored all manner of new playscapes. We tried gender play, strap-on fucking, and heavy dominance and submission, as we built our relationship from the bed up.

Even with this extensive plethora of play options available, something was missing. We fantasized that we *were* other people, and that we were *with* other people who watched, ordered, and judged us in bed. Since so many of our recurring fantasies featured other people, we eventually wanted to move forward and actually *find* other play friends. We talked ourselves blue in the face discussing potential consequences and ramifications: What were our ground rules? Would we be jealous? How would we handle it? Would we need new pajamas?

The few experiences we had together with single females we met online were great, but we got sick of having to work so hard to find people, e-mail back and forth, and verify that people were serious about getting together. It was a major hassle, but what other options were there? Converting vanilla friends risks friendships, with uncertain results. We don't like bars, partly because inebriated people can't give real consent. We thought we were stuck.

We spent New Year's Eve at swing club in Chicago, and I had the novel experience of singing "Auld Lang Syne" as a crowd of people watched Charlie fuck another girl with her silicone cock. This sealed it for us–we were doing exactly what we wanted to be doing. We moved in together in St. Paul, and decided that we wanted more extracurricular time. We wanted to join play parties here in the Cities and have a buffet of partners to choose from.

We kept our ears close to the ground. People we met in chat rooms told us about a great swingers personals Website. We signed up, and immediately were invited to a great hot-tub party. Talk about quick response! The people on the site were cool, hot, and funny: everything a pair of young perverts could ask for! Or so we thought then.

On this particular swinger site, you had four orientation options: Straight, Bi-Curious, Bisexual, and Gay. I chose Bi-Curious, because, for all my bluster and desire, I was a bi-virgin. And I was tired of being a bi-virgin. I wasn't going to lie about my curiosity and, damn it, I wanted my first time, but I didn't know how I would feel about it afterward. Sure, I was little nervous about revealing it to strangers. Swinging, we had learned, seems to be largely driven by women in heterosexual relationships wanting to play with other women. I didn't want to make the bi-male stuff into the focus of our play, just one component.

Naïfs that we were, we thought that any group so sexually free would be liberal in other ways. In *any* other way. Needless to say, to our horror we discovered that swingers really are representative of mainstream America. Most are white suburban social conservatives, except when it comes to fucking each other's wives. In the Website forums, the same itchy topics recurred, like epistolary herpes: "Bi males brought AIDS into the Lifestyle. . . . Men can't possibly enjoy anal play. . . . Bi men are sluts that can't keep their hands to themselves. . . ." It was the same homophobic bullshit that I hear everywhere else.

Then we started getting some nasty response letters: "We'd love to know you better, except for the whole bi thing." What the fuck was that about? Are men really that insecure that they can't get it up knowing that there's someone in the room that *might* be enjoying looking at their beautiful naked body, or be thinking about fucking *them* instead of, or in addition to, fucking their wife? If that scares them, how will they react when they find out about the Bisexual World Domination Society and our secret volcano lair?

In our local swinger community, the only thing more offensive than being gay was being a political leftist, and I was both. "But look what we have going for us," I told Charlie. "We're young, hot, smart, funny, and kinky. What else would people want?" Well, as it turns out, lots of people don't like kinky, and they only like group sex as long as it doesn't involve boys wanting to shuck, suck, or fuck another cock.

## A GOOD CATHOLIC BOY RESPECTS HIS BODY

As a good, straight-edge, Massachusetts Catholic son of an alcoholic chain-smoker, there were some issues to be resolved before I could transform into the hedonist I am today. I was told my body was a temple to be respected, not abused. I was told that some sins ruin your soul forever. This was tempting to believe because it made it so easy to judge and condemn other people. I was spotless: drug-free, unpierced, and a virgin. Well, there was that masturbation thing, which I conveniently ignored. At that point in my life, drugs were wrong, period, and booze was only for loser people who wanted to be independent, exciting, and free, but were afraid to be themselves while sober. *Everyone* made fun of fags, except fags. Dykes weren't liked much better, and bi girls were just dykes that wouldn't admit it.

In my freshman year in high school, there was *one* out lesbian and *one* out gay man. They were sophomores and best friends who started our school's Pride group, which, perplexingly, allowed straights to join. None of us could understand the point of this; allies weren't well known in my school in '93. And these particular queers . . . welcome to stereotype city! He liked musical theatre and was fat and fey. She was on the wrestling team! Being out and flaming saved them some direct harassment, because they were threats to no one, and no self-respecting bully would choose such easy targets. Even so, it must have been lonely. Even otherwise smart kids knew better than to risk their reputations by being close friends with them.

I met them through the Model UN team. They were cool and nice, and friendly. Months passed, we talked occasionally, and one night they invited me to a *Rocky Horror Picture Show* viewing at his house.

I was naïve (shocking!), but curious. I had heard some stuff about *RHPS*, but in those pre-Internet days (at least at my house), how would a fourteen-year-old find out more? Rumors of the underground world percolated slowly, spread from person to person in dubbed mix tapes and dog-eared copies of *Naked Lunch*. My underground education was emerging but incomplete. I knew about the Violent Femmes and the Cure and the Smiths but not Bauhaus or Television or Patti Smith. I could have rented *Rocky Horror*, but I didn't have a car, a job, or money, and it is R-rated.

They told me it would all be better in the dark–if *I* were in the dark. So I arrived, in time to see our host dressed as Rocky, and everyone else putting on makeup and fishnets, and I was shocked. It was one thing to know of such things, but to see it in the flesh? *In the flesh?* This was another thing entirely. Now I wonder how much bi activity begins with reckless viewings of *RHPS*?

Soon, a jagged V traced its way across my forehead in magenta lipstick, and I sat with bated breath as the movie began. They knew the callbacks, and my mouth hung open. Toast was flung, Frank bedded Janet, Frank bedded Brad. My mouth hung open. I laughed. They laughed at me for not knowing who Meat Loaf was. The video seduced by proxy. This was a test, and I was failing, and enjoying failing. Should I have been surprised when he started touching me, not sexually, but sensually? Did I notice? What is part of the ritual, and what isn't? Bacchanal reverie filtered through celluloid. Did I enjoy it? The corner of the veil lifted, and what lay beyond rationalism was terrifyingly alive. It didn't care about self-justification, or rules, or sin. And, in the moment, neither did I.

Did the party *advance*? It tried. Did I panic? Of course. When he actually propositioned me, using unambiguous words, I panicked. I sped home on my bicycle, smearing the scarlet letter on my forehead into a red stain. I was ashamed, and conflicted. He called and I said some hurtful, homophobic, and callous statements that I still regret. We never talked in any real way again.

I never got to talk to him about what he saw in me, or whether this was an unusual event. Was I special? Was he desperate? Did he confuse my openness to being friends with a gay kid with attraction? Teenagers are afraid. He could have been a good friend, which I'm sad I missed out on.

So, my first real bi experience (or potential bi experience) was not a particularly successful or positive one. Looking back, he wasn't my type, and my rejection came as no surprise to him, but I was impolite. I was wrong. I doubt he stayed home and cried, but I proved myself to be a coward and weak, and worried that God wouldn't like me if I had gone any further.

I've learned a lot since then. I hope that my bi-activism and general pro-sexuality help make it easier for scared kids like me not to be jerks when reacting to other people's desires and needs. This conspiracy of silence and fear makes for bad situations with confused and failed expectations. Teenagers will always have awkward moments and fears, but I hope that having their partner be of the wrong gender won't have to be among them.

## OUT AND LOUD

Considering my own early homophobia, I felt a little funny about getting *so* pissed off that people on the site were being so stupid. Then again, I had dealt with and owned up to my stupidity, so why couldn't they? Maybe they just needed encouragement.

When we began looking for other play partners, I would have felt odd calling myself bisexual, because I hadn't gone "all the way." I had a girlfriend, and was cruising by pretty easily on heterosexual privilege. Most people in the vanilla world didn't know I was bi, unless they asked, and I didn't make a big deal out of my attraction to other men. It didn't happen that often, anyway, and most were too straight or too monogamous for it to matter.

Then, I started working on the *BiCities!* television program. As the months went on, my Imp of the Perverse yelled at me more often and more loudly. Fuck closets. Bi men need to be heard. I like being in the eye of shit-storms, generally, and this was a perfect opportunity to start one. I decided start listing myself as bi in our personals listing and to challenge every piece of biphobic propaganda on the swinger site.

What took me so long? For a while, I didn't really feel bi. It just wasn't a part of my identity. All I cared about was bisexual *behavior.* Who cares whether the boys that do it call themselves bi, straight, genderqueer, or down low? I just wanted to get laid. Also, I didn't really want to be *the* face of the bi maleness. Eventually we decided that anyone who wouldn't play with us because I'm bi was a jackass anyway, and not worth playing with, even if they were beautiful, had a high-end Sybian sex toy, or would fly us to the Caribbean for a weekend getaway. If they want to pass up fucking my beautiful partner because I've kissed a few guys, it's their choice and, in America, making dumb choices isn't a crime–yet.

So I decided to come out. Our personals ad was the first stop. All it took to come out there was selecting *I'm Bisexual* from the pulldown menu, and clicking *Save Changes.* If only other aspects of my identity were that easy to change! Almost immediately, people noticed. We also added a picture to our profile of the two of us doing strap-on play. We started posting more heavily in the forums. We pointedly brought up the

Lifestyle double standard that women are presumed bisexual (at least passively), while men's interactions are limited to talking about sports, cars, and computers, and trying to avoid touching each other.

Not everyone was happy for our change. We still got rude e-mail responses. Coming out was no panacea for all that ailed us, but some wonderful things happened. Other bi men online came out. Discussions about risks of bisexual STDs (sexually transmitted diseases) took on a much more factual tone. People wrote to thank us for being out. The obvious hate speech disappeared, or was challenged. Straight men were more out about liking anal and strap-on play.

Secretly, I hoped that coming out was getting us more tail. Statistician that I am, I wrote a poll to find out.

| Poll Choices | *Votes* | Percentage |
|---|---|---|
| Having a bi male means we won't contact you | 12 | 18.18% |
| Having a bi-curious male means we won't contact you | 5 | 7.58% |
| Knowing that there's bi-male history means we won't contact you | 4 | 6.06% |
| Having a bi or bi-curious male makes us want you more | 12 | 18.18% |
| We won't play with you two because you're jerks | 1 | 1.52% |
| The bi-male thing makes no difference either way | 21 | 31.82% |
| Liberals don't deserve group sex | 3 | 4.55% |
| All of the above | 1 | 1.52% |
| None of the above | 7 | 10.61% |

I guess that on the whole, it's all a wash in terms of fuckable hours. But I feel so much better and more honest, which makes all the difference. I don't ask guys if they play with boys: I just ask them to play with *me*. Or they can ask me, without fear.

The most satisfying part of coming out is playing up my identity as a bi-male predator. I'm not an aggressive bi-male, but making people who are uncomfortable with gay male sex squirm is like shooting fish in a barrel, and a guilty pleasure. Heaven knows that a little payback is warranted.

These days, there's a small but loud bi-male-friendly community within our local lifestyle scene. We aren't asked to every party, but we can talk openly about the fun of anal play and strap-ons and exchange knowing winks. Then we meet back at our secret Bisexual World Domination Society volcano lair, kick back, and have a few hard ciders. After a long day of making straight boys suck cock, thereby making the world a better place, what more could we ask for?

# To Fuck and Be Fucked

*Arch Brown*

[Haworth co-indexing entry note]: "To Fuck and Be Fucked." Brown, Arch. Co-published simultaneously in *Journal of Bisexuality* (Harrington Park Press, an imprint of The Haworth Press, Inc.) Vol. 5, No. 2/3, 2005, pp. 171-177; and: *Bi Men: Coming Out Every Which Way* (ed: Ron Jackson Suresha, and Pete Chvany) Harrington Park Press, an imprint of The Haworth Press, Inc., 2005, pp. 171-177. Single or multiple copies of this article are available for a fee from The Haworth Document Delivery Service [1-800-HAWORTH, 9:00 a.m. - 5:00 p.m. (EST). E-mail address: docdelivery@haworthpress.com].

**SUMMARY.** A gay playwright in Chicago looks back on a highly sexualized relationship with a promiscuous married man whose difficulty reconciling his desires leads to a confrontation between the author and the married man's wife. *[Article copies available for a fee from The Haworth Document Delivery Service: 1-800-HAWORTH. E-mail address: <docdelivery@ haworthpress.com> Website: <http://www.HaworthPress.com> © 2005 by The Haworth Press, Inc. All rights reserved.]*

**KEYWORDS.** Bisexuality, bisexual men, heterosexual women, "outing," closeting

I possess a bizarre predilection for meeting bi married men. I've known several over the years, as friends and lovers. I seem to connect easily, and screwing a married man is a major turn-on for me. Living in late-seventies Manhattan, my lover Bruce and I enjoyed occasional separate baths nights: he to St. Mark's and I to Everard, where I met one monster-meated married man, Mel, who added many notches to my macho-meter.

He was lounging provocatively on a narrow bed in what laughingly was called a "room" at Everard. I gave him my best sexy smile and he spit in his palm and began proudly stroking his partially erect cockus-colossus. As I closed the door behind me, he spread his muscular blonde-furred legs and, reading his cue, I slid my hand beneath his heavy balls. My fingers slipped into a pre-greased hole. My kind of man.

No talking or foreplay. We fingered, fucked, and fellated for more than an hour. He was hot, humungous, just a tad kinky, and obviously open to experimentation. Finally, we climaxed in a single moment of ass-pumping ecstasy. After our hearts stopped pounding, we cuddled and talked. I told this handsome hunk that I had been a writer and director of gay porn. He joked strangely that he was too shy to see one.

I commented that I had never seen him before and he openly admitted that he was married. "I have a wife and young son and don't get out much. If I have time, I stop in here on my way home. She's at her sister's in Jersey tonight with the kid. Name's Mel, by the way."

A couple months later I again found him in a cubicle: again no talk, just incredibly rough, hot mansex leading this time to two spectacular climaxes, the second in my very sore pie-hole. We had even taken a break in the action so I could go back to my room for a few toys. We obviously had that mysterious connection beyond simple chemistry.

After my breath returned, I said, "How've you been, Mel?"

He looked into my eyes and mumbled, "Have we met before?"

"A couple months ago. The name's Arch."

"Right, Arch . . . you make films or something."

"So you *do* remember. How's the family?"

"Great. Look, I really gotta get going. I should have been home twenty minutes ago. Hope I see you again sometime."

I began leaving earlier for the tubs in hopes I might run into this sexy-eyed hunk with a killer smile and dick of death. Over the next year, the exact scene repeated itself five more times. Each time, I'd wait till we were through balling–same scene, same toys–and then would ask how he'd been. He'd ask if we had met before and I'd just swallow my pride. It didn't really matter that I had to bite my lip again and again; he simply excited me more than anyone had in years. His memory loss bruised my ego: was it possible he had this much fun with everyone he met? He had to feel the incredible mutual energy. Why couldn't he admit to it? My married-man-at-the-baths stories soon became hits at dinner parties and Bruce found the entire saga sweet and charming, like a sad soap opera.

Then one night I spotted Mel across the room at the Ramrod Bar. It had been months since we had last fucked, but I had never seen him anywhere but at Everard. I was out with Kevin, a good friend who had heard my ongoing series of Mel-the-married-monster-meat stories, and I said, "Watch this. See the guy in the suede jacket by the cigarette machine? That's the married guy who never remembers me. I'm gonna go over, cruise him and take him home, and he's not going to know who the hell I am."

Five minutes later, I was exiting with Mel on our way back to my place, as Kevin convulsed with giggles in the corner. On our ten-block walk north, what little we said was focused on the upcoming scene and little else. He didn't seem to recognize me and I played along.

But this was a much longer and more complex session. We were now in my playroom with my toy chest! We played game after game. He was open to anything I suggested, the kinkier the better. The wife must be away again, I thought. Finally, after several hours and a couple of mutual cummings, I said, "How you been, Mel?"

"I thought you looked familiar. From the baths, right? What's your name again?"

"Arch," I said staring him down. "And that's the last time I'm gonna give it to you. I've had enough of your amnesia act. We always have a ball-banging time and for some weird reason you're not able to deal with it, or me. So before you leave, I'm going to give you my name and number. If you wanna save the cost of a cubicle, give a call. And if I *do* run into you again anyplace, you will remember my name! Or, no fun and games for the Mel-boy. You got it?"

He smiled shyly. "I swear, I'll remember . . . Arch!"

And so began more than a year of continued mutual pleasure. We never talked about that weird need to erase me from his mind, but I was willing to avoid the topic, as long as he continued to need me to be weird as well. The male version of the English word *mistress* is *master*, and that suited me just fine. He seemed to enjoy the subterfuge, and he swore he quit the baths and I was the only man he was seeing.

He'd call once or twice a month and show up at home soon after lunch, ready and willing to let me do piggy things to his beautiful fuzzy blonde body and big fat-headed boner. He'd be gone by the time Bruce got home. There were few sexual boundaries, but there *were* limits to fact-telling. As months passed, he slowly became more open and comfortable enough to tell me about daily events at what I surmised was an architectural firm specializing in kitchen and bath renovations. He said he was born in New Jersey and had three younger straight brothers. He had a B.A. from Fordham, a flat in the East Eighties. and a three-year-old son, Eldon. His last name was Schmidt but his wife, Cynthia, an actress, used Cyndy Shmitt because of a name conflict at Actors Equity. That was all I learned about him. When facts *were* exposed, it caused him some guilt or confusion, so I never pressed for more.

He even had me over to his apartment one evening. Cyndy was away overnight, and he "didn't want to waste an opportunity." So, I finally got to meet Eldon and helped put him to bed before we barricaded his door and had our usual scene. Banging his hairy butt with a huge dildo in the same bed he banged his wife nightly gave me the biggest and hardest butt-banger of my life!

Although very affectionate physically, he never exposed his emotions, at least to me. So no matter how good a time I gave him, I only got a thank-you kiss at the door. But who cared? I was in pig-heaven. He didn't have to use devotional words of love. I was very happy with the occasional "oh yeah" and "more, sir!" Life was good!

During that year of incredible erotic gratification, I finished writing my first play. My stage director buddy, Kevin, showed it to a friend whose theater company mounted a workshop production. Another producer saw that production and wanted to move it Off-Broadway. His only stipulation was that we replace one of the two non-union actresses.

A full Off-Broadway production using non-union actors is rare and, not having the luxury of time to first select from piles of mailed-in headshots, we were swamped at one-day cattle call auditions with 150-plus actresses.

As actress sixty-five or seventy read the same monologue, my mind became numb. The director and producer weren't doing much better either. But we still hadn't seen the right actress for the role and we plodded along with bleary eyes and unfocused brains. The producer, Barton, handed me a headshot of one lovely blonde actress who was delivering a decent reading, and pointed a finger to her résumé, stating she was an Equity member. After she finished the speech I said, "Do you realize you cannot be hired for this job?"

"Yes, I know . . . but. . . ." she said, suddenly very nervous.

"Then why did you bother to audition, Miss–?" I looked at her name for the first time. Cyndy Shmitt! My throat was choked as I asked, "Ah, have you come for perhaps another reason, Miss Shmitt?"

Silence. Barton, Kevin, and I clearly saw her hands shake and smile faked. Barton, the producer, asked, "What's going on here?"

My entire body flushed hot as I said, "I believe Cyndy is here to see me, to look evil in the eye." She nearly imperceptibly nodded behind the manuscript. "You see, I've been having an affair with her husband, Mel, for two years. Remember that night I left with him from the bar, Kevin?"

More silence. Perhaps I was as calm or as blunt as I was because my mind was muddled from the monotony, and her completely unexpected presence took me over the edge–into truth, of all things. After she left quickly, swallowing tears, I fell apart. I was literally quaking, but my extremities were numb and leaden. My heart was pounding so hard I felt unable to breathe. From the look on Kevin's face, I gather I looked about to faint. He poured me a Scotch, informed the remaining actresses we were taking a ten-minute break, and related the sordid details to Barton. Kevin kept up casual, supportive conversation, telling me how brave I had been. I hadn't even told my parents I was gay after living with Bruce for thirteen years. Telling Cyndy the truth had been horrible, but revealing; I was an addled mess: half guilty-child and half proud-lover, but I wasn't sorry.

We managed to complete the auditions and find the right actress. As we were clearing up the piles of headshots, the phone rang.

"Hello," I said.

"Did you have to tell her it was two years?"

"Well, it's been at least that. Closer to three, if we go back to the very first night at the baths. You know I would never do anything to harm my relationship with you, but she admitted she had come just to see me. She wanted the truth. No?" I wasn't sure exactly what I said. I didn't have a script prepared for that scene. "Sorry, I guess I just had diarrhea of the mouth!"

"Telling her how long I've known you hurt her the most! Can't you ever leave out the punchline?" He hung up with a bang! I knew instantly that Mel was out of my life.

But life went on. I met another occasional fuck-buddy, a florist who was bright, funny, and mucho fun in the sack. Bruce also had found a new part-time pal.

One afternoon two years later, my phone rang.

"Hi Arch, it's Mel."

"Yes. I know your voice when I hear it. Ah, what a surprise!"

"I guess it is. I was hoping you might be free Thursday or Friday afternoon. I'd like to come over."

"Thursday'd be fine," I heard myself say. I hadn't taken even a second to think carefully. The thought of having him in my arms blinded me from anything as mundane as sanity or logic. So it started all over again: the calls from work, the sex at the same incredible intensity.

Cyndy had divorced him. He joked with a shy smile that she had even used my name and "confession" as evidence. I was now a legally defined home-wrecker.

In the two years he'd already remarried and had his second son. When I asked why, he said almost too casually, "I fell in love." We never had a real talk about this need for both men and women. We even had a couple of nonsexual lunch dates, but if he'd see I was acting curious, he'd cleverly and subtly change the subject. He used his charisma to easily manipulate me. I'd never met such a bright man with such strong bi needs to fuck and be fucked–even turning my top act around on me a couple of times. Yet at age 35 he was unable to spill the beans about those needs to anyone, not even to me.

I never got his full story. This second wild cycle lasted less than a year. He said he'd met another married man with a cruel countenance and a foot-long wiener of his own. And there was this new terrible disease around the gay community, so they were going to be sexual exclusively with each other–and with their respective wives, of course.

The four-sided form of monogamy must work for him: I've never seen or heard from Mel again. Although it's been more than twenty years, I'd still give my left nut for one weekend alone with him locked in my playroom, with his prime plumbing fixtures *and* my toolbox.

# Bicurious Husbands
# Online Discussion Group

Available online at http://www.haworthpress.com/web/JB
© 2001 by The Haworth Press, Inc. All rights reserved.
doi:10.1300/J159v05n02_22

[Haworth co-indexing entry note]: "Bicurious Husbands Online Discussion Group." Co-published simultaneously in *Journal of Bisexuality* (Harrington Park Press, an imprint of The Haworth Press, Inc.) Vol. 5,
No. 2/3, 2005, pp. 179-194; and: *Bi Men: Coming Out Every Which Way* (ed: Ron Jackson Suresha, and Pete
Chvany) Harrington Park Press, an imprint of The Haworth Press, Inc., 2005, pp. 179-194. Single or multiple
copies of this article are available for a fee from The Haworth Document Delivery Service
[1-800-HAWORTH, 9:00 a.m. - 5:00 p.m. (EST). E-mail address: docdelivery@haworthpress.com].

**SUMMARY.** In online discussions, bisexual and gay men come to terms with various issues surrounding coming out, family and marriage concerns, and bisexual identity. Excerpted from "When Bicurious Husbands Come Out," in *Bisexual & Gay Husbands: Their Stories, Their Words,* Fritz Klein, MD, & Thomas Schwartz, editors, 2001. *[Article copies available for a fee from The Haworth Document Delivery Service: 1-800-HAWORTH. E-mail address: <docdelivery@haworthpress.com> Website: <http://www.HaworthPress.com> © 2001 by The Haworth Press, Inc. All rights reserved.]*

**KEYWORDS.** Bisexuality, bisexual men, Internet communities, gay men, GLBTIQA community advocacy, heterosexual women, coming out

### *FROM: MANDY*

As a (formerly married) now out-of-the-closet gay man, I have a question for the group that can perhaps help me understand my bisexual brethren here. I just realized that there's perhaps a point of confusion in our language.

When you (those of you who describe yourselves as bisexual married men) all use the word "bisexual," I realize that I don't know if you mean that you:

1. are bisexual in the sense that you could be sexually attracted to another man (this would be my minimum definition of being bisexual),
2. or, are bisexual in the sense that you could be sexually "and" romantically (as in "a relationship") attracted to another man,
3. and, can these gender-neutral attractions occur concurrently? Can you wish to have sexual contact (and also relationships) simultaneously with both a man and a woman?

I had occasion to have an online conversation with a man (not on this list) this weekend who identifies himself as "straight," but is sexually attracted to other men. It made me realize that the words and labels we use may have very different meanings from one person to the next.

On the concurrent relationships issue (which, it would appear, at least some are interested in here), it seems to me that we're going beyond a discussion about just being attracted to both sexes (i.e., not having a preference for either), but now we're entering the territory of issues of sexual monogamy and polygamy, which are not limited to just bisexuals, but are issues for straight and gay couples as well.

Seems to me there are married straight men who wish to have sexual encounters with other women on the side, in addition to their wives. Those who do it covertly are "cheating on their wives" (according to "traditional values" about marriage). Some wives know and accept it (this is more common in Latino and other cultures), and then there are some marriages where the husband and wife both openly play around, called "swinging." (Please excuse me if I've over-generalized or not used the PC language to describe these positions.)

It seems that if bisexual men are interested in having dual or polygamous relationships with either or both sexes, then one just simply needs to find partners who share these values.

If we're talking about married men who just wish to "get a little on the side" with another man, then is this situation any different than what straight men face, who wish the same (but with women, obviously)? What support groups do straight men in those positions find? Perhaps the equivalent support group, were there one, would be CHOW–Cheating Husbands Out To Their Spouses. ("Cheating" implies this is happening behind their wives' backs, which is not always the case with them, nor with bisexuals here.)

I guess what I'm driving at here (and I can hear the flames coming already) is that I wonder if some bisexual married men don't think their situation (wanting a variety of sexual contact, not just with their wives) is somehow unique and different, because they're bisexual, and that this factor somehow licenses them or entitles them to go behind their wives' backs. If they were straight, society would simply see them as a horny man cheating on his wife.

I know this will fall on some deaf ears, but I am NOT one who advocates marital fidelity just for fidelity's sake, nor for reasons of traditional moral values, etc. My concerns are more about personal honesty and integrity. It's what you agreed to up front with your spouses. Yes, lives and relationships change, and certainly a partner in marriage on his wedding day may not realize what he'll want in twenty years. But when it becomes apparent that he has "changed his mind" about sexual monogamy, or even about wanting to love more than one person concurrently, then wouldn't the wife need to (1) know about that, and (2) agree to and accept that, in order for the marriage to be considered a good, healthy marriage?

I think many of you here *are* *out* to your wives, and are in the process of redefining your marriages with your wives' knowledge and input.

And I think it's great to hear the stories where this is happening, where wives have grown in the relationship too, in the same direction, and are okay with "open marriages," and dual or multipartner relationships. I have to say that I am interested in the reactions of wives who never saw it coming, and who themselves are not interested in exploring sexuality with their own genders, or entering into other sexual relationships themselves. Interested in how they accept their husband's desire to seek out others. I think these are the stories that are too rarely posted here.

I hope my questions are not seen as "antibisexual married men." Though I am not one, it is an issue I'd like to better understand, and that is why I ask the questions.

I'm also thinking about the individual who earlier today posted a message about his disappointment in the group session he went to, with all the unhappy husbands. . . . Perhaps bisexual married men would find more in common and more support from straight "swingers" clubs and groups, or from polygamous groups?

I hope you'll forgive what to some will seem like obvious or dumb questions, in my process to better understand this issue.

## *FROM: DALE*

Mandy wrote: > *Can a bisexual man be satisfied with one sex or the other, at any moment in time, or across a lifetime?* <

The "natural" man, as other kinds of natural creation, exists in wonderful and seemingly unending diversity as well as a good deal of concurrent uniformity. My understanding of personality issues supports that some people find the sexual part of their (bisexual) personality will be expressed serially (in sequence) and will vacillate between male and female but not necessarily both at the same time. Others will find equal attraction at all times to both genders at once. Yet others will hover (within a range) at some point between equally attracted to both genders and an attraction skewed to the male; others similarly hover (within a range) with the skew being toward female. I haven't seen much evidence that would support there's one "universally" correct or normal way to be bisexual.

> *Is it a matter of a bisexual man finding his one life partner (and whether that will be a woman or man, who knows), or, does bisexuality imply an attraction to both concurrently, and a need to satisfy both desires concurrently?*<

For a given personality it could well be expressed in that model. For another, not. Again I believe profoundly diversity is the norm rather than binary absolutes.

One way of looking at the term BI-sexual is to recognize the prefix "BI" implicitly means two. So, BI-sexual can simply mean being somehow attracted to and able to have satisfying sexual relations with both genders. It doesn't HAVE to have a quantitative rating for the distribution of that attraction between the genders.

I happened to say in a therapy session early on in my wife's and my struggles with all of this, "I'm a gay man who happens to be married." At that particular juncture it was a VERY threatening thing to my wife for me to say that because "gay" translated that she would ultimately be excluded from my life as time passed and I inhabited the M2M side of my personality more directly and openly. She needed at that juncture to label me "BI-sexual" because it supported there was an ongoing place in my life for her.

I, on the other hand, made the statement at that time (and possibly still now) because: I knew that I'm only about one woman short of gay! I don't feel sexual attraction to women in general and the logical side of my mind supports the concept that if I were truly "BI"-sexual I'd be more broadly attracted to women.

Since that time I feel a little more comfortable acknowledging "BI" in its academic sense even if it's only ONE woman I'm attracted to . . . and my wife has become MUCH less threatened by the label "gay." We both find honesty and comfort, though, saying that I'm "not straight." The one thing certain about us is that both individually and as a couple we continue to be works in progress!

My self-analysis and description of my personal status: I am attracted to ONE woman in the universe (my wife) and to men more broadly. I feel profoundly "connected" to my wife as my female life partner . . . can't conceive of myself being so attached to any other female so long as she's alive. I would LIKE to find a male with whom I also can feel this kind of "life partner" connection. I/we (my wife and I) continue in a kind of search mode with a variety of exploratory contacts happening as time passes but so far haven't found what feels to be a personality interested in "coming in" to my/our life in that fashion for an extended period of time. The one thing certain about the search is that if I/we stopped looking we're certain NOT to find anyone!

My recommendation is to explore and experience as best you can, all the while paying close attention to what strikes the most resonance with your underlying personality and personal style. As you collect a variety of experiences you should find your most positive responses to "cluster" together, which will give you the most reliable insight into what your personal realities are. I think you'll find the most reliable definition of yourself within yourself. What I think you'll find about yourself is that you are both different from and similar to a lot of other guys . . . but not ever a carbon copy of another personality! That's just the way God made us all, I think!

### *FROM: CHUKKY*

Funny, but I disagree with most of what was written. I haven't had sex with my wife since my coming out a year ago. Ummm, actually I never enjoyed sex with her or any girl I dated and slept with . . . but performed more to keep up the appearance. In my relationship now . . . the sex is wonderful . . . and words can't describe the feelings I have for him . . . in bed and away. Looking back, even on my honeymoon, I remember walking the beach and looking at the guys . . . and never felt the same about the women. In addition, I remember being friends with a few guys whom I really wanted . . . and hinted to but didn't come out directly because of their being straight . . . however, I thought they weren't . . . or let me say . . . I hoped they weren't. I would masturbate thinking about them . . . or a handsome stranger who I met or spoke briefly to. I cannot believe that a guy can be attracted to and love a guy and girl the same. . . . I know I am going to get blasted for that statement . . . but I just don't think it is possible. One has to be stronger than the other . . . and/or the people that say that are lying to themselves–either out of not being able to face the true fact or just being merely afraid.

I know in my situation, I lived knowing my true feelings since I was 18 (I am 40 now), but would NEVER admit to anyone I was gay–no, not BI–Gay! I always thought as a kid that gay was feminine . . . and tried to repress my feelings for men . . . It does not go away. In addition, because of the relationship I am in with my wife . . . and my lover, I realize I was never able to love a woman or feel the things toward her that I can and do feel for a man. I was never the guy who had a one-night stand with anyone, in my gay or straight life. I was never able to be affectionate unless I felt warmth or, in this instance, deep love. Thus, for me, I could never understand cruising the forest preserve or bookstores, etc. Before I had anyone, I would rather masturbate to my fantasy than be with a stranger. For me, the feelings, the emotion was far more important than the sex. However, the sex is so great due to the emotions–if that makes any sense. I hope I didn't offend anyone . . . just my own views I had to share. I guess in my own way, gay or straight, I'm untraditionally traditional!


### FROM: DALE


Chukky wrote: > *I cannot believe that a guy can be attracted to and love a guy and girl the same. . . .* <

Based on your personal experience, I agree it would be impossible for YOU to be attracted to and love a guy and girl the same and/or that you may have some company in your position. You have no authority, though, to project your personal experience onto the rest of the universe as a given. I wouldn't deny you whatever your experience and insight is . . . but neither would I deny the guy sitting next to you whose experience supports a slightly different convention. Just because you can't project yourself into another "flavor" of sexual orientation other than your own doesn't mean it doesn't exist or isn't likewise as undeniable a reality for THAT person as yours is for you.

I can't say I haven't ever indulged in black and white thinking–feeling there MUST be some kind of universal "right" or "only" way things must be. Time and again, though, just when I was certain I had seen or experienced all the diversity there was in the universe, and that there couldn't be anyone who was XXXXXX–wait a little while and sure enough–along would come someone whose reality is XXXXXX! So, I feel I've made some progress toward being a better citizen of the world as well as a less stressed personality by trying to learn to give others permission to be whatever way they need to be to express and affirm themselves. Where I begin to fight back is when someone else expects me to take on THEIR reality for no better reason than they can't understand or tolerate mine!

## FROM: KENNETH

I am in a love relationship with a married man. I feel that it would be improper for me to attempt to tell him how to relate to his wife. All I can do is tell him what I want in terms of being with him; the rest is up to him. He is the only one who can possibly know what he wants. When he decides, he must tell me. I absolutely cannot be of support to his wife, since I am the very person who most threatens their relationship (from her point of view).

So, don't ignore your needs and wants–express them. Respect your lover's. Then decide where YOU will go from there. Forget about supporting them as a couple–the whole idea is completely noncongruent (unless you wish for them to succeed, in which case you will always be the "fifth wheel").

## FROM: DALE

Kenneth wrote: > *Forget about supporting them as a couple–the whole idea is completely noncongruent* <

I would challenge the idea of framing the idea in a way that makes it seem as if it were a "given" for the universe! It may be a challenge to construct such an arrangement. From my own experience, I can say that if all the parties are present at the construction process and committed to the idea, it can be done . . . has been done . . . and is being done.

> *(unless you wish for them to succeed, in which case you will always be the "fifth wheel")* <

This feels to be another perception, perhaps grounded in your personal experience, but a perception nonetheless. Again–keeping all parties acknowledged and fulfilled in a triadic relationship is likely to be its own set of "different" challenges–but no more inherently impossible than a dyadic relationship. In some ways working out a triadic relationship could be more challenging and more complex . . . in other ways it could well be an easier scene because of the resources the additional person brings with them.

It's been my experience that self-held perceptions can be an effective predictor of success (or lack of it). "The whole idea is completely noncongruent" and "you will always be the 'fifth wheel'" are perceptions that would preclude you (or anyone else who takes them on) from ever having much success trying to construct a triadic relationship. I see them to be examples of polarized (and polarizing) thinking.

### *FROM: WOODY*

Dale couldn't have echoed better how I feel! I came out to my wife as a bisexual, but four months later, and a lot of self analysis of my own feelings, I told her I felt I was gay, but leading a bisexual lifestyle. Now, THAT WAS threatening to her, for the same reasons it was to Dale's. I now use the "one woman short of gay" phrase also–it seems so descriptive. I have no sexual attraction to any other women. As a matter of fact, I don't have as much sexual attraction to her as to most men to whom I am attracted (this has been amazing . . . for a 59 year old!). But–I do love her. And want to stay with her as long as she wants me.

Yes, you have to decide in your own mind what you think you are, what best to label yourself and be comfortable with it if that's important to you. It doesn't matter what others think.

haiku:

*blood on fence post*
*stonewalls echo*
*coyote-howls*

### *FROM: SCOTTY*

Wow . . . well, we are all entitled to our own opinions, and often they are based upon our experiences, but how can anyone make generalizations?

I view this situation not as one where I am competing for my boyfriend, but where he is fortunate enough to love and be loved by two people, and if those two people can come to care about each other, then we have created more love in the world and in our own hearts. I know this goes against the entire "scarcity paradigm" that our society is based upon, and that it is challenging, but I also believe that, if we want this, it is possible.

It is, in fact, entirely congruent for me to want their marriage to succeed AND my relationships with both of them to succeed. My self-interests are not only defined by what feels good to me but also by living out my ideals, which include a sense of fairness and caring for others as well as for myself.

I certainly question myself about this arrangement. There are emotional risks being taken by all of us, and that feels good . . . we all have much to lose and much to gain.

One of the things about being outside of the status quo is it gives one an opportunity to experience one's own life in different contexts. There isn't a lot of cultural support for that, as we all know, so we find it where we can. I like the idea that we are capable of creating support for each other.

*    *    *

### FROM: STEPHEN

When someone gets critical of the goals (such as a triad or dual monogamous relationships) of those of us who are fully bisexual, they are operating out of ignorance and entirely from your own sexual perspective.

Someone being exclusively gay doesn't have a clue (based on their own emotional and sexual life) that we bisexuals can indeed be absolutely turned on and go into heat over both men and women at the same time, depending on the situation. But that, my friend, is the fact. I do it all the time. :-) Like the song says, "Love the one you're with"–and I do.

I have actually left the arms of a great man and taken a shower, then gone home only to find my wife to be so loving and desirable that my batteries take on a full charge and I do it all over again and fall asleep with my sexuality fully and completely realized. It's an absolutely wonderful feeling to have both parts of my sexuality satisfied. For me that is true contentment.

My ultimate goal is to find one loving man and make of him a lifetime lover while at the same time keeping the love and respect of the woman I am married to. This is not and never will be easy. I never expected that it would be. But it is what I want and what I am working to achieve. I know that my wife will be the least of my problems. She knows that I have dual needs and that I am not worth a shit unless they are both being met. Now, I need to find a man who is as willing to share me as my wife has told me that she is. She realizes that there is part of my soul that no man can ever reach. A part that is hers alone, and she is willing to give the part that does not belong to her back to me, so that I can share it with a man. The one thing that I know is that there is more than enough love in any human being to fill the entire universe. The only limitation on one's ability to love is in thinking that there is a limit.

And so my friends, instead of quarrelling with those of us who are switch hitters, why not just continue on your own path of self-discovery like we all have to do? In the end each of us must be the judge of how he conducts his life. And, each of us must pay the price for doing so. There is no free lunch. : –)

Billy wrote: > *"Why is it that heterosexuals feel that they have the right to sit in judgment of us?" That is an interesting question. I myself am surrounded by extremely conservative fundamentalist Christians.* <

When I came out to my wife I told her to tell anyone she wanted to tell if she thought talking to that person would make it easier for her to cope with the news. She told a dear and longtime lady friend from church. She was met with absolute silence. She did not get the support she had thought would come. I was hurt for her because she thought her announcement had cost her a friend. I made up my mind to test that supposition. We were going to be near the home of the couple in question and I told her to call and tell them we were going to be in the area and to ask if they would like to see us. I was delighted to hear that they wanted very much to see BOTH of us.

My thought was that when my wife told her about me that the lady was so stunned that she didn't know what to say because the news was so far outside her experience in life. I was right. They were very gracious and welcomed us with great warmth. After dinner her husband (a member of The Promise Keepers) and I went for a walk. I got the "I hate the sin but love the sinner" spiel. And then I got the surprise of my life. The husband confessed to me that he was not in a position to throw rocks at me because he had had a thing for pornography all his life, and that it was a real struggle for him considering his religious life. So I guess that there are two lessons to be learned here. (1) Some people take comfort from despising the gay community because it makes their own emotional baggage feel lighter. (2) It is human nature that most people NEED someone to look down upon so that they can feel good about themselves. Which perhaps explains why so many straight and gay people have such a hard time even believing that there is such a thing as a bisexual. I have been told so many times that as a person who identifies as a bisexual I am really nothing more than a gay man living in denial that it doesn't usually even faze me anymore.

Although I would not expect such ignorance from anyone on this list. In all fairness I must tell you that the same bigoted remark was made to me by a top ranking official from the National Gay and Lesbian Coalition.

And so, with regard to people being judgmental about your life I say, "Fuck 'em." This is your life, and your adventure. You KNOW what to do, JUST DO IT!

### FROM: KENNETH

Frankly, I don't think I am operating out of my "sexual perspective," but out of a lifetime of learning about human nature and what works and what doesn't. Every reality isn't relative. I hope you believe that, too. For example, I would hope that you believe that honesty in relationships is always the best policy, regardless of whether there are two or three people involved. By the same token, the capacity of an individual for intimacy is limited, whether that person is BI or hetero or gay. We're all still people and limited in time and energy.

I would like to quote from a book called *Intimacy Between Men*, by John H. Driggs and Stephen E. Finn. The book is based on a combined fourteen years of experience as cotherapists leading short-term support groups for gay men in Minneapolis. They write, "There is the issue of time and energy. Intimacy is so challenging, especially in sexual relationships, that no one can simultaneously do justice to two intimate sexual relationships. One or both of the relationships must suffer."

That is all I was saying.

### FROM: JAMES

I have a different take on this. . . . I agree (oh, boy, do I agree) that we are people and limited in time and energy. But I have learned a wonderful thing (at least wonderful to me) since coming out three years ago. I have learned that I have an incredible ability to love . . . and to love a number of people. Recently, I was trying to explain to my wife why I can love a number of men . . . really love them . . . in very different ways. I have thought of the three words in Greek for love and appreciate the need for different words . . . and I might even add another one or two. But I do not find that my time or energy limits me in any way when it comes to loving. The heart . . . at least mine . . . has the ability to expand and expand and expand with love. It used to scare me how easily I love

. . . but not anymore. Where I would introduce the word or concept of energy is how I relate to those I love. There is where my limitations kick in . . . but my ability to love seems to flow on endlessly . . . (sigh)

## FROM: STEPHEN

I was openly gay before I decided to get married, so I think there are guys here who can relate to your situation. I pained over the decision for five years (we both did), had lots of couples' counseling, and finally decided it was right. While it is challenging sometimes, I have never regretted it. I do sometimes wonder if we "mixed-orientation couples" have any harder a time than any married couple. I just think marriage is challenging and requires tremendous maturity no matter what your background or history. A big difference is that I grew up in a pretty liberal, accepting environment. I wasn't keeping secrets. I wasn't choosing marriage as a way of conforming to heterosexual norms. In fact, I still think my mom, to whom I'm quite close, would prefer me to be gay. Less competition. I chose heterosexual marriage because I loved my wife and felt we had more going for us than I had ever had with a guy. I wanted the challenge and surprise of heterosexuality after years of homosexual relationships, which for me were great but also predictable in a way. Undoubtedly that was the men I was attracted to, not generalizable to all gay men's experiences. For me with guys the romantic spark was just never there, although they were great buddies and I still love some of them.

## FROM: SCOTTY

I have been reading the posts of the last few days. The issues about whether a person is bisexual, or why stay married . . .

I think that fear is what we are really talking about. Fear of rejection. I can't judge someone for holding onto the cultural acceptance of (apparent) heterosexuality. There are a lot of goodies that go with that. One of them is that you don't have to deal with being a reviled person . . . no small thing.

Before I finally came out and stopped trying to be bisexual or heterosexual I was terrified that everyone would hate me if they knew. *I* hated me. I thought my feelings were disgusting. When I finally came out it was because I couldn't stand the pain of hiding anymore. I woke up in the middle of the night one night . . . in my sleep I had pushed the woman I lived with out of bed and was hitting her, all while asleep. I am not a batterer . . . I wasn't beating her up . . . no one was hurt . . . but the message couldn't have been clearer.

Since coming out a discovery I have made is . . . I HAVE the safety and approval I was afraid I would lose. No, I do not have a wife I walk arm and arm with . . . but I have my own approval and dignity in ways I didn't before and that is priceless to me. If someone yells "faggot" at me (which happened once) I just think they are an asshole . . . I don't feel ashamed of myself anymore.

Without going into my whole life story, I want to share with you all that the danger is FEAR, NOT LOVE. The more we trust our fears to guide us the more separated we are from our true loving nature. That doesn't mean you can come out to everyone and they will be delighted . . . but it means you have got to delight yourself by BEING yourself. Look at all the pain that comes from trying to be other than you are.

I do not presume to tell anyone what they should do. I do not mean to imply that any one course of action is best for everyone. I am just saying . . . look your fear in the face, remember who you really are inside, love yourself, and see where that leads you.

If the shoe fits, wear it. But if it doesn't fit, don't.


### FROM: SHAWN

The description of what it feels like to have the capacity to love both men and women erotically reminds me so much of my own experience. Some people don't want to believe that we are BI simply because they have not had this experience. The thinking seems to go . . . "if I have not experienced it, then it must not be for real. Thus, I will ridicule and doubt the word of those who say they are 'BI.'" BI the way, have you read, "BI Any Other Name"? Recommended reading.

I have come to the conclusion that I will not accept the fear and prejudice that might be hurled at me by anyone, whether it is because they hate my bisexuality, dislike my hazel-green eyes, dislike my Jewish great grandparents who hardly spoke English, or whatever it is about me that someone might fear or misunderstand. Life is too short for all that foolishness and a lot of us are moving on. The fearful and hateful and judgmental can stay behind in the dust if they so choose. I wish that they wouldn't. They're missing such a good time and I do wish them well. They are, after all, still our brothers and sisters. The Rev. Dr. Martin Luther King Jr. said it so well when he referred to the white hate-mongers (who were so busy shedding innocent blood) as "our sick white brothers and sisters." He still called them brothers and sisters!!!

To some degree we all choose our spiritual, emotional, and relational destinies by the attitudes we adopt and cling to. We all have been given the choice, however, to move on to a higher level. My hope and prayer is that the cultural shift now occurring will take our society to a better place than we've ever been heretofore.

## NOTE

Excerpted from "When Bicurious Husbands Come Out," in *Bisexual & Gay Husbands: Their Stories, Their Words*, Fritz Klein, MD, and Thomas Schwartz, editors, 2001, The Haworth Press, Inc.

# The Slash Fanfiction Connection to Bi Men

*Raven Davies*

doi:10.1300/J159v05n02_23

[Haworth co-indexing entry note]: "The Slash Fanfiction Connection to Bi Men." Davies, Raven. Co-published simultaneously in *Journal of Bisexuality* (Harrington Park Press, an imprint of The Haworth Press, Inc.)
Vol. 5, No. 2/3, 2005, pp. 195-202; and: *Bi Men: Coming Out Every Which Way* (ed: Ron Jackson Suresha,
and Pete Chvany) Harrington Park Press, an imprint of The Haworth Press, Inc., 2005, pp. 195-202. Single or
multiple copies of this article are available for a fee from The Haworth Document Delivery Service
[1-800-HAWORTH, 9:00 a.m. - 5:00 p.m. (EST). E-mail address: docdelivery@haworthpress.com].

**SUMMARY.** A straight female author of Western romances discusses online subculture of "slash fiction" and fans who reinvent pop-culture film and television characters as bisexual men. The author explores the underground nature of women's interest in male sexuality and argues that bisexual men have a central place in the imagination of a small but growing women's community. *[Article copies available for a fee from The Haworth Document Delivery Service: 1-800-HAWORTH. E-mail address: <docdelivery@ haworthpress.com> Website: <http://www.HaworthPress.com> © 2005 by The Haworth Press, Inc. All rights reserved.]*

**KEYWORDS.** Bisexuality, bisexual men, heterosexual women, slash fan fiction, popular literature and media, men's erotic fiction, Internet publishing

In the 1920s, an underground group of gay fans of the new technical sensation, cinema, created a new way of seeing the unfolding story. Changing the starring characters to their own sexual orientation, they began writing stories to illustrate their own life experiences and fantasies, while maintaining a close similarity to the personae originated by the actors. Evading copyright restrictions through disclaimers and amateur publication, these daring authors filled underground gay newspapers with risqué "fanfiction" tales, incorporating their favorite screen characters.

Jump forward eighty years. Television has become the mainstay of nearly all fanfiction, and the Internet is its cosmic freeway. This literary genre has blossomed into three major categories. "General" fanfiction places the characters in new situations of adventure, romance, or mystery, sticking canonically to the source material. "Adult" fanfiction tells heterosexual romances and erotica, often referred to as "Mary Sue" or "Mary Jane" stories, where the female writer places herself in the storyline as the love interest of her favorite male character. This category can also contain adult adventure stories, too violent or intellectual for anyone under eighteen.

"Slash" rewrites mainstream media into erotic gay fiction, eliminating existing heterosexual eroticism, or placing it in the background. The characters metamorphose into bi males if they have women in their lives, or gay if they appear sexually ambiguous in the original material, leaving the writer to conjure up stories to fit their new sexual identities.

The "Slash" connotation comes from the packaging of the paired characters, separated by a slash mark or virgule, such as *Starsky/Hutch*.

Though some Slash writers (referred to as "Slashers") are gay, the majority today are liberal straight women. No matter the Slasher, we take our stories beyond the norm, to new heights of loving, caring, and sexual bonding of two men, whether they have, or never had, women in their lives. We focus almost entirely on the coming out of a bi male/gay, or a bi male/bi male sexual relationship. Slash is a literary form in which men come to terms with, and act out their need for, sexual and meaningful encounters with other men.

No character can escape the attention of a Slasher. Only an interest in the show is required, and the words will be written and read repeatedly, by those living in Boise, Idaho, to Tokyo, Japan. Slash "fandoms" (a television series, a movie with sequels, or, more rarely, a novel series) include: every *Star Trek* Roddenberry production (Kirk/Spock are a favorite pairing, neither having long-term female attachments, and thus treated as gay); *The Magnificent Seven* TV series (Chris/Vin are a bi male/gay pairing, one having been married, the other sexually ambiguous); *Hercules* (Hercules/Ares are both treated as bi men for obvious reasons); *Babylon 5* (Stephen/Marcus, again are bi male/gay, as their sexuality remains unknown, except one is a virgin in any sexual arena), the *Lethal Weapon* movies (both bi male, both being married), and the vampire novels of Anne Rice (the characters aggressively exhibit bi male tendencies). The telling of these characters' sexual exploits and adventures goes on and on, as does the list of Slash Web sites, which are just as long as every television series made (including cartoons!). Since the evolution of the Internet, any TV series can continue eternally in fanfiction.

Slash writers are an unusual mix, considering those who created the genre. We are now comprised mostly of straight women and gay men, but the Slash genre, even when written by women, overflows with masculine energy, profanity, explicit male/male sex, rape, sadism, life and death adventures, and endless other adult male-oriented subjects.

Readers include three very distinct groups: bi men, gays, and straight women. These groups share a love of fantasizing about the sexual activity and relationships between male characters, left unfulfilled by mainstream heteronormative entertainment. They all suffer from the same tired boy-plus-girl story formulae, concocted by those fearful of pushing a few harmless buttons. Slash provides adult, creative, thought-provoking fiction for bi males and gays, regarding their own sexuality, or a portion of it, and how one lives with it, as well as the many women who fantasize about male bonding, desiring something besides a few tame comedies. When will "Will" spend a half hour in bed with a lover?

Straight women are possibly the best and most prolific Slashers due to their interest and love for men, all men. E-mails from my readers suggest that women look at these characters in different ways, from lovers to sons, but are only willing to share them with men, not with half-their-age female co-stars. Women develop true love affairs with certain male pairings, and become so involved in ongoing stories that they sometimes e-mail an author before they even finish reading a long tale, to ensure the fictional twosome get out of their difficult situation. Besides being sexually attracted to these characters, women also mother these men, and adore them no matter what they do. Quotes from e-mails I have received from female fans of *The Magnificent Seven* illustrate their deep caring for the characters:

> *. . . you worked a lot of stuff from the episodes into the storyline . . . things that would have hurt Vin and he'd have never said a word . . . the sex was wonderful . . . with those two men, how could it not?*

> *. . . poor Vin, tortured like that . . . well done with your storyline of the multiple personality that ensued . . . totally credible, since he is so kind and gentle . . . and paradoxically so deadly. . .*

The social aspect of Slash is extremely strong among women, who constantly discuss the characters in the most loving and explicit ways via e-mail, dissecting each new story. One conversation illustrates how bi men and gays are admired and respected in this fantasy world, in fun, as well as with serious concerns for their welfare. Ginger sent me a note, joking about an evening with Vin and Chris: the men would giggle, wrestle, and exploit each other for our amusement, then Ginger would take Chris for her own heterosexual fun and I would lull Vin into another fantasy, all in mirth and good faith, including flowers, candles, seductive music, and much laughter. Women cherish slashed characters, as much as a fictional character can be loved, and it "is the character" who they love. Put the actor into another role, and he may not be looked upon in the same manner.

What about bi male and gay readers? Attending a GLBT writers' conference recently, I discovered how many bi and gay men do read good Slash, if they can find it, as they are more discriminating in their choice of stories, and their reactions to the characters, both within the storyline and the sex scenes. A letter from Tim, who reads Slash every night, illustrates a good review:

> *I am gay and in love with* [one of the actors] . . . *went through the same helpless anguish Chris felt . . . you fulfilled my fantasy about Vin and Chris . . . you described everything I wanted and needed to see, feel, and hear.*

The 1970s sci-fi TV show *Battlestar Galactica* highlights an important point about Slash: people in Hollywood are reading this underground genre, and not liking it. Slashers and readers are responding strongly to a new cable movie, based on the *Galactica* series, which changed two of the main male characters into women. It appears the producers hoped to stop the bi male overtones exuded between Apollo and Starbuck (who were both involved with women, but were also bonded together with Krazy Glue). An uncaring executive or writer turned Starbuck and Boomer (a third guyfriend in the original) into female characters–a scenario that any fan of the series would find ridiculous. The word is spreading through all fandoms to write disparaging letters and to boycott this disturbing and homophobic casting tactic.

All fans are willing this film to fail, with its many ass-kicking women (yawn) leaving no possibility of gay sexual activity, except lesbian Slash. They have left nothing for bi males, gays, or straight women to even fantasize about! We want Starbuck/Apollo back together, in their caring and yearning relationship that could not be dismissed. As the saying goes, "no guts, no glory," and the American entertainment industry is truly gutless.

Slash shows the power of an active audience to remake things in its own style, and to take its interests elsewhere if a show or cast fails to intrigue them. Hollywood better get a grip soon as to this business reality, although their habit of antagonizing audiences is a bonus to Slashers. Entertainment industry marketing surveys track only active viewers; they prevent producers and advertisers from tracing lost viewers who have the money to purchase what they're selling. These lost viewers have turned to the Internet, looking to their computer for adult entertainment. In one instance, several actors on a show complained that the audience viewed their characters as gay, and demanded additional heterosexual love scenes. Too bad! Those actors had successfully titillated a lot of people before the producers caved in, creating the worst of episodes and the lowest of ratings, which led to the cancellation of the show.

On the down side, the intense world of Slashers and readers can feel intimidating to some. Tim, the gay fan who reads Slash every night on his computer, seems unable to participate in the round-robin discussions with some of the women who run the chat lists and Web rings (two types of e-mail communication between fans). Gay and bi male readers remain very quiet, and seldom acknowledge they read Slash. Many Slash Website holders are extremely shy, working in cybershadow; others are tyrannical, omnipotent creatures–some even scare me!

As with any creative art form, audience tastes vary, and bi male readers may be the hardest audience to satisfy, even though the stories are about aspects of their lives. It is much easier to accommodate other readers. Simply put, gay men wish to read gay sex, whether it's Slash or good literary works of any type. Lesbians have their own erotica. Straight men would rather be burned at the stake than to read anything like this, although I do have a few straight male readers who simply like the Western adventures, skimming over the sex. Straight women are an anomaly: either they behave like most hetero men (giving you the cringe and shiver thing), or they have fallen in love with this genre. Bi men, however, generally want both gay and hetero pairings, which proves difficult to incorporate into M2M Slash in its current form, considering it is based strictly on male/male pairings.

Female Slashers exclude almost all heterosexual activity from their stories. As with gay readers, straight women would rather see their favorite male characters exclusively with men, not with other women. Hints of past straight relationships are required, but our goal in writing Slash is to discount the existence of these *other women*, in order to pair the male characters. Strangely enough, one heterosexual erotic scene can kill a Slash story, as gay men do not want to read it, nor do straight women. By discounting bi characters' heterosexuality, however, we may be doing bi men a disservice in portraying them unrealistically as homocentric.

There must be room for bi men to become involved and contribute to Slash, as readers and writers. Most female Slashers would have little problem discussing the characters, who we all love personally, erotically, and humorously, with gay or bi men via e-mail. Bi men's input, and sharing of knowledge, would be extremely valuable, as well as fun. Gay or bi male readers could ask someone, such as myself or a gay Website owner, to add a Web ring link to our Websites, for their own discussion group, which they could turn into a large chat room with a membership of only bi men, or bi and gays. Anything is possible, as these stories are written for and about bi men.

Slash is truly a bisexual literary art, a truly wondrous world for a writer to try her/his hand at erotic storytelling with short stories or epics, for bi male, gay, and straight women readers to enjoy, and when warranted, with immediate feedback. If you capture an audience of thousands, your stories have hit people in the heart, the brain, and the genitals.

# Bi Now, Bi Tomorrow

*John Egan*

[Haworth co-indexing entry note]: "Bi Now, Bi Tomorrow." Egan, John. Co-published simultaneously in *Journal of Bisexuality* (Harrington Park Press, an imprint of The Haworth Press, Inc.) Vol. 5, No. 2/3, 2005, pp. 203-211; and: *Bi Men: Coming Out Every Which Way* (ed: Ron Jackson Suresha, and Pete Chvany) Harrington Park Press, an imprint of The Haworth Press, Inc., 2005, pp. 203-211. Single or multiple copies of this article are available for a fee from The Haworth Document Delivery Service [1-800-HAWORTH, 9:00 a.m. - 5:00 p.m. (EST). E-mail address: docdelivery@haworthpress.com].

**SUMMARY.** A Canadian gay male scholar and activist ponders the transformations in his own thinking about bi male identity and GLBTIQA community politics over time. The author posits a four-stage process of social, legal, and cultural acceptance of sexual minorities and compares the civil-rights progress made by gay men and lesbians to that still being made by bisexuals. *[Article copies available for a fee from The Haworth Document Delivery Service: 1-800-HAWORTH. E-mail address: <docdelivery@haworthpress.com> Website: <http://www.HaworthPress.com> © 2005 by The Haworth Press, Inc. All rights reserved.]*

**KEYWORDS.** Bisexuality, bisexual men, gay men, lesbians, Canada, GLBTIQA community advocacy

Several years ago, a dear friend gave me a magnet. Stenciled over the obligatory rainbow background, it said "Bi now. Gay later." Ostensibly one of those innocuous *petit cadeau*, supposed to invoke mirth and solidarity, from one queer to another. I smiled and put it on my fridge, but I felt distinctly uncomfortable about it, although I couldn't immediately put my finger on it. Once I got the joke–today's confused, self-deluding, self-loathing bisexual will undoubtedly become tomorrow's gay man or lesbian–I no longer felt that it was funny.

I am an Old Skool gay activist. I've been working toward substantive change for gay men and lesbians for nearly two decades. I started in New York in the mid-1980s, shifted to Vancouver in the early 1990s, and continue now in Sydney. My migration from the U.S. to Canada in 1989 resulted in significant philosophical and tactical shifts in the nature of my activism, but the initial goal–to fight for my own human rights as a gay man–has remained central throughout. Like most activists, it has been mostly unpaid work. Antigay violence, coming out, same-sex domestic violence, substance misuse and addiction, mental health, immigration and legal reform are some of the specific issues upon which I've worked. Case manager, hotline answerer, justice advocate, peer counselor, media liaison, and litigant were among my various roles. Most recently my activism has been research-based at universities and in my local community. Years of contact with persons whose interests in queer material issues ranged from incidental to adversarial led me to conclude that researching ourselves is fundamental to achieving the sort of tectonic shifts we need in discourse and public policy. The irony of working at leading international universities, having earlier railed against institutional hegemony and embedded patriarchy, is not lost on me.

Although I find many aspects of social theory about queers extremely problematic, the work of Bruce MacDougall, a Canadian expert on queer legal issues, is a gem. His four-category rubric on the progression of discourses on queer rights in Canada strongly resonates with me as an activist. According to MacDougall, legal discourses on homosexuals ranged from condemnation (rejected and vilified), through compassion (tolerated and pitied) and condonation (accepted, though not normal) and ultimately to celebration (valued and honored). Though a historical analysis of queer rights in Canada and the U.S.–both in a legal and a sociological sense–won't reveal a linear or static progression between these stages, in a general sense I think the rubric fits–for gay men and lesbians, especially in Canada. For bisexuals?

I used to think that the fight for lesbian and gay rights constituted a *de facto* fight for bisexual rights. Now I believe that while there are some carry-over benefits for bisexuals when gay and lesbian (or same-sex) rights are protected, bisexuals has unique–and legitimate–issues of their own. Using MacDougall's work to examine bisexuals' experiences seeking justice, all too often bisexuals find little more than compassion–particularly from their gay and lesbian "allies." What follows is a reflection on my own practice as an activist, examining how the role of bisexuals (and bisexual issues) has evolved–particularly with respect to how lesbian and gay activists have responded to bisexuality.

## CONDEMNATION:
## BISEXUAL PRIVILEGE

When I got involved in lesbian and gay activism in 1986, the pressing issues of the day were HIV/AIDS, HIV/AIDS, HIV/AIDS, and gender relations between gay men and lesbians. The body count in many North American cities led lots of dykes to put aside their "misterogyny" and tend to the sick and dying. Countless lesbians wiped asses, cleaned and cooked for, and transported men who couldn't do it themselves. They also taught us how to organize and resist, in the face of government inaction. The community response to AIDS among gay men would've failed weren't it for the unique combination of political and organizational savvy (lesbians mostly), personal and material resources (gay men mostly), and the stark reality that mainstream society wasn't at all upset to see homos dropping dead in the street. Sadly, had the roles been reversed I'm not convinced gay men would have responded in kind for lesbians. Well, actually we haven't, with respect to violence against women or breast, cervical and ovarian cancer, or lesbian custody rights, or . . .

In the late '80s, relations between gay men and lesbians weren't always good (in all honesty they were often quite tenuous), but principles were prioritized over personal issues, and a begrudging relationship between (some) homo men and women evolved. At New York's Gay and Lesbian Anti-Violence Project and at the Gay and Lesbian Switchboard, work was mostly gay male- or lesbian-specific. I can't recall anyone at the Switchboard self-identifying as bi. Most probably because an openly bi person would've found it "a hostile work environment," not perhaps characterized by enmity, but certainly not warmth.

Because one of the few things most gay men and lesbian activists could agree upon was that bisexuals were dissable. Most often, the discourse was one of bisexuals "passing with privilege." Bisexuals passed as hetero when they wanted to–particularly when they had an opposite sex partner–and could "choose" to appear straight. Bisexuals didn't fight for gay rights because they didn't have to–and wouldn't: bisexuals who claimed to challenge heteronormativity and heterocentrism were liars. Among my cadre of activist peers in New York, bisexuals rode on our backs. At best.

## COMPASSION:
## POOR CONFUSED SOTS

By 1990, I had moved to Vancouver, Canada. In Vancouver, bisexuals were nominally being added to the list of inclusive terms batted about (we were by then the LGB community), and occasionally specific bisexual issues would be added to calls to action, but little of substance changed. Gender issues between lesbians and gay men continued to evolve, however, and many of us had developed professional and personal relationships across gender lines. Many of us found working between the gay male and lesbian communities valuable, pleasurable and often pretty easy, though at times we did still treat the other as Martians. "Can you explain to me again why you might have sex with five guys in one night at the tubs?" "Sure. Can you explain to me why you'd move in with a girl after the second date–even when the sex wasn't so good?" Ouch.

Okay, perhaps from different sides of the same planet. But that para-doxical sameness and differentness allowed us to (more often than not) work and live together pretty easily. Back then the odd "compassion-ate" homo might espouse a view of pity towards those claiming to be bi-sexual. "Nice" bisexuals were often confused about their sexuality. "Strident" bisexuals also deserved our pity because they were just self-loathing homos who haven't yet accepted who they *really* were. But what did not change was a resistance to bisexuals (and trans folk, who were often kept literally outside LGB spaces) being considered genuine peers and allies. Bisexuals were welcome if they played by our rules and if they behaved nicely: in other words if they ate a lot of crap passive-aggressively fed to them, without complaint. And if they only discussed or displayed same-sex partners. "Don't ask, don't tell," or "it's acceptable if you're bi, just don't rub our faces in it," regardless, the expectation that bisexuals in the movement would have to remain closeted about any opposite gender relationships was clear.

In the early 1990s I became involved in a Canadian Human Rights Commission (CHRC) case about immigration sponsorship for foreign lesbian and gay partners of Canadians. I had entered Canada on a work permit; by 1991 I was in a partnership with a Canadian man, and my work visa had expired. Others in similar circumstances had begun meet-ing in Vancouver to mount a legal challenge to immigration policy and to offer support and information to those in similar situations. In 1992 my partner and I filed an application for my permanent residence as a "spouse," under vaguely defined Humanitarian and Compassionate (H&C) grounds, and joined a CHRC class action. We gave depositions, filed mountains of additional paperwork, and met with other couples (and lawyers) to strategize. In addition, we contacted our local Member of Parliament, Margaret Mitchell of the New Democratic Party, who immediately used her parliamentary privilege to query Immigration Canada about our application. I was granted my permanent residence before the human rights complaint was adjudicated, but in 1994 the Federal government acquiesced to our complaint. Acceptance of same-sex partners under H&C became official immigration policy, something only a handful of countries had implemented in the early 1990s.

The Canadian partners involved in this process always saw the result as inevitable. Canada's Charter of Rights and Freedoms didn't explic-itly include sexual orientation, but Section 15 (1) requires government (elected officials, civil servants and the courts) to ensure all in Canada have "equal protection and equal benefit of the law without discrimination." To our Canadian partners it was evident that if a case could be made that a group was discriminated against, the Charter would be interpreted to protect them–meaning we as gay and lesbian couples would win. The non-Canadian partners–particularly those of us from the U.S.–found their optimism (and impatience) admirable, but perplexing. In my years of activism, I'd not encountered any government that acquiesced to any of our agitations, unless they ran out of ways to delay it. The response from Immigration Canada to our CHRC complaint remains the most tangible evidence of my success as an activist–and clear evidence that many Canadians are concerned with being fair more than winning or losing. In relatively quick succession sexual orientation was "read into" the Charter: judges established legal precedents that identified gay men and lesbians as a group of individuals who experienced discrimination, though partner rights were initially excluded. Québec added sexual orientation to its human rights code in 1977–the first provincial or state government in North America to do so. By 1998 sexual orientation had been read into most Canadian provincial, territorial, and Federal human rights codes.

## *CONDONATION:*
## *QUEER (LGBT) HERE*

In 1994, the Government of British Columbia reconfigured its health services from one organized in strict geographic terms (regional care) to one that employed a population health model, where services are modified to reflect specific communities' needs. In greater Vancouver, a multicultural structure of advisory committees was created that included women, children and youth, Aboriginal peoples, the disabled, and seniors. Gay men and lesbians were not afforded such a committee, but by 1996, using the reading of sexual orientation into the Charter as an integral part of their rationale, a group of activists successfully argued for its creation. This committee was conceptualized and operated as a *lesbian, gay, bisexual, and transgender* health advisory committee. When I became a member in 1999, my rather narrow sphere of queer activism–gay men and lesbians–was instantly broadened. I realized I had catching up on a lot of nongay and nonlesbian health issues.

My bisexual colleagues on the queer health advisory committee amply demonstrated their knowledge and commitment to queer health. They worked hard to represent their own constituencies as bi folk and as queer men or women, and served our committee as excellent ambassadors to civil servants and the public. They engaged critically with health workers and advocated effectively for more accessible and sensitive services. They dealt with other committee members' hetero and bi-phobia, often without a trace of rancour. In short, they modeled the sort of dignity and integrity to which I aspired as a queer activist. They stuck to the high road, and they got the job done, even when ignorant homos like me sometimes got in the way.

I came to believe that I was not (primarily) bi-phobic: I was heterophobic. I clung to the idea that bisexuals were self-loathing, manipulative homos posing as heteros. Thus, I responded to bisexuals not as bisexuals, but as het interlopers to queer spaces. They were to be mistrusted, scrutinized, for eventually they would reveal themselves as "really" gay–or more likely, straight. I couldn't accept that sexual orientation was less compartmentalized for others than it is for me–so I rejected anything but a simplistic homo-or-hetero binary. In other words, if it didn't reflect my life, it mustn't be true, or important.

The hypocrisy of being a social-justice activist yet holding so tightly onto such an ignorant and prejudiced view of bisexuals appalls me now. In 1986, I would have argued that gay rights automatically included bi rights. Today I see fighting for the rights of all queers–gays, lesbians, bisexuals, transpersons, and others–doesn't reflect a singular set of issues that constitute the entire agenda of these different constituencies. We have plenty in common, but each has unique, equally important health issues. Together, I'm convinced, we're natural, formidable allies.

## CELEBRATION:
## NOT QUITE THERE YET

Since 2003 same-sex marriages have been legally performed in three Canadian provinces (Ontario, British Columbia and Québec), giving nearly three-quarters of Canadians access to legal same-sex marriage in their province of residence. Same-sex marriage is important not only in what it substantively means (couples can legally wed who were previously unable to do so in Canada), but the very wording–*same-sex* rather than *gay*–reflects that some who enter into such unions are not gay or lesbian. The inclusivity of all persons who would marry someone of their own gender is an important step, materially and discursively. As MacDougall argues, same-sex relationships are being legally recognized–celebrated–in Canada, in Massachusetts in the US, and in a number of European countries.

But does the shift towards a "same-sex" discourse with respect to marriage hearken the celebration of bisexuals as full members of the "lesbian and gay" civil rights movement? Sadly not. Just as many Canadians hold sentiments with respect to same-sex marriage ranging from discomfort to rejection, so do many queer activists hold opinions on bisexuals' role in our community from condemnation to compassion to condonation. Relatively few gay men and lesbians see same-sex marriage as anything but a "gay" issue.

## *BI NOW, WE SHOULD BE OVER IT*

Many years ago, I was explaining to a non-activist friend why a specific issue was a genuine and legitimate human rights question: the question escapes me, but the substance of the conversation remains important. "How do you know if what these people say is even true?" she asked. Her question caught me off-guard and resonated with me and my own doubts about claims of injustice. My reply caught me equally off-guard, and served as one of those uniquely powerful teachable moments: "My experience has been that whenever some group or community claims it's being treated differently by mainstream society, there's always some degree of truth to it. When I shift my focus away from *when* discrimination is acceptable to me, and towards *whether* discrimination is *ever* acceptable, it's clear to me what needs to be done. I can perpetuate injustice or I can help fight it."

Bi now the gay male, lesbian, and feminist communities and social movements should be immune to the very same dynamics of hateful homophobic, heterocentric society that devalue other queer persons. Bi now we should be able to distinguish between our allies and our enemies. Bi now gay men and lesbians should be rejecting the hierarchy of queerness, where gay and lesbian issues are considered superior to bisexual or transgender ones. Bi now we should be transcending this very notion that bisexuality is transient, inferior, or mythological.

# Magic Man

Julz

[Haworth co-indexing entry note]: "Magic Man." Julz. Co-published simultaneously in *Journal of Bisexuality* (Harrington Park Press, an imprint of The Haworth Press, Inc.) Vol. 5, No. 2/3, 2005, pp. 213-220; and: *Bi Men: Coming Out Every Which Way* (ed: Ron Jackson Suresha, and Pete Chvany) Harrington Park Press, an imprint of The Haworth Press, Inc., 2005, pp. 213-220. Single or multiple copies of this article are available for a fee from The Haworth Document Delivery Service [1-800-HAWORTH, 9:00 a.m. - 5:00 p.m. (EST). E-mail address: docdelivery@haworthpress.com].

**SUMMARY.** A bisexual female activist declares her love and affinity with bi men and explores the complexities of relationships between bi people. When both men and women in a relationship are bisexual, some popular assumptions about male/female couples are over-turned, but others persist and must be negotiated with grace and empathy. *[Article copies available for a fee from The Haworth Document Delivery Service: 1-800-HAWORTH. E-mail address: <docdelivery@haworthpress.com> Website: <http://www.HaworthPress.com> © 2005 by The Haworth Press, Inc. All rights reserved.]*

**KEYWORDS.** Bisexuality, bisexual men, gay men, bisexual women, GLBTIQA community advocacy, polyamory

Oh, the music of my misspent queer youth! When I heard Heart's song "Magic Man" on the radio as a teenager, I was certain that one of the hot babes in the band, like me, was sneaking off to suck face and be felt up by a guy who called himself gay because "bisexuals don't exist." (Gawd forbid if any of his friends in the college "gay" had group found out that he had girl cooties!)

Then, as now, few understood my attraction to queer men. I was an adventurous gal even then, and had swapped spit and been fondled by a variety of boys and girls by the tender age of sixteen. But why could this allegedly gay boy make my knees tremble like no other? Sure he was smart, and could dance better than straight boys, but that wasn't it. We could talk on the phone until dawn and walk around his campus singing Jacques Brel songs, but that wasn't it either. In some intangible way, we understood each other. He scared my mother to death, and I got all sorts of dire warnings about how my heart would ultimately be broken, because "he'll never feel the same as you do." Yet my heart remained intact in his care, and eventually he faded gently out of my life, married a nice Latino boy, and bought a house in the Chicago suburbs.

Flash forward twenty-two years. I want to write a wonderful essay about the joys of being in a relationship with a bisexual man, but time has tempered these joys with some cautious experience. Rest assured, though: I still prefer bi men when I have a male partner. I am in a long-term polyamorous relationship with one, and any other man I have chosen to be with has been bisexual as well.

I am not one of those unfortunate women who found out her man was bisexual by accident after a long relationship she assumed was strictly heterosexual. Such women have their own tales to tell, often painful ones, but that isn't my story, so I can't speak to it. I have known since day one that he was bisexual. I am too. What a world.

This story is also not about the woman who meets the man, finds out he's bi, and since loves conquers all, learns to accept it. I have a friend or two for whom this is their story. I, however, am an unabashed girlfag.

Let me define that. Girlfags are women who identify with queer men, somewhat feel that we are queer men ourselves, and often are sexually attracted to queer men. We are not faghags. Faghags are usually straight women who enjoy the company of gay men.

Many girlfags are bisexual women who dig our own kind. But there are straight girlfags, too, so it's more complicated than that. Some girlfags say that they are gay men trapped in women's bodies. For me, it's more as if the traits of the queer man I was in a past life assert themselves.

Whatever I call myself, and whatever the reason, my attraction has always been to other queers of both genders. And since I'm a functional grown-up who abhors rejection, bisexual men are my best option for queer-boy action. I believe gay men when they say they aren't interested in women, and have no desire to change their minds.

There is a not inconsiderable number of us girlfag folk. As a bi activist, I hang out with a lot of women who are partnered with bi men. We not only accept but also embrace the bisexuality of these guys, a fact that should encourage all the men I know who despair of ever meeting a woman they can be honest with.

Who are we, these women who knowingly and willingly enter relationships with bisexual men? We are mothers, musicians, health-care professionals, activists, nerds, teachers, or any other thing you can imagine. Though the sample of my grrrl-posse may be utterly unscientific, it appears that many of us are bisexual ourselves, or pioneers in some other fashion. Having sorted out our own identities in an often-clueless world, we tend to prize honesty over convenience. It matters to us to know who our partners really are and what they want, even if it leads to a more complex relationship. And if you ask us why we love bisexual men so much, there is usually a certain smile, and a sigh that accompanies it.

I wanted to delve deeper into where that smile and sigh come from. What is that gut-level tug we feel toward these men that we rarely, if ever, feel with straight men?

My friends and I talk about the humorous postcoital conversations we've had comparing fellatio techniques, or the pleasures of the bisexual pastime of multi-gender cruising together. These are good for giggles but not the stuff relationships are made of.

One friend sweetly states, "Well, I like watching guys get it on with each other, and if I date a bi man that's probably more likely to happen." This is more common than people may suspect. Everyone jokes about how men like to watch two women get it on. Some women like the same thing in reverse. The porn industry simply hasn't thought to make millions off of it.

When I probe deeper with that friend and others, and within myself, however, we touch on a profound sense of being understood by bi men in a way that most monosexuals can't. I spoke to one bi woman who was marrying a bi man in two weeks. She spoke of the deep sense of relief she felt the night she and her partner came out to each other. She described a sense of possibility and potential unknown to her before. She gave the example that she had never considered having children before being involved with him, but because he was looking at their roles as partners in a fluid way, she felt freer to imagine what parenthood would look like.

She hits on one of the real beauties of relationships with bi men: the ability to reinvent gender roles with another. Of course, straight folks can bend gender rules too. But since, by our very existence, bisexuals have already rewritten the sexual "man meets woman and lives happily ever after" script, it seems more possible to keep editing it to meet our needs. We may, or may not, want our happy endings less conventional, but while "happy" may look different, it's still a goal.

Another common thread seems to be that as bisexual women, we are often misunderstood by straight men, and the old myth of the "hot bi babe" rears its ugly head. Alas, most bi women are not hypersexual, perfectly manicured porn chicks, dying to have someone "watch." As one woman put it, "My bisexual male partner knows that I am a 'real, complex bi woman,' and loves me for it." Bi men usually understand that we want to get it on with other women for the same or similar reasons as theirs. There also seems to be a shared queer sensibility, cultural and political, that matters to us greatly. "You mean you love Ani DiFranco too?"

Many bisexuals on various lists and Web logs I've read say something like "I love people not genitals; gender doesn't matter." Though this is a common theme as well, I'm not sure what they are talking about because to my "bi-man-loving" women friends, and to me, genitals matter a great deal. We love these men because, among other things, they are men. One of my favorite bi women, Dr. Geri Weitzman, did some research on the topic of gender and partner choice among bisexuals. She found that while a majority of bisexual folks (70 percent in her research sample) saw bisexuality as the capacity to love people of both genders, not a need to have one of each, gender still often played a part in partner choice.

With that brief outline of what women like me enjoy about bi men, let's move on to thornier questions, such as how our relationships work, between each other and in the world at large. My mother, alas, still has kittens when thinking about my involvement with bisexual men. "You're going to get a disease, you know," she says, handing me another newspaper clipping. But I know how to play safe. Indeed, I'd hate to scare her, but the folks I know who have gotten "burnt" recently are straight. I, on the other hand, watched half my social network die during the '80s. I got the hint. And not to blow my own bi horn, but my straight girl friends have much more trouble negotiating safer sex than I do. "Dude, wear a condom." I have yet to have a bi guy react badly to that. The reaction is usually, "Goody! She wants to do something with me that involves a condom!" From what I hear, many straight men still can't adopt a similar attitude.

Mom's other fret, echoed by some of my straight friends, is, "He will leave you for a man." Some bi women don't have any insecurity about this. Unfortunately, I do. Since it feeds the monster in my anxiety closet, it is unhelpful when people say this. My rational, not oppressed, mind, however, tells me that a straight man could leave me for a woman, and a man's being bi makes him no more or less capable of breaking promises than anyone else.

We can also get lost in the "bisexuality does not require polyamory" discussion. The fact is that I personally am both, my lover is both, and I don't happen to know any monogamous bisexuals. I know they exist, just as polyamorous gay and straight people exist and all have different stories to tell. But I can only tell my own, with some corroboration from my peers.

I admit, I don't know many women whose bi male lovers are actively dating other men. Their fellas seem to get their same-sex groove on by tricking or casually playing at parties. I am guessing that there may be less long-term processing this way, because one doesn't have to figure out how to include the other person in their lives. Sadly, it's not always easy for some of us when our male partners hook up seriously with other men. Sometimes it's even painful. For either or both of us, and for a variety of reasons.

Among other things, my own lover has dated some gay men who have treated me, and my relationship with him, with scorn and derision. Fortunately, these guys get voted off the island quickly now. In speaking with another bi male friend who has concurrently dated men and women, this experience is not unique. Some gay men can be mean about considering women partners a "phase" they are eager to help our fellas get over. And some gay men don't want to bother with real, "out" bi men. Some guys seem happier interacting with closeted cheaters with unknowing wives at home, and cannot parse the concept that another guy might be choosing both a woman and a man honestly.

That said, where do our men find other men who can deal with this all? One might conjecture, "Bi men should just date each other." But in my experience, the bisexual tribal dance is a complex one. Put bisexuals together in social situations and it often resembles an eighth-grade dance: some opposite-gender canoodling and a lot of awkward wall clinging. None of us was probably very well supported in "same-gender" flirting growing up. My man has sometimes despaired of meeting another man who "really gets it."

And that brings us to our relationships with each other, and I must get very personal. Because getting "it" means "me," I have a lot of complicated feelings about my lover's difficulty finding boyfriends. He says "it" is more than just "me," but that is how it sometimes ends up feeling: that I'm the barrier to his ability to meet other boys. It's not a pleasant feeling, but it's not uncommon among bisexuals: worry that we hold each other back, and resentment at the thought that our partner might resent us.

Another complicated feeling that can arise is that of threat. An observation made by one of my cohorts resonates with me: "It's always harder when he goes off to play with a guy if my self-esteem is already low from something." Some, though not all, women can be competitive, and sometimes competing with men feels like a no-win situation. Yet for bi men, the fear that women partners will feel threatened and not want to deal with their sexuality may be the biggest issue that keeps some men from coming out to those women partners. Will the feeling of competition be too much? So the threat can feel mutual, and in some ways that's actually comforting, and helps bring us together. And ironically, gay men often say that they feel *they* will never be able to compete with a woman for a bi man's affections, as well. So it isn't bisexuals alone who have to work through these issues. To muddy the waters further, some bisexual and polyamorous folks are less threatened by their partner having a same-gender lover than an opposite-gender one. There is no "one size fits all" or even "most" answer. We all have our relation-ship demons to confront, and polyamory and bisexuality can be the faces of those demons for some people.

In my own case, well, my boy and I fight a lot. We fight, we cry, we fuck, and we fight again. We fight about insecurity and inequity, but also about the bathroom mirror not being hung correctly, like any long-term couple. We clumsily hurt each other as we try to make our passion work in a world that has no rules or reassurances for us, that a bi woman and a bi man can actually make it. We also sometimes are stub-born dysfunctional morons who pick fights because after thirteen years all couples, regardless of orientation, can fall into bad habits. My rela-tionship with this particular bisexual man is a tumultuous one. Many of my friends have very serene relationships. Maybe bisexuality has both nothing and everything to do with the conflicts.

I know lots of bi men who despair of ever having an honest, healthy relationship with a woman. I am here to say that there are people doing it, and doing it well. Possible yes, idyllic no, but the monosexuals don't get idyllic either, so why should we? Every relationship has its own set of problems and challenges, and everyone is their own story maker. But yes, guys, there are women who will not only love you in spite of your being bisexual, they will love it as part of the whole package.

In bi men, women like me find fellow transgressors who don't color inside the lines and who share our glee in believing that those lines may exist for the sole purpose of our delight in violating them. We have found others willing to share our corners of the world without compul-sory boxes. It's beautiful, volatile, and potent magic. Strange and com-bustible, hope and possibilities, as well as risk and potential for pain, like with all love between differing individuals, that we deep down know is worth it. That's the best kind of magic, man.

# Mission: Lighten Up!

doi:10.1300/J159v05n02_26

[Haworth co-indexing entry note]: "Mission: Lighten Up!" Chvany, Pete. Co-published simultaneously in *Journal of Bisexuality* (Harrington Park Press, an imprint of The Haworth Press, Inc.) Vol. 5, No. 2/3, 2005, pp. 221-229; and: *Bi Men: Coming Out Every Which Way* (ed: Ron Jackson Suresha, and Pete Chvany) Harrington Park Press, an imprint of The Haworth Press, Inc., 2005, pp. 221-229. Single or multiple copies of this article are available for a fee from The Haworth Document Delivery Service [1-800-HAWORTH, 9:00 a.m. - 5:00 p.m. (EST). E-mail address: docdelivery@haworthpress.com].

**SUMMARY.** Longtime bisexual male activist pokes fun at stereotypes of bi men and women while revealing his own process of self-acceptance through humor. The author argues that a sense of fun is essential to thriving as a whole person, even in the face of painful stigmas and misunderstandings. *[Article copies available for a fee from The Haworth Document Delivery Service: 1-800-HAWORTH. E-mail address: <docdelivery@ haworthpress.com> Website: <http://www.HaworthPress.com> © 2005 by The Haworth Press, Inc. All rights reserved.]*

**KEYWORDS.** Bisexuality, bisexual men, coming out, humor, bisexual stereotypes

I'm on a mission to make bisexuality fun again. Heck, I'm on a mission to make any sexuality fun again; I'm not picky.

But seriously, folks. I'm reclaiming a sense of humor. In fact, I'm *developing* a sense of humor, about myself and the world around me, for the first time in years. My bisexuality is a driving factor in that process.

When I first came out several years ago, I couldn't have said this, alas. Like many bisexuals, I bloomed late: my early thirties, which is almost retirement age in queer years.

I was aware of attractions to men and women somewhere around the age of twelve. Something about admiring the bejeezus out of The Bionic Woman and thinking she was a cool chick, and yet getting in a sweat over the Six Million Dollar Man, should have been my first clue. Or did Lieutenant Uhura and Captain Kirk predate that? But like many queers, and many bisexual queers in particular, I didn't know what that all meant, or how to deal with it.

How could I be straight if I was masturbating over cigarette ads featuring open-shirted hairy-chested men . . . ads in *Playboy*, no less? [Mr. Chvany? Um, Mr. Chvany, this is *Playboy*, not *Playgirl*: the boobies are on the *next* page.] But how could I be gay if I liked making out with girls and wanted to go further? How could I lose my virginity with an attractive woman, and enjoy it, but not have that decide my fate? How could I have my first boyfriend and feel "wow, this is it!" but not have "it" be all encompassing? How could I risk coming out and losing my entire family and network of friends (so I thought, so most people my age grew up fearing) if I wasn't getting over my interest in women, seeing as how gay men and lesbians seemed to think bisexuality was "just a phase" and talked it down a lot and were mean to bisexuals, but my bisexuality didn't seem to be a phase?

Oh the confusion, oh the depression, oh the sadness! Waah! No wonder I turned into such a dour, overly sensitive young man.

And whoops, there went my teens and twenties, mostly in a haze of wistful celibacy (although I did wank a lot. Why yes: I have a strong right hand.). I didn't know how to deal with sex of any other kind. Bye, wasted youth, don't forget to write. At least I got other stuff done: a brief stint in the military, where I got my first taste of adult responsibility; taking care of an elderly relative through her last few years of life; the first couple of years of graduate school. I wasn't happy, exactly, but I was growing and learning.

And then I got really tired of worrying about myself and wondering who I was, and came out. I had figured out at least this much: yup, I'm probably more attracted to men than women, without being completely unattracted to women. So, all right. And when exactly does life start? Because I'm nearly thirty-three, and I want life to start sometime. Hey, what about now? Sure!

Hooray for 1996, the Year Pete Came Out.

I started hanging out in the queer community (via a GLBT science fiction convention at first; yes, I'm a complete nerd, but never fear, I only use my powers for good) and quickly discovered that there were chicks who dug bisexual men and dudes who either dug us too, or didn't care who else we slept with, as long as we could suck their cocks decently. Which it quickly proved I could (go me!).

My sex life improved tremendously at that point, mostly because I acquired a sex life.

But my sense of humor took a bit longer to develop. This was because, as just about any bisexual person will tell you, a lot of people don't "get" bisexuality.

As with most misunderstood social groups, there is fear and stereotyping and sometimes outright harassment and violence directed at bisexuals. Even after years of dedicated activism by bisexuals and our friends within the GLBT community, there are many settings where it's considered perfectly appropriate to say ridiculous, nasty things about bisexuals. ("You're bi? Aha! Your father was a hamster! And you'll leave me for a woman! And you smell like a monkey! And . . .")

Many straight people are just as bad. If they're homophobes, of course, they don't consider being bi much of an improvement over being gay, unless they think our "heterosexual" feelings are a lever they can use to turn us "straight." But even non-homophobic straight people, who have oodles of gay and lesbian friends and can sing along with "YMCA" or "Come to My Window" without getting self-conscious, can find bisexuals a little threatening.

So unless you have "I'm bi" tattooed on your forehead, people sometimes say terrible things about you, in your presence, not realizing they're about to devastate your tender shy flower feelings. (Nobody ever assumes there's a bisexual in the room with them, unless they're at a bi event. And maybe not even then, because people's power to believe that There Are No Real Bisexuals passes all understanding.) But really, there are nicer things to tattoo on one's forehead.

Not to mention the true-life horror stories it seems everyone can tell about such-and-such a person they used to know who was sexually confused and ping-ponged between men and women or kept Big Secrets, and then did something horrible (infected a lover with something deadly, betrayed a trust, behaved like a total flake, et cetera and so on).

I don't mean to minimize the horror of some of those True Life Tales. I've heard more than a few myself. They're very sad.

It's just that, when you're openly bi, one of the first things people need to do is tell you those horror stories, as if they think you had something to do with it, or as if you can fix it for them. Which leads to conversations like, "But no, can you tell I'm not the confused bisexual chick who dumped you forty years ago? Because I was, like, totally only one year old at the time, okay?"

It's a bit like going to confession: bisexuality makes people get their feelings about gray-area sexualities off their chests.

Actually, confession isn't the word for it. Bisexuality is more like cough syrup: being out as bisexual often loosens the yucky, phlegmy stuff people carry inside themselves about sexuality (their own or someone else's), and they need to spit it out at you. Little sex-panic loogies . . . duck! Ewww, got me!

When you put it that way, it doesn't sound like much fun to be bi. If bisexuals aren't slimy ourselves, we sure sometimes feel as if people slime us. I spent several years powerfully attuned to all the negative messages about bisexuals that constantly circulate through queer communities and the culture at large. All of which I took personally and felt just awful about, even though I totally didn't have to. And once I stopped feeling so awful about those stereotypes and harsh words on my own behalf, I continued to burn about them for my bisexual friends and lovers, all of whom are fantastic, wonderful people who've stood by me and deserve nothing but the best. [I love you guys! Group hug!] I spent several years being Pete, Crusading Bisexual Superhero, doing my bit to combat those negative ideas about us.

Oh the injustice! Oh the humanity!

Oh, God, how boring after a while.

I mean, it's a good thing to be a Crusading Bisexual Superhero. People have told me, to my face, just how much my Crusading Bisexual Superhero words or deeds meant to them. Pretty good stuff, that.

It only partway helped me feel better about myself, though. Eventually, I realized I needed to work on self-acceptance via other means, as well.

Truth is, it *is* fun to be bi. Exactly as much fun as it is to be straight, or gay.

Truth is, many bisexuals wind up having a fabulous sense of humor about sexuality, partly as a defense mechanism, but partly because people's "stuff" about bisexuality just goes to show how complex and silly human nature is, no matter how many (or few) sides of a "fence" you happen to be on.

The more I interacted with bi people who had good heads on their shoulders and a snappy quip on the tip of their tongues, the more I wanted to be one too.

It's taken a lot of practice, and I'm not all the way there yet. Ask any of my friends whose heads I've bitten off, on days when my martyr complex was showing, and they'll tell you I haven't dropped all of my baggage. Whoo, baby. But angst is a nasty puce color that clashes with my blue eyes, and baggage gets very hard on the arms after a while, so the practice is worth it.

And people give humor-inclined bisexuals plenty of great material to work with.

For instance, people are always asking bisexuals, "How long has it been since you slept with (or had a serious relationship with) a man (or woman)? Are you sure you're still bi?"

Jeez, it's as if they're checking our Bisexual Freshness Date. Am I a human being, or a bottle of milk? My sexuality doesn't expire after a certain length of time. I know celibate gay people, and boy do I know straight people who go for years without a date. Some of them are my very dear friends. Please love them. But ask *them* if they're still who they say they are, even if they haven't gotten any lately.

So comments like that are annoying from heathen outsiders. But get a bunch of bisexuals together, and we start playing jokes like these for all they're worth.

"Oh God," I've been known to say to friends, "I haven't slept with a woman in two years. I . . . I can't even remember what a vagina looks like. My freshness date is almost up! I'm spoiling! Help me, Eve Ensler, you're my only hope!" I raise one arm and press the back of my hand to my forehead, like a damsel in distress. Since I'm a six-foot-three, broad-shouldered, two-hundred-thirty-pound guy, that's a lot of distressed damsel. Most people who aren't stunned into complete silence are surprised into laughter. (For the cultural-reference challenged, Eve Ensler wrote a play called *The Vagina Monologues:* she must know from vaginas.)

We also joke about our "bi cards," which are like a combination library card and those frequent-coffee-drinker cards they give you at the java shop ("Get your seventy-ninth cup free!") only with different spaces to punch out depending on whether you just slept with a woman or a man. There's much discussion, in my circle, of what forms of bad behavior count towards getting your "bi card" revoked. "Oops, I slept with a woman and felt completely fulfilled, didn't fantasize about men once: revoke my bi card!"

Bisexuality is also like an amusement park ride: you must have had at least this many male and female lovers to call yourself a True Bisexual!

Or I'll be in bed with one of my male partners, and we'll be doing something involving whatever it is two men do together (if you don't know, I'm not telling you. I'm not sharing; I'm keeping every guy on earth for myself, all three billion. Bisexuals are greedy, don't you know.) And I'll say, "Oh, wow! This is so great! I've totally forgotten about women! I see the light now! My confused sexuality is cured! Thank you, Jesus, thank you! By the power of the penis, I am healed!" And then I'll start mock sobbing, like on one of those faith-healing programs.

Since my primary male partners are also bisexual men, this usually results in a mutual fit of giggles and more hijinks. And the next day, we put on our business clothes and go out into the world and act just like "regular" people, with jobs, and pets, and sometimes kids, and we make useful contributions to the universe, and we help old ladies across the street, and we love pretty flowers, and sunshine, and fluffy bunnies.

Because really, kids: it's just sex and sexuality. Everyone has a sexuality, and as far as I can tell, upwards of 99 percent of people have one that is perfectly fine and harmless, among consenting folks who remember to stay on guard against nasty germs or unwanted pregnancies.

And sure, bisexuality looks strange and different through the lenses of a mainstream culture (a mainstream that, by now, pretty much assumes that homosexuality is an ordinary thing, even if some people still can't stop being upset about it). But the strangeness and difference is part of the fun. At least, it's part of the fun for many of us, even those of us who aren't bisexual.

Some of us find life interesting and sex comic (though also powerful and fulfilling and necessary). So what if some of us, when we say, "Take my wife . . . please?" actually *mean it*? (Not that bisexuality is the same thing as partner swapping or polyamory. Necessarily.)

Lighten up. That's the phrase I repeat to myself lately. Just lighten up. And life gets better the more I put that idea into practice. I commend it to others as a decent approach to human existence.

If you're bisexual, lighten up. Hey: women are fun, men are fun, so go have fun: do right by others, expect them to do right by you, be honest, but lighten up, and have fun. And if you're not bisexual . . . well, hey! Women are fun, men are fun, you don't have to do anything in particular about either one of those facts (and neither do us bisexuals, actually: repeat after me: bisexuality is an option for bisexuals, not a requirement!) but lighten up, and have fun. Be a good and worthy person. Your sexuality is part of that, but a good part. Even if other people don't understand you. It's okay.

Now, sure, it's taken me eight years of being out of the closet to be able to say that, and two supportive families (my family of origin, and the one I've put together for myself since coming out), and a community of bi and bi-friendly people, and yada yada yada. But it's been a philosophy and way of life worth striving for. There are, after all, more important things in life to deal with than "who's sleeping with who?"

Having a sense of humor feels ever so much better than moping all the time.

And here's an example. About a year ago, a gay man I'd been getting acquainted with told me that as far as he was concerned, bisexuals were like unicorns.

In the past, that kind of dismissal would have felt devastating. And I'll admit, even a year ago it rankled a bit . . . we had seemed to be getting along well and I'd done nothing to merit any nastiness from him. In general, I would like to live in a world where I get along with everyone (and buy a winning lottery ticket and eat ice cream every day without getting fat, too). It was a letdown to realize that here was someone who just couldn't see the real me, nice guy that I am, as long as my sexual identity stood between us.

But, sense of humor intact, I merely replied, "Well, I guess that means you won't be stroking my horn anytime soon, since I don't exist. Pity, because I think you're kind of cute."

He didn't reply to that. But I had a marvelous time chuckling to myself about it. And life went on.

It's okay. Lighten up. Have fun. And kiss a bisexual. We like it.

# Adam's Treehouse

*Adam Ben-Hur*

Available online at http://www.haworthpress.com/web/JB
© 2005 by The Haworth Press, Inc. All rights reserved.
doi:10.1300/J159v05n02_27

[Haworth co-indexing entry note]: "Adam's Treehouse." Ben-Hur, Adam. Co-published simultaneously in
*Journal of Bisexuality* (Harrington Park Press, an imprint of The Haworth Press, Inc.) Vol. 5, No. 2/3, 2005,
pp. 231-238; and: *Bi Men: Coming Out Every Which Way* (ed: Ron Jackson Suresha, and Pete Chvany) Harrington Park Press, an imprint of The Haworth Press, Inc., 2005, pp. 231-238. Single or multiple copies of this
article are available for a fee from The Haworth Document Delivery Service [1-800-HAWORTH, 9:00 a.m. -
5:00 p.m. (EST). E-mail address: docdelivery@haworthpress.com].

**SUMMARY.** In a gay man's aerie apartment in the San Francisco Bay area, weekly nude gatherings for men at various stages of sexual and self-exploration create a unique environment where men's private longings are allowed to flourish. As the men open up to each other and discover a primal way to relate without the barrier of clothes, their archetypal roles as both lovers and warriors show forth in unexpected ways. *[Article copies available for a fee from The Haworth Document Delivery Service: 1-800-HAWORTH. E-mail address: <docdelivery@haworthpress.com> Website: <http://www.HaworthPress.com> © 2005 by The Haworth Press, Inc. All rights reserved.]*

**KEYWORDS.** Bisexuality, bisexual men, gay men, California, nudism, coming out, Bear subculture, mythopoetic masculinity, men's support group

Seven years ago, I began hosting weekly afternoon get-togethers for a handful of bisexual married buddies whom I knew or who had personal contact with someone who knew me. This proverbial "small circle of friends" banded together in my second-story one-bedroom apartment, just a short walk from downtown Walnut Creek in the San Francisco Bay area.

Once inside the apartment, with its steeply slanted wood-shingled roof, surrounded by eucalyptus trees, safely away from public streets, you felt a step closer to nature. A welcoming spirit of playfulness pervaded the space. Several hundred wonderful men in Northern California will light up with a big grin if asked if they ever "played in Adam's Treehouse."

When the group began, I had known some guys for many years and gladly introduced them around. It started as a very relaxed, low-key group of mature men who wanted a little extra contact and excitement in their lives, and who could arrange an afternoon off. These good men spent most of their lives helping others and had rarely asked for anything back.

I worked at home, which made it convenient to host them. I always looked forward to seeing everyone. I enjoy playing host and helping people relax and open up to each other. These men weren't looking for a "relationship," but they did want the safety and security of seeing other men like themselves with whom they could easily relate.

This was new territory for many. Aside from satisfying their natural physical desires, they sought out the company of other men who, like themselves, found the idea of guys having sex together perfectly normal or were curious about sex with men. It's common for a happily married bisexual man who desires another man sexually to wonder if he's a freak of nature, out on the edge of society. But my experience is that most of them are far above average in their ability to create a successful life for themselves and their families.

I cannot adequately convey how cozy and pleasant this man-space was. The tight quarters of my "Treehouse" helped everyone get physically and psychologically closer. My place was so small, you could hear in the kitchen whether another man's pee was hitting the water or the porcelain in the bathroom. Guys would enter the Treehouse, introduce themselves to everyone, undress, grab a beer, and find a place to sit, often enough right next to someone they never met before. I almost always stretched out on the carpet with a pillow at my side so the other guys could snuggle on the couch. After the couch filled up, other guys would join me on the floor, resting a leg or an arm against another man's body in friendly lassitude.

Nudity is a metaphor for transparency where a man can let himself be seen as real by others, aside from its effect of being easy on the eyes and a natural relaxant. At some point, a man's own spiritual life force reclaims ownership of his nervous system, disentangles it from inhibiting frameworks, and gives it the authority to fulfill its needs to get real with other men.

Some experience this change like a hyperdrive shift into outer space. For others, it seems more casual and easy: "What the heck! May as well give guys a try." Rather than letting a social image dictate whom they love and how they express it, they simply find the appropriate companionship and a bit of privacy, and disport themselves like great lions and tigers of pleasure. Every man integrates his essential bisexuality into his masculine self-concept at his own pace, but the process accelerates being with friendly open guys whose essential nonjudgmental acceptance of others allows them to "just go for it." Ironically, men become simultaneously tenderer and more masculine in their own naked company.

Many Treehouse gatherings stretched calmly, sensually through the warm afternoons toward dusk. Without self-consciously intending to become a formal men's support group, these men helped and supported each other through emotional separations, divorces, love affairs, injuries, surgeries, family deaths and births, job changes, financial ups and downs—whatever kind of weather affected the other guys' lives.

Within two years, solely publicized by word of mouth, this circle of men easily grew to forty. At least seven men showed up each week, and almost everyone would drop in monthly. Most men arranged their own workdays. They could have dedicated the same time to a golf game or volunteer community service or the pursuit of some favorite hobby.

I mentioned before that no one was looking for a "relationship." This is true. But there have been a surprising number of lucky coincidental friendships that started as a result of two guys showing up at the same time who took to each other mutually and immediately, had various interests in common and had no problem allowing a discreet relationship to occur. We'd hear that they had taken off for a bed-and-breakfast weekend in Mendocino or run off to Palm Springs for a holiday or a camping trip in Yosemite. We wouldn't see them for a few months because they were out having fun together. I was always happy when this kind of thing took place. I've always thought of my Treehouse as a place of friendship and understanding, where people can open up at their own speed of self-discovery, and feel good about themselves in the process.

Gradualness is important. People have many different layers, filters, and screens that they need to maintain their sense of identity, privacy, and anonymity. As people feel more comfortable and at ease, they gradually let down their social mask. A man would reveal on their fourth or fifth visit, "You know, I like you guys, but I have to confess: my name isn't really Mark, it's Drew. I gave a false name because I wasn't sure how I'd fit in, if I'd like you guys or if you'd like me, but anyway I can drop that now. Just call me Drew." These occasional group breakthroughs brought everyone closer into a new male intimacy.

I've known Paul, one of the founding fathers of the Treehouse, for eleven years. He's a man's man who plays semipro polo and organizes scuba-diving trips to places like New Guinea, Tasmania, and the Red Sea. Professionally, he manages construction sites throughout the San Francisco East Bay. A mutual friend introduced us.

Before he joined the Treehouse crowd, Paul and I privately saw each other. I was the second man Paul had ever had sex with. He'd visit after work on a winter afternoon and I'd build a fire in the slate fireplace for my Marlboro man. He'd stretch his powerfully framed, work-muscled body out on a towel or blanket in front of the fire and I'd massage his back with warm oil for about an hour before gently turning him over to begin sex. Paul was a very warm and personable man, but he had no desire to reciprocate. He was comfortable only with allowing himself to experience one kind of sexual expression with another male. Sexually, he could only imagine himself as passively receiving oral sex from another guy, and I was more than happy to oblige.

Once, we were resting by the fire in that pleasantly mindless post-orgasm afterglow that is the reward of the blessed. As the pine logs hissed and sizzled, I watched the fire flicker in his gray eyes while idly tracing the wide welt of his triple bypass scar upward from his groin and across his belly and chest. Apropos of nothing, he asked me if I'd ever kissed a guy—what was it like?

I affirmed that kissing another man was wonderful, but only with the right guy. He said he could *never* imagine kissing another guy. He just didn't think he was wired for that kind of intimacy. I just smiled, knowing that in this case "never" probably meant "sooner or later." I knew that this gradualness would eventually open his sexual perspective. Paul and I continued to see each other every other week for several years, and he relaxed more with each visit and, interested in meeting my friends, began coming to the Treehouse.

One afternoon, the first person over was Jerry, a knockout dreamboat who looked like he jumped off the cover of *GQ* magazine. In a live-action version of *Sleeping Beauty*, this guy could play Prince Charming. Jerry had told me that had an argument with his boss that morning and wanted to get away and change the tapes in his head. He got naked, then rested on his side on the couch, reading a novel.

Then Paul arrived for an afternoon romp with the guys at the Treehouse. I noticed that my older friend was immediately taken with Jerry, awkwardly dropping his boots and work jeans. I was distracted with finishing some work and, aside from getting them something to drink and putting my favorite erotic film on the VCR, I stayed in front of my computer in the living room and tried to focus on my work. They began a normal introductory conversation.

A few minutes later, I saw them fondling and caressing each other. A few minutes later, they were making out like teenagers. I smiled quietly, reluctantly returning my attention to my computer screen. For a man who claimed he would never get close to another guy, my tough old macho buddy suddenly showed an amazing natural talent for French- kissing other men. When the couple finally slid to the floor in a romantic 69 position, I suggested they take over the bedroom and I'd make sure they weren't interrupted.

As other guys arrived, they immediately noticed the sounds of amorous romping drifted through the closed bedroom door. The men present were curious who the lucky dogs were. I explained that our Marlboro man had finally met the right match to ignite his dormant erotic fires, and that they'd join us when they'd finished burning up a few sheets and scorching a pillow or two. The couple didn't reemerge for three hours.

Eventually, the bedroom door opened and they slipped into the shower together chuckling, which I thought was a very good sign. Showering together after sex is always a sign of genuine attraction, of wanting to continue the rapport and intimacy you experienced in bed. From their affectionate laughter in the toilet, we knew they had hit it off.

They entered the living room beaming, continuing to dry each other off. Since the couch was already full, they cuddled up on the floor, purring on their pillows together like Bengal tigers in the aftermath of their hunt. Prince Charming tucked up nicely into Marlboro's man's strong shaggy arms as quiet kisses were pressed into the back of his neck and shoulders, and his perfect butt molded into my older buddy's contented groin. We spent about another hour like this before everyone dressed and stepped back into their usual Clark Kent timelines and personas.

This vignette, one of many stories from the Treehouse, dramatically illustrates how someone gradually makes a major shift in their earlier sexual stance. Paul's years of contact with me and the other guys let him show his affectionate side and see himself in a different sexual role or position with a man.

That afternoon, Preparation met Opportunity and shared a pleasant afternoon naked together. In the course of our lifetime, it's very likely we will explore many forms of sex. Most guys eventually change how they express ourselves sexually, in the same way they change jobs or careers in order to experience themselves in new ways and discover new aptitudes.

It's important to accept other people and to respect the boundaries or limitations that may constrain them at the time. People can tell when it's time to shed one of those layers, when it's alright to draw aside one more screen, when it's safe to try something new.

One afternoon at the Treehouse, nine men were lounging around naked, having a great talk and telling stories, and the experience reminded me of the classic film epics *Spartacus* and *Ben-Hur*. These "sword-and-sandal" flicks featured, in addition to mid-twentieth-century moral edification, voluptuous breasts bursting out of diaphanous, low-swagged gowns, and meaty, squared-up pectoral muscles, oiled and gleaming in the Technicolor sun. The scene in my living room that day transported us several thousand years into the Greco-Roman past as good-looking naked guys, younger and older together, enjoy their own lusty, good-humored company in a eucalyptus-scented villa by the Aegean Sea.

On the couch, Don and Eric's outstanding gladiatorial physiques embraced and entwined as tightly as morning-glory vines, their hard muscles covered by soft flesh revealed in each other a living sculpture of Eros at play.

Joe and Frank, who served together in Vietnam, told enthralling war stories, like uncles home from the war sharing Ares' tales of valor and heroism with their nephews.

Randy, radiating smooth-skinned, pink-nippled, curly-haired Celtic genes, poured Scott a glass of wine from a pitcher of dappled hand-blown Italian glass and then nestled on the floor, his white arm draped across Scott's shaggy thigh. From a Portuguese background, Scott looks like a Roman senator with a massive hairy chest, graying brown hair, and a handsome, chiseled, patrician face. It was like the naked Irish slave boy serving wine to the master at a summer villa in Capri. Or Ganymede at the feet of Zeus.

The dull veil of everyday life gently parted and the eternal soul identity of each person suddenly shone radiantly, like faces in faïence. I pictured a gold horseshoe torqued around Randy's neck as Scott idly caressed his autumn-burnished hair and fondled his curved white and freckled shoulder.

These thoughts made me grin ear-to-ear and I blurted out, "You guys look like a bunch of extras from *Ben-Hur!*" Everyone got the picture and roared in laughing agreement. It was absolutely true.

# Part Four: Bridge-Building in Bisexual Spirit

## Choosing Not To

*Michael Ambrosino*

Available online at http://www.haworthpress.com/web/JB
doi:10.1300/J159v05n02_28

[Haworth co-indexing entry note]: "Choosing Not To." Ambrosino, Michael. Co-published simultaneously in *Journal of Bisexuality* (Harrington Park Press, an imprint of The Haworth Press, Inc.) Vol. 5, No. 2/3, 2005, pp. 239-246; and: *Bi Men: Coming Out Every Which Way* (ed: Ron Jackson Suresha, and Pete Chvany) Harrington Park Press, an imprint of The Haworth Press, Inc., 2005, pp. 239-246.

**SUMMARY.** A bisexual male coming-out manifesto. The author recounts his trial-and-error process, lessons learned from gay men, lesbians, and other bisexuals, and the stages of his coming out. The author ends with a message of hope to aspiring bi men and affirms the role of bisexual men's communities. Reprint from *Bi Any Other Name: Bisexual People Speak Out,* Loraine Hutchins & Lani Ka'ahumanu, editors, 1991.

**KEYWORDS.** Bisexuality, bisexual men, gay men, coming out, personal transformation, lesbians, GLBTIQA community, spirituality

Coming-out stories can have a particular eloquence to them. Purposeful and frightening, coming out begins an awkward journey. Filled with courage, scrutiny, humor, and hatred, many eventually celebrate, having absorbed the power reclaimed by finally owning themselves. I've read about and watched men and women finally embrace their sexual preferences and then carry on with what seems to be an endless task of informing friends, family, and acquaintances. There's a clarity here, a purpose sustained by the individual's emerging sense of self and the support the lesbian and gay community offers those who dare to reach for it.

Comparatively speaking, my own emergence was vague and ambiguous, a private affair full of disappointments and a klutzy sense of trial and error. Because of an uncertainty about bisexuality, friends and family blinked nervously, shrugging in their minds and hearts, not quite understanding what kind of animal I was declaring myself to be. Lesbians and gay men also experience the litany of annoying questions, stupefying attitudes, and sentiments born of ignorance that, via violence and discrimination, literally kills so many women and men. Many whom I told about my bisexuality saw only the possibility of my becoming infected with the HIV virus. Some cried uncontrollably, seeing my life racing toward a final countdown.

Most responded with glibness, confusion, or anger fueled by stereotypes of bisexuals as traitors to one pole or another, misfits, or sexual dyslexics–people who can't make up their minds. For many I was the first "real" bisexual they had ever known. "But you're so happy!" "Do you ever have successful relationships?" Twisted facial expressions accompanied those questions about what my sexual preference entailed. Most people were disbelieving, very skeptical, checking for change, and constantly thinking someday I would "straighten out" or "queer up."

I knew very few bisexuals; landmarks found in most lesbian and gay communities do not exist for us. So it was off to the gay bars with a naïve vision of brotherhood, which, I quickly learned, translated into a feast of hands and not much more. Gay men have enriched my life; in a world all too tolerant of violent, insensitive, shortsighted males, gay men have provided me with a refuge. For much of my initial coming out, the choices were few. Searching for the words to convey my feeling of being "home" among gay men, I recall mostly the images: so many rounds of laughter, so many stories of suffering, so many men who, against the constant chant of "faggot," evolved into some of the wisest, most human and resourceful men I know. That we do not honor these men, that this world refuses to see the peace implicit in their ideals, disgusts me. With AIDS, the patriarchy has finally found a cure for the challenges gay and bisexual men have thrown in their faces: quietly kill them.

Finding a balance between those masculine traditions of our upbringing that have merit and those we develop in resistance to the more absurd and often deadly values of the patriarchy is often a confusing and lonely journey. In my search for self, gay men have always been primary role models, examples of an alternate grace and beauty. I've seen carnivals of perseverance in the face of a society that approves the killing of gay culture (while tapping into its profitability), their emotional and political gifts to the world, and even the men themselves. Unfortunately, when it comes to supporting my bisexuality, many have failed, even to the point of being unwilling to talk about it.

After ten years of struggling to find myself within this strange psycho-sexual soup, only in the last year and a half have I felt at home with my bisexuality: accepting it thoroughly, giving myself the space to live with the imperfections, fears, and delights of being emotionally, physically, and sexually open to both men and women. I'm out in as many situations as possible, standing up against biphobia in my communities as I work for an AIDS social services agency staffed overwhelmingly by lesbians and gay men.

My emergence as a bisexual man has consisted of three definite stages: (1) acknowledging my attraction to men and then acting upon it; (2) realizing that I was bisexual and actively trying to define and learn more about myself as a bisexual man; and (3) realizing that I could be in a relationship with either a man or woman, and yet still consider myself bisexual. In other words, I didn't have to prove the "legitimacy" of my bisexuality to anyone.

Bisexuals have just begun to establish themselves as unique, as different and alike as any other established group, yet with their own public and private idiosyncrasies. Countless times I find myself turning to bi men or women, knowing their experiences will provide me with a more understanding and constructive critical platform with which to discuss my life, politics, and sexuality. We die, get beaten up, are discriminated against (especially by lovers, straight or gay), passed over (omitted from countless so-called liberation day parades), and blatantly discounted and misunderstood even as our numbers increase, diversifying what is now beginning to be known as the community of sexual minorities. Upending traditions along the way, paving our acceptance by solidly pointing out the limits placed on loving, sexuality, sexual pleasure, and sexual experimentation in both cultures, bisexuals now are helping to set a new agenda for the lesbian and gay community.

Acknowledging only the "heterosexual" side, bisexuals are perceived by gays as being immune from the discrimination and violence that face all sexual minorities. Our "heterosexual privilege" somehow outweighs those times we get chased from bars, beaten in parks, infected with HIV, or are rejected by our biphobic lovers. Three acquaintances have committed suicide because of the confusion and anger their bisexuality created in their lives. Obviously, biphobia has devastating consequences on the ability of bisexuals to lead healthy lives.

Scared and unaware of any possible alternatives, many "gay" men refuse to explore either a resurging urge to have sexual relationships with women or the heterosexuality they might have felt all along. It's just too difficult to deal with a shifting sexual vocabulary. They take the words they know and use them in a community that provides many of them the only safety and comfort in their lives. Without adequate support systems, to leap into what is initially perceived to be a confusing, ambiguous void seems all the more dangerous. Straddling lives, pulling taut the lines of communication between two very different worlds, finding rare and often claustrophobic pockets of acceptance is what awaits bisexuals who come out.

True, there are more pressing issues facing humanity than the fate of bisexuals, our history, our sense of culture and community. But if we are to stand for the liberation of all peoples, carefully listing the "isms" as they come and go in our lives, then we must acknowledge biphobia: the fear of bisexuals, bisexuality, and our rightful place in straight, gay, and lesbian environments.

Without a sense of purpose, without a clearly defined perspective, many bisexuals fail to recognize the political implications of their sexual preference. Lack of awareness, lethargy, and the fact that the diversity of our population is tremendously hard to organize have all contributed to the slow-forming sense that a bisexual community exists. Cutting across all social strata, bisexuality thrives, potentially comprising the largest pocket of the sexual minority community. But organizing bisexuals has been one of the most frustrating and least productive endeavors in my political experience. Our inability to organize build our own resource centers, periodicals, and political action groups has often been a reflection of our limited sense of ourselves. Nonetheless, we continue to prosper, primarily because so many bisexual women have plunged in, pioneering the formation of small groups that have slowly emerged across the country.

Lagging behind our sisters, bisexual men have been slow to act on organizing ourselves into a productive coalition. For men wishing to find and sustain supportive environments in which we can begin to realize some sense of being other than the models this country dictates, the search brings few results. Is it impossible to claim those abilities of men that cultivate our strengths and still be feminist and gay and lesbian positive? Must so many men either attack feminists for realizing their power or completely subordinate themselves to feminist philosophy, not recognizing the desperate need for us to take responsibility in creating our own systems of progressive principles? Within our own circles, I feel we can develop alternatives to those aspects of being male that we dislike most, working out the misogyny within the tradition of masculinity, realizing our responsibility to each other in ways in which we have rarely dealt.

I flip-flopped for years about how men can address these issues. I've grown simultaneously weary of coalitions among men and respectful of those willing to work together toward the recognition of how our behavior both betrays and sustains us. Central to the ability of men to organize around our common struggles is the ability of men to surmount and overcome internalized homophobia.

I see my vision of love between men as incredibly subjective; men do love each other traditionally and untraditionally all over the planet, whether or not we choose to express and share these complex feelings in healthy or constructive ways. In my experience, the most intimate relationships I've seen between men have been those of gay or bisexual men. Still, in the four cities I have lived in over the last decade, bisexual men have been far more apathetic or lethargic in terms of defining our needs and working together to satisfy them.

Any struggle toward a finer recognition of ourselves will be a slow, arduous task. Years of covering up–falling back on cultural norms that allow us leniency toward our natural response to pain, confusion, and sorrow–is one reason we flinch when offered the opportunity to grow. My own record of rejecting those who would have helped me overcome some of these obstacles is dismal, and I recognize the man in me and other men who only works for change when desperation forces us to do so. Denial–working through issues around rape, violence, and the patterns ingrained after years of attempted recruitment into a society that discards those not white, male, and middle class–is a battle in which we must temporarily give up a need to control, trusting that other men might help provide a new sense of love and direction.

AIDS statistics have plunged bisexual men into an unprecedented limelight. Each month the Centers for Disease Control reports on the growing number of bisexual men living with and dying of AIDS. At the height of AIDS hysteria, bisexual men, along with gay men, Haitians, and prostitutes, became the expendable scapegoats with which to bait the American public. Portrayed as promiscuous and irresponsible, bisexual men were the dangerous infectors, living a veiled life of sexual conquests, spreading the disease by keeping secret the reality of the "other half" of their sexuality.

Positioning us as statistics, the push in AIDS educational materials has hardly focused on bisexual male behavior, leaving us adrift along with people of color, lesbians, and adolescents as to what we can do to protect ourselves. Slowly bisexual men are being integrated in the literature aimed at preventing the spread of AIDS. While acknowledging that a good portion of the anonymous sexual activity in any given metropolitan area is among men who either do not identify as gay or who have sexual relationships with both women and men, HIV educational programs specifically designed for these men have been slow in coming. Given this, bisexual male invisibility increases while the number of bisexual men dying from the disease increases exponentially.

While gay men have fought to uncover and chronicle the voices of gay PWAs, the histories of bisexual men afflicted with the disease are much less common. Where are these men? Dying in the cities? Closeted in gay ghettos? If anything it is a testament to the general invisibility of bisexual men, our personal histories, and the contributions we have made. Here again, lacking political clout, with few organized channels, bisexuals must create their own arenas with which to challenge those who stereotype or omit us from important historical periods. Our history is huge but scrambled; the books that really represent us have yet to be written.

Men will always offer me a brand of love and affection that is different from but complementary to the love of women. To have been able to experience both in a lifetime has been a gift and a guiding force in many of my ideals. To have never been able to experience both, holding these thin threads together, would have deprived me of a greater sense of love and life. Growing as a bisexual has been frustrating. Sometimes I begin to wonder what the big deal is, resenting the middle ground I'm forced to represent in a bitter fight between two warring opponents. Too often lives are on the line and, if forced to choose, my heart easily sides with the lesbians and gay men who have shared so much of themselves with me. It is within their vision that I find a healthier state of being. But it is among bisexuals and those who would support us that I feel most comfortable, most productive, and most free to express the full range of my personhood. The fact that bisexuals are beginning to band together to represent ourselves is the most positive element I've seen among bisexuals in many years.

Until bisexuals believe that they have as much right to exist and to prosper, that our position in a sexually segregated society is a vitally important alternative, then we will remain a silent majority, the ineffective middle ground. As bisexuals we can offer such a variety of progressive alternatives to the mainstream. Building upon what has already been accomplished, confronting skeptics and bigots alike, we envision the day when bisexuality is not the least understood of sexual preferences, when it becomes comfortably approached as a norm.

There are certainly some who have encompassed my bisexuality in wonderful ways. They remain a minority, though, and it is usually with a personal reaction of disgust and a practical application of patience and consistency that I have gained the trust in those suspicious of how my bisexuality might taint my priorities or intentions. In affirming our bisexuality, we honor our individual experiences, holding dear those graceful and clumsy selves who represent the achievement of having forged a unique person in the context of a society of rigid alternatives. We choose not to.

## NOTE

Reprint from *Bi Any Other Name: Bisexual People Speak Out*, Loraine Hutchins & Lani Ka'ahumanu, editors, 1991. Reprinted by permission of Alyson Books.

# Ex Exodus

*Ed Boland*

Available online at http://www.haworthpress.com/web/JB
© 2005 by The Haworth Press, Inc. All rights reserved.
doi:10.1300/J159v05n02_29

**SUMMARY.** A gay man recounts his oppressively religious upbringing and experiences with "ex gay conversion therapies." He affirms the
complex but essential place of women and male bisexuality in his life
alongside his gay identity. *[Article copies available for a fee from The
Haworth Document Delivery Service: 1-800-HAWORTH. E-mail address:
<docdelivery@haworthpress.com> Website: <http://www.HaworthPress.com>
© 2005 by The Haworth Press, Inc. All rights reserved.]*

**KEYWORDS.** Bisexuality, bisexual men, gay men, Christian funda-
mentalism, Exodus International, "ex-gay conversion therapy" ministries, heterosexual women, sexual exploration, personal transformation,
spirituality

I was born and raised in central Kentucky, the youngest of four children in a devout Southern Baptist household. I was taken to church for
the first time about a week after I was born and for the next twenty years
I was there an average of three times a week. I attended Sunday school,
church camp, and sang in the youth choir. I participated in Bible Drill,
which was a memory exercise in quoting scripture, and was a state
champion three consecutive times between ages nine and eleven. After
making a profession of faith in my early teens I became very serious
about it. I attended hardcore Bible studies classes and was an evangelical. I witnessed to my friends in school and did a lot of community work
along the same lines, but during these years the hormones raging
through my body were doing some really confusing things to me.

I'd always known I had an attraction to men, but I assumed it was because Daddy was cold and Mommy was overbearing, and I just wanted
someone to pay attention to me. I first used the word *gay* in reference to
myself at the age of nine in the fourth grade. I told two of my friends
during lunch at school. They went home and told their parents, who in
turn told my teacher. She pulled me aside and had a chat with me, carefully trying to determine if I'd been abused or molested. I hadn't, and I
was terrified that the teacher would tell my parents, which she did, although nothing was ever said at home about the incident until my mom
finally told me many years later that she'd dismissed it because I was so
young at the time. She "thought I didn't know what the word meant." I
reminded her that at the age of eight I scored so high on my SAT that I
was offered a full scholarship to a small, prestigious university in our

area, so I certainly knew what I was talking about. Ahhh, the power of parental denial.

During my teens, I suppressed my attraction to men as just an obsession with masturbation, which I indulged in frequently. I had a few meetings with my youth minister to talk about what was bothering me, which I still remember as being painfully embarrassing and awkward. He told me to pray more. This sort of off-the-cuff, vague religious solution to a normal, universal, biological activity contributed to my dominant mindset in the coming years: God will change me if I pray and, if that change never happens, then I'm not praying hard enough or I'm just not worthy. If the change never comes, that means God doesn't love me.

I dated a couple of girls in high school but, because the Bible teaches that it's wrong, I was conveniently able to dodge the bullet of premarital sex until my freshman year in college. Then I met Rose. Rose was a fifth-year senior graduating with a degree in psychology (read: self-diagnosing). She was active with the campus Baptist Student Union and was attending my church. We soon became powerfully codependent and, one snowy winter night, she threw herself at me sexually in the parking lot of a Mexican restaurant. I was stunned and my initial response was to recoil.

For the next few weeks, I received letters of hateful, spurned-lover spew. I agonized for six months over the whole affair until I decided to spend that summer working as a missionary in southeast Texas just to escape the pain. For ten weeks, I attended vacation bible school and youth group meetings just south of Jasper, Texas (where some years later, James Byrd, Jr., a black man, was murdered by being dragged behind a truck). I was completely removed from my friends and my familiar surroundings, and found myself with too much free time to do nothing but live with my own thoughts. As I was lying in bed one night, having just finished jerking off, crying because I felt something was wrong with me and God wasn't changing it, I finally admitted to myself the real issue: "I'm gay." The next logical question was "Now, what?"

Upon my return to Kentucky, I arranged a meeting with my pastor, a very affable guy named Mike. As I sat on the sofa in his office and self-identified as gay for the second time in my life, he could sense my agony. To his credit, he didn't try and pray it out of me or tell me I was a sinner, he just said that it was a bit out of his league and wanted to know how he could help me. I wasn't sure what he or anyone else could do, so he referred me to a guy named Bruce who ran a program called Crossover Ministries. Crossover was the local arm of Exodus International, an organization that believes that through prayer and group therapy gays and lesbians can become straight. "I can do all things through Christ who strengthens me" (Phil. 4:13). In recent years, Exodus has been touted by conservatives as a viable solution to being gay.

Bruce was a member of a local Pentecostal congregation and arranged to meet me at his church during lunch one day. He was warm and friendly, somewhat bearish, and passionate about his faith and the work Crossover was doing. He himself had been "in the lifestyle" while a younger man, but had now been married for six years to a woman. In an odd twist of fate, my older brother turned out to be one of the first people Bruce had sought help from. We talked, then prayed. I cried. Bruce invited me to join the group.

As I walked into my first meeting I was a nervous wreck. Bear in mind I had just turned nineteen and I was still a virgin. I had never been exposed to gay culture, and there I was walking into a room full of men at least a decade older than me and openly identifying myself as gay. The group met every Thursday night at the Pentecostal church and over the next few months I grew very close to Bruce and others in the group. I continued to pray and to study. I supported those around me as best I could and received love and encouragement in return. The weekly meetings became a great source of comfort to me, but I couldn't sense much of a change. I always felt horribly guilty over nothing more than my natural urges but I kept pressing on. At one point, I decided that the problem was too much secular influence, so I sold my enormous record collection and listened to only Christian rock. It didn't help, and I remained for the most part joyless.

In the summer of 1990, Exodus held their week-long North American convention in San Antonio, Texas. Two thousand ex-gays and ex-lesbians from all over the U.S. and Canada were meeting for seminars, support, and fellowship, and I wanted to attend, but I couldn't afford it. I explained the situation to my pastor, and he went to the deacons in our church and said, "There is a member of our congregation who needs a special therapy, and I can't tell any of you what or who it is, but would you be willing to help anyway?" Someone anonymously stepped forward and donated the money for me to attend.

My roommate at the convention ended up being one of the very few straight men in attendance who came to support two of his friends. He was a nice enough guy from Boston and we chatted a lot during the week. I mostly hung out with two guys from my own group, plus a fellow from Maryland who we met the first night. It was a confusing week. On the one hand, I was throwing myself head-first into every possible seminar and prayer group in efforts to change my orientation, and on the other hand, I was a *fucking horny nineteen-year-old virgin surrounded by gay men.*

While sitting and singing in the final worship service, I watched the people around me very expressively standing and raising their hands in praise. I looked around at the new friends I had met that week: here were these diverse, intelligent, incredibly talented men and women, all of whom absolutely loathed themselves for being gay. Many had stayed in the program for years, yet still struggled every day with their sexual orientation. I felt I had been completely open to the healing power of Christ, yet I felt no change, just cold and bitterness because years of prayer and sacrifice hadn't brought about any change in me, or them.

Suddenly I had a revelation: maybe I was OK–and maybe all of these people were OK, too. Maybe I hadn't experienced any change because I wasn't supposed to. I realized I was running away from something that I didn't understand. The only way for me to find out if I should become straight or not was to learn what I was up against.

I made the long trip back home in almost total silence. When we arrived back at the church in Kentucky, I grabbed my bag, told my friends I loved them, hugged, and left, never to return to the program. That next Sunday I skipped church. I didn't return the Sunday after that, nor the next, nor ever again.

It still took me over a year to lose my virginity. During the next year, I immersed myself in my art courses at school and began to make gay friends. One of the local bars had an after-hours dance where they didn't serve alcohol, so eighteen-year-olds and older could get in. I very slowly began to explore this strange new world, and to face my fears while doing so. Finally about two weeks before I turned twenty-one, I asked an older coworker of mine–a beautiful blond bear of a man–if he would show me the ropes, and we had sex. I've never looked back.

The fifteen years since I left Exodus have brought about some interesting developments. Michael Bussee and Gary Cooper, two of the founding members of Exodus, left the organization and their wives to begin a relationship together. They now renounce all forms of so-called reparative therapy. My local group leader, Bruce, tested HIV-positive–it turns out he never stopped having risky sex; he just drove to another city to do his cruising. His wife subsequently tested positive and divorced him. I saw him on *Geraldo* telling his story and never felt more betrayed in my life. I still occasionally run into friends from Crossover; none of them are currently attending the program or church. We usually hug hello and with a laugh ask ourselves, "What were we thinking?"

*   *   *

You might be wondering why a self-identified gay man has a story to tell in an anthology about bisexual men. I've never identified as bi–not even during that iffy period that bridged my going to church and going to bars. I never identified as ex-gay while in the Exodus program because I had never been out before I joined. For all of my advanced teenage maturity, I was clueless about any culture outside the church and even the basics of my own sexuality. My attraction to men was in place as far back as I can remember, yet women have played an undeniable role in my sexual development.

There are numerous passages in the Bible about lust being sinful, but what boy in the throes of puberty doesn't think about sex every few seconds? I was taught that it was wrong to have those thoughts and feelings so, around the age of thirteen, my fantasies took a turn. Instead of playing a role in them myself, I often visualized people I found attractive having sex with someone else. In some twisted logic, I considered it less of a sin if I wasn't actually participating. Virtually all of the men I was attracted to at this age were married teachers, coaches, and ministers and, because I always wanted to be the one getting fucked, it just made the most sense for these figures to be having sex with their wives, the way God intended. Isn't that how sex was meant to be?

Adding to the effect, a friend got his hands on some X-rated straight videos, and those images fueled my imagination. Seeing female genitalia and expressions of female sexuality never turned me off; rather, they usually amplified the masculinity of the men engaging in sex with them. For this reason, the two ideas became intrinsically linked in my mind, and I still visualize the masculine, bearish men I find attractive having sex not with each other but with women. While I have no desire for children of my own, the virility of these men and their potential to father children makes the women in my fantasies just as important. It's like trying to define "good" without the word "evil": they need each other. Some may argue that this is internalized homophobia or the results of trying to brainwash myself into becoming straight, but I don't see it that way at all. I feel no shame in being gay, and I think a great many more people have fluidity of sexuality than admit it.

I experienced sex with a woman only after I came out. Having grown up in such a repressed environment, I vowed never to deny myself new experiences–especially sexual. I'm not overtly attracted to women–I can appreciate their beauty, yet I don't find myself checking out tits and ass. My first heterosex experiences happened in a bisexual setting with a bi couple, and I discovered that I enjoy both forms of sex a great deal. I consider myself a "Kinsey Four" in that respect, and a lot of my gay friends don't understand this. They insist that because I can be fully functional with a woman, I am bisexual, but I disagree. There is so much more to my sexuality than just the mechanics of fucking. While I might be able to have a fantastic, sweaty, fulfilling romp with a female fuck-buddy, I can't fathom having a relationship with one. I am one hundred and ten percent interested in men when it comes to relationships, therefore I consider myself emotionally gay, if not physically bi.

# Loving Without Limits

Bob Vance

Available online at http://www.haworthpress.com/web/JB
doi:10.1300/J159v05n02_30

[Haworth co-indexing entry note]: "Loving Without Limits." Vance, Bob. Co-published simultaneously in
*Journal of Bisexuality* (Harrington Park Press, an imprint of The Haworth Press, Inc.) Vol. 5, No. 2/3, 2005,
pp. 255-262; and: *Bi Men: Coming Out Every Which Way* (ed: Ron Jackson Suresha, and Pete Chvany) Harrington Park Press, an imprint of The Haworth Press, Inc., 2005, pp. 255-262.

**SUMMARY.** A bisexual man explores varying shades of intimacy between himself and men and women. An update, written fifteen years later, notes the complexity of enacting a holistic sexuality in a sexually repressed society. Reprint from *Men and Intimacy: Personal Accounts Exploring the Dilemmas of Modern Male Sexuality,* Franklin Abbott, editor, 1990.

**KEYWORDS.** Bisexuality, bisexual men, sexual exploration, male intimacy, personal transformation, heterosexual women, spirituality

Their first night together was just his second sexual experience that included insertion. The first, with a woman at home, had been initially exciting, but finally frightening as they were both virgins and she bled quite a bit. He felt he had "done it" wrong, had hurt her, and so he left rather quickly, feeling failure and ineptness at his own inability to understand what he should do in this situation. This, in the mountains of Vermont, was different. They were both happy, infatuated, wanted to share this feeling with everyone they met and were able to in small ways the entire time they spent together. The Vermonters and other tourists smiled and greeted them warmly with knowing looks and good-natured humor. Their sex felt like the most natural relationship possible between two people. He thought: this must be what love is about, comfort and intertwining ecstasy.

The second night it rained again. That day they had traveled throughout the state, found waterfalls draped over slick grey-green rocks, followed twisted roads through narrow green valleys. The clouds were low and full and fingered down the sides of the mountains. The organic smell, the damp fertile air and the undulating land itself became projections of the sexual tension between them. He had a hard-on nearly the entire day. She would notice and laugh, just acknowledge, or they might stop for a while to play.

They would sleep in a lean-to shelter that night, the inside of the small tent too wet from the night before. In the lantern glow, deep in the trees, they made love again. She slid down over him, moved slow and steady in excruciating ecstasy that he could have held on to forever. He had never felt anything like it. She said later that some men didn't like to make love that way. He couldn't imagine why not–had always been frustrated by the expectation that *he* be the mover.

*   *   *

Sitting in the teacher's classroom had become a disturbing exercise in nearly ecstatic learning mixed with intoxicating fantasies; a nearly hypnotic connection with the teacher that he could never determine the source of. Was it just a trick? A product of his infatuation? It seemed too electric, like plugging into and completing the circuit for some advanced mental power tool. He had never thought so clearly, been so aware of his own mental acuity and ability for critical examination. He wrote down everything, took notes voraciously, along with short comments that, more often than not, attributed this, he thought new, ability to understand to his teacher.

He visited the teacher's office weekly; another exercise in ecstatic torture. The man's eyes were the most incredible green he'd ever seen. And they were not frightened of staying on his own.

"This is it," he thought, "I must be queer." What to do? Well, he surmised that first he ought to tell the woman he was currently sleeping with. Then he would need to tell the teacher (as if the man didn't already know). He would find out if his perceptions were right and they would have, or not have, a relationship. That's what one did if one felt this strongly about someone. You told them. At least that had been his experience with women he loved. Having had no real experience loving other men in this way, he supposed it could not be very different.

So he confessed his infatuation to the teacher. The teacher smiled broadly in acceptance, but openly questioned the student's conclusion that he must be homosexual. Apparently the teacher had a roommate once who had decided he was homosexual in much the same way the student had, but then changed his mind very soon after. Perhaps, the teacher suggested, he was bisexual.

Though this meeting went well, a definite beginning, things got more confusing and painful from then on. He became very conscious of the necessary secrecy surrounding such a love. The teacher seemed to want to put off an after class meeting until after the term ended. He took that as a rejection, and doubted the wisdom of having told the teacher his feelings in the first place. His love grew stronger, more fierce for expression than ever.

Then he flunked the midterm exam, an event that sent him crashing. Other things in his life had taken a decidedly unbalanced turn. He impulsively quit his job (because he felt he was applying the ideals he was learning in the class), had gotten a woman he slept with once pregnant.

There was an abortion. The midterm was the final straw. The teacher told him not to worry about it, but none of anything he was hearing, feeling or experiencing made any sense. He doubted the reality of everything and there was no new reality that he could find to take its place.

He dropped the class. Luckily the teacher was with someone when he brought in the drop slip, so there was no discussion: just a horrible cracking of the teacher's otherwise beautiful face. His life continued to fall apart, but with a strength he felt at the time must be superhuman, he rebuilt it. A year and a half later he left that city for another. He heard through a friend that the teacher quit teaching at the same time. He thought this must be what love is about: devastating passion and chaos.

\* \* \*

Everything in me resists packaging my sexuality in a word and using that word as a part of my identity. This does not mean I do not believe sexuality to be a part of one's identity, but rather that the words used for such definitions seem arbitrarily assigned and, ultimately, harmful. Choosing one or another and relying on it exclusively to define a very important part of me seems stifling, a serious understatement about a part of me that is always in flux and too mysterious and integral to be named (namely, the Tao that can be named is not the eternal Tao).

I chose the stories that precede this essay as a personal example of what has been my experience of sexuality with women and men. That is not to say that I haven't had experiences with women I have loved that seemed to threaten annihilation and overwhelming passion, or that I haven't had warm and comforting relations with men I have loved. I have, but I think the point is that, because passion and physical expression of love between a man and a woman is expected and reinforced in our culture, I've been able in most cases to follow my instincts toward sensual/sexual connection with women easily and without the blocks one encounters in a budding same sex relationship. My long-term relationship with my female partner (a nearly ten year linking, at this writing) has often taken on the sometimes frighteningly passionate aura of love's chaotic side. But we have been born in a world that is safe for most heterosexual expressions of love, healthy or no, and the process of healing and affirmation of our love is embraced and given direction and assistance through freely exchanged and inherited cultural myths and stories about loving one another. This is hardly so for male/male love.

For one thing, I think men in general are not taught to love anyone very well. We are raised as warriors to the detriment of our other psychic parts. Warriors do not love. They fight, they fuck, they follow directions unerringly. That our culture chooses to ignore the sensual/ sexual side of male/male bonding, that it has censored all or large parts of our culture's rich heritage of same sex love stories, has damaged our ability to form healthy attachments to each other and resulted in a fearfully homophobic population of men who can only subvert their natural feelings for bonding and cause them to react superficially or violently toward each other even while, in reality, loving one another deeply. Because our natural urge is to love and care for each other, parts of our cultural story that might teach us how to do this have been chopped out in order to serve the sickest of us who want to direct and subvert that urge and use it to produce soldiers who will fight for their petty and selfish goals of conquest and ownership.

My favorite story in literature that, I think, comments on the inability of two men to find direction or expression for the passion they feel toward each other is in a short story by D. H. Lawrence called *The Prussian Officer*. In this story the two men who feel strong passion for each other eventually create a situation that kills them both. Although this is an extreme example, and not what has to happen, it is what can happen on both an individual and societal level, unless we, as men, actively stop denying ourselves access to each other's natural inborn abilities to love and comfort others we are drawn to. We need to rediscover, unbury, and reinvent our myths and our history of loving one another. Different people can choose to do this in different ways. I have chosen to be, as others define it, bisexual. I believe it may be the best way for me to proceed on my quest toward learning how to love others.

This does not mean I will be, or will want to be, sexual with everyone I love. It means I am committed to being open to the possibilities that shared sensuality and sexuality present to me. I will not limit myself to those few physical experiences deemed appropriate because of artificial barriers that serve no useful purpose but to prevent unity among people and engender fear and warfare between peoples.

I could never believe physical attraction to others can only be considered for purposes of eventual reproduction. As generally furless creatures, we have had to depend on each other to stay warm and safe in a sometimes cold and hostile world. It is our heritage, our birthright, to want to be physically involved with others of our species that we love. I refuse to deny this for purposes of conforming to unproductive and artificial concepts of normal human behavior. I will try to approach it honestly and without subverting its potentially cooperative, peacemaking, ecstatic, and spiritualizing nature.

## *UPDATE*

When first approached about including "Loving Without Limits" in this anthology, I wondered how current it could be, fifteen years since Franklin Abbot first asked me for a piece for his *Men and Intimacy* anthology. Much in my life has changed . . . spiritually, emotionally, and in the sentient world as it directly and indirectly relates to and affects me.

Soon after writing the essay, my partner, Susan, and our son moved to a small town: the smallest, least urban, least diverse place I have ever lived. I went into this move open-eyed. I had taken a kind of inventory of the things I might have to leave behind or about which I would need to adjust my expectations. While I loved the prospect of living very near to some of the natural areas I like to explore and walk (if I have anything that could be called gods, Lake Superior ranks high on that list), how I would actualize my normal manner of relating to others in terms of my sexuality/intimacy construct topped of the list of probable adjustments. It equaled my expectation of change in the opportunities to participate in above-average contemporary theatre, as well as my ability to find other poets who shared a modicum amount of my sensibility about that oldest of art forms. As it turns out, I have been able to sate my desires for much on that list. Surprise, surprise.

One thing to add about that, however: finding sex is the easy part. Sex is always the easy part. Sex with men in particular is as easily had here as anywhere. I have met an astonishingly wide variety of non-straight men from an equally astonishingly wide variety of backgrounds and occupations: fundamentalist preachers, restaurant managers, local politicians and government employees, nurses and doctors, contractors, dry-wallers, church managers, computer analysts, et cetera and so on. Even a small number of hairstylists. Many of these men are married and have ongoing sexual relationships with their wives that they enjoy. The level of fear that many of these men have about the male/male sex they want, seek, and enjoy is sobering. And truly, the nearest gay bar, the only place for non-heterosexual men to meet openly (if that can really be said to be the case about any gay bar, as opposed to "the bar" being an enforced kind of ghettoization), short of taking at least a four-hour drive, is almost one hundred miles away. Also: the level to which many of these men are willing to engage in unsafe sex practices, particularly anal sex without condoms, frightens me.

Sex is the easy part. And if I have learned anything at all in the past fifteen years, it is in the concrete realization that sex without intimacy becomes boring quickly. Furtive, fast, lunchtime meetings, with closeted, married men who may have a handful of children, and whose fear, outside of the room where they beg to be fucked, is painfully palpable, get tiresome. Being in the closet has always to me seemed to entail far too much suffering, as well as having a disabling effect on the quality of sexual expression in and outside the confines of whatever ongoing heterosexual relationships there may be.

"Loving Without Limits" is surprisingly current in how it portrays my thoughts and feelings even after fifteen years. I remember having a small precognition as I wrote it that it had inadvertently turned into a kind of personal manifesto in that it was able to net, bring together and solidify, the kind of inner and outer work I had been doing around issues of sexuality and intimacy since my late teens and early twenties . . . that is, now thirty years ago. I am able to see it even more clearly in that aspect.

## NOTE

Reprint from *Men and Intimacy: Personal Accounts Exploring the Dilemmas of Modern Male Sexuality*, Franklin Abbott, editor, 1990, Freedom, CA: The Crossing Press.

# Whereto, My Beloved?

Ganapati S. Durgadas

Available online at http://www.haworthpress.com/web/JB
doi:10.1300/J159v05n02_31

[Haworth co-indexing entry note]: "Whereto, My Beloved?" Durgadas, Ganapati S. Co-published simultaneously in *Journal of Bisexuality* (Harrington Park Press, an imprint of The Haworth Press, Inc.) Vol. 5, No. 2/3, 2005, pp. 263-273; and: *Bi Men: Coming Out Every Which Way* (ed: Ron Jackson Suresha, and Pete Chvany) Harrington Park Press, an imprint of The Haworth Press, Inc.. 2005, pp. 263-273.

**SUMMARY.** A Jewish Puerto Rican man examines his bisexuality in terms of Eastern spiritual traditions, equating the search for holistic sexuality with his spiritual aspirations. Reprint from *Blessed Bi Spirit: Bisexual People of Faith,* Debra R. Kolodny, editor, 2000.

**KEYWORDS.** Bisexuality, bisexual men, Judaism, Latinos, personal transformation, GLBTIQA community, multiculturalism, Hindu yoga meditation, Eastern mysticism, spirituality

I have been so many selves–a pastiche of personas, some projected upon me, others chosen. Puerto Rican or Jew (through my parents), fat man and working-class slob, hippie and radical, street person and dope head, neo-pagan and Buddhist, activist and therapist, heterosexual and homosexual, even male and female. I smile and shake my head when I look at all the different people I have appeared to be, both to myself and others.

Sometimes I think I've been too many people in too short a time. At other times I realize that I've been portraying different roles in a play directed by an essence of me. In Hindu parlance, this essence would be called the unperceived perceiver, the unheard listener, or the unnoticed witness.

Yet, throughout my life, and within all of these characters, there flow twin streams: spirituality and sexuality.

## *CHILDHOOD IN THE MAELSTROM*

When I was growing up within my parents' interpretation of and indoctrination in the Judeo-Christian tradition, these streams stood in opposition to each other. Sexuality seemed to be spirituality's subversive foe. Spirit loomed over sex like a secretly frightened bully, intimidating sexuality into a corner crowded with shame, whispers, and tugging hungers, dankly clutching at me with want and confusion.

During my childhood I had a long-held fondness for rocking myself in bed, singing songs aloud, songs in which I transported myself to faraway lands, became and interacted with a myriad of "make-believe" characters: some from television, others from comic books, still others from mythology. The worlds I explored were vivid and alive with an intensity not just inside my head but also in the very air of my Brooklyn bedroom. My father thought I was crazy. He complained aloud and abusively about it. I was sent to a headshrinker through grade school. I eventually learned to drop my story singing, my inner world making, and became ashamed of my rhythmic body shaking amid the Gods. It was childish, nutsy, even worse, girlish. I realize now if I had been born in a different age or culture I might have been groomed to become a griot, shaman, or bard. I realize now that I had been shouted and shamed out of my spirituality as well as my sexuality. I was queer in each way. I had been duped into thinking they were separate from each other.

My father viewed me with distrust. During one of his periodic rages at my mother he told me point-blank that he seriously doubted I was his biological offspring. I suspect what rankled my father was my not being the man he was. Fact was, I only had a vague notion that I was a "boy," some pervasive social category into which I was supposed to assimilate myself, but was doing a halfhearted job at best. From the start I was possessed by a sense of maleness being something imposed from outside and not from within. I was aware of having a self, of being someone in a body, but not necessarily a boy child's body governed by a "male" character. I remember a definite interior feeling of girlishness. I knew I could not afford to let anyone discover it, though I feared it would be betrayed by the feminine fleshiness of my childhood fatness. Nonetheless, I tried hiding with indoctrinated shame.

I can't say I felt a complete "female" because I didn't know what that was any more than I knew what a complete "male" felt like. But I was terrified to realize that I was on the borderline, somewhere in the middle. I frightened myself into secrecy.

For my Puertorriqueño father, maleness was a God-given, predetermined repertoire that he expected would be automatically passed on with his genes. He was repeatedly enraged that I did not meet his expectations, acting as if I purposely refused to accede to them.

## COMING OF AGE–BREAKING FREE

In spite of this, or perhaps because of it, I rebelled when able. I chased after sex to avenge myself upon spirit, which I had associated and confused with my parents' religiosity of learned guilt and twisted aggression. With innumerable male and female partners I felt like a shifting, shimmering presence within their embraces: a screen onto which they projected their own definitions of maleness and femaleness. What surprised me was their apparent certainty of being a man or a woman. I resented their sometimes implied, sometimes directly expressed demand that I reflect this same certainty. Almost every one of my lovers, with a few notable exceptions, had a surprisingly rigid inner gender schema, sprung upon me within the first moments of initiated intimacy.

Parallel to this sexual self search was a spiritual one. Coming to terms with my bisexuality and my conscious refusal to "be a man" helped me to realize fully both psychological and spiritual components of my being. A hopeless bibliophile, I sought solace in books during periods of isolation: Jungian psychology, gay liberation manifestos on genderfuck, bios of androgynous pop stars, and coffee-table photo books full of "she-males." I ransacked stacks of mythology featuring twin-sexed gods like Dionysus and Yemaya-Olukun and discovered anthropological ancestors like the *hijra* and the *berdache*.

For me, the Divine was a "she-male." God appeared to be most at home in that borderland between male and female. I believed that most human beings had fallen into a spiritual exile, mistaken for reality, at either supposed gender extreme. For this reason occultism and mysticism developed a seductive hold on me. I began practicing meditation and mild yoga, and studied Eastern philosophy after a long fling with neo-paganism.

Once, just as I was entering sobriety following a heart attack, I found myself depressed and angry in a Tibetan Buddhist monastery, facing the abbot, Khenpo Kathar Rinpoche, sitting there wondering what I could possibly ask him. A male friend and occasional sex partner had brought me atop this mountain overlooking Woodstock. Maybe he thought just being there would help me. I doubted it then because the Rinpoche could barely speak English. Stupid me. I thought up some question, as that is what I understood was expected. Khenpo Kathar Rinpoche remarked that there is an unknown, invaluable treasure deep inside ourselves, and that I could find it only by making the effort. At that point, emerging from the drug and alcohol haze I had hoped would cloud and medicate my self-dislike, this was a key that gradually unlocked a me I could begin to love and respect. It led to twelve years of meditation and life as a Buddhist.

Despite the scope of this journey, the reconciliation I sought between spirit and sex could not fully manifest itself for me until the person created by those warring streams had died. A trip to San Francisco in the summer of 1990 catapulted me into the next phase of my rebirth.

I had been "in the life" for more than two decades by then, a counter cultural veteran, overjoyed to have discovered a vibrant bisexual community dedicated to restoring the radical sexual politics that had been one of the mainstays of a gay liberation movement not yet turned bourgeois. Those ten days in San Francisco had a phantasmagoric quality. I shuttled from conference to street demo, from sex club to bookstore, subconsciously searching for an explanation for the HIV-devastation around me. I kept remembering my friend Bill's commentary: "Don't you realize, most of the men our age in this city are dead or dying?" As a member of the AIDS direct action group ACT-UP, as a psychotherapist working with addictions, and as a queer, I had many HIV-infected persons in my life: clients, comrades, and sex partners. But on this trip something snapped. Maybe it was the protective wall of denial I had unconsciously erected. This time I truly felt the atmospheric presence of AIDS. Bill told me that more than fifty percent of the gay and bisexual men in the Bay Area were HIV-infected.

Sex and death were inextricably enmeshed here. I became a *Bhuta*, what in Hindu and Buddhist lore is called a wandering soul, lost among the *Pretas*, the hungry ghosts doubling as people caught up in the dance of desire and risk, outward defiance and inward quiet desperation. I had thought that I could synthesize calm Buddhist insight with angry queer street politics, and thus could handle anything, but it wasn't true. I was overwhelmed. I burned out.

When I returned from San Francisco I was disconsolate. Both Buddhism, which had opened me up to so much of life, and queer culture and politics, which had held so much promise, seemed to have failed me. Lost again, I wandered aimlessly.

The end of a disastrous affair, years after that fateful trip to San Francisco, completed my shift. My last fling in the face of encroaching middle age? Very likely, to some degree. Yet what had been loving three-way sex play soured into the poison of mutual manipulation and recrimination. He tried turning me against her; she turned against him and toward me, then returned to him. He ended up a year later psychiatrically hospitalized. She landed in a twelve-step program. I ended up emotionally spent, watching in the background. The affair seemed to have been a final catalyst. Somehow its death pairs with the pall of death in San Francisco.

I remember the day after the relationship finally collapsed. The week before had been full of burning, sleepless nights. I had felt as if my soul had poisoned itself. Sitting in the taxi riding to Albany's one Hindu temple, I felt the gentle warm breeze sweep in through the cab's open windows that early May morning. It had rained just before dawn, and the sun-kissed roads were still water-streaked, shimmering. The image of

Mother Meera, an avatar, or recognized incarnation of the Divine Mother, appeared in my mind. Her image comforted me. I felt a sense of calm, an accepting and embracing love sweep over me. I felt strangely safe, almost ecstatic.

## *A SOUL REBORN*

On that day I recalled what my guru, Gurumayi Chidvilasananda, had once stated. To paraphrase her: Our most searing emotional agonies are often the effects of the burning away of a conflicted ego's most painful habitual patterns–patterns that the neurotic small self, the ego, tries to maintain in order to hold fast to the illusion of permanence. The alternative? Accept the impermanence of our patterns, and thus comprehend our true relationship with–call it what you will–Reality, Life Itself, or the Divine.

My first contact with Gurumayi Chidvilasananda had been in the late fall, after my return from the summer 1990 International Bisexual Conference and the ACT-UP demos in San Francisco. The *ménage à trois* affair had not yet begun, and I was a sexual freewheeler, with no attachments. Our initial conversation took the form of a confession. For no reason, except to be honest and to acknowledge my growing dissatisfaction with my sex radicalism, I revealed to Gurumayi my bisexuality and what effect that fateful summer in San Francisco had had upon me. Maybe I was expecting–at least, maybe my ego was expecting–a "logical" answer. I did not get it from her. What I did get puzzled me. My bisexuality was what I was anxious about. For me it was right in the middle of the mix of my spiritual and psychological crisis. Gurumayi simply called it my search for God, each and every bit of it. It sounds like a cliché, but the apparent simplicity of it caught me unawares, and even now it speaks an infinity of wisdom to me. Once again, a well-put, simple truth awakened me when I least anticipated it.

Now I had discovered my True Beloved.

I converted to Hinduism at that time, and in the process dropped out of queer activism. Though I had been living as a Hindu for five years before my taxicab experience, somehow that May morning marked a turning point in my practice. I realized then that God's love for us never decreases, unlike human love, and that the latter can only persevere if it is informed by the former. This is one of the main messages in the Hindu tantric understanding of sexuality, and may be the truest sex radicalism of all. I learned that declarations of and attempts at sexual revolution uninformed by God are just self-deceptions and quickly degenerate into replays of culturally conditioned fears, aggression, greed, and narcissism. If one's heart is not as open as God's, then the ego quickly belies all our high-flown rhetoric. The three of us may have started out as lovers, but we were really only in love with our small selves, our egos, our images of ourselves as sex radicals. Our inner dishonesty polluted our self-images, so that the basest ego-driven needs took control and corrupted the relationship. The affair's end taught me that only by opening myself fully to the Divine could I reflect liberation in the world—sexual liberation included.

I found, amazingly so, that much of what was taken away from me in childhood seems very present within Hinduism, its way of life so vast and polycentric, all the "experts" have trouble defining or categorizing it. A lot like I do, I guess. In it I see the Beloved I have always searched for, but only vaguely knew it until now. For you see, my Beloved is Lord Shiva, the God who is half woman. My Beloved is Mother Kali, who is sometimes female, sometimes male. Together they constitute the world's oldest deity.

I discovered Tantrism, the branch of Hindu and Buddhist spiritual practice characterized by shame/guilt-free sexual symbolism and an open acceptance of androgyny, which was shunned and suppressed in the West. Tantra is more than an assortment of schools of thought or an ancient collection of apparent sex manuals (as some Western popularizers might have it). It is a mind-set, a way of life, in which one gradually withdraws from a learned dualistic and compartmentalized perception of ourselves and the universe. In withdrawing from false, imposed dualisms that attach constrictive and alienating identities upon us, Tantra offers a philosophy and a set of practices that enable us to merge with the underlying Divine Wholeness. Tantra returns one to the borderline between male and female, not as a "mistake of nature" but as an emanation of Sacred Reality. It was with tantric Hinduism that I finally felt as though I had come home.

Hinduism thrives heartily upon contradictions. The most ascetic sects live alongside the most sensual, with nothing more than a mild philosophical debate between them. More a way of life than a religion per se, conservatism coexists with the broadest sorts of acceptance. You can find the most sharply delineated sex roles assigned to biologically defined men and women. You can also find changes exerted by feminism and modernism. And, along with both of these realities, you will find a sanctified caste of transgendered people. All of these are accepted within the same spiritual social spectrum.

I can get away with wearing multiple earrings and nose rings, cosmetics and extensive jewelry (not to mention a chest and two arms full of god/dess image and yantra tattoos) along with my dhoti (a waist-gown, usually of cotton or silk) within a religious context. It doesn't hurt that Hinduism's main deities, such as Shiva, Durga, and Vishnu, are omni-erotic and pan-gendered. I achieve a fulfillment in Hindu community, in Hindu practice, in Hindu belief, that I never felt before. On the few occasions when I had come close, I had also felt hemmed in by a fear created by the clear and present fact (and danger) that such fulfillment was countenanced only among fellow outlaws. In my life as a Hindu I am given tacit spiritual approval. Sometimes I am even given explicit approval.

I feel I have somehow come home. For years I grieved the loss of my family to domestic violence, drugs, and racism. Now I find myself adopted into a family of immigrant South Indian Brahmins, my name changed legally, a member of the local Hindu community. I experience a sense of connectedness, a feeling of belonging I never felt before.

Therein lies my dilemma. I know I could easily disappear from visible queer life by entering fully into the Hindu community, cutting off all ties to the identifiable lesbian, gay, bisexual, and transgendered community. It is very, very tempting. My disillusionment with the latter community leaves me quite ready to abandon it. I find myself increasingly out of sync, if not alienated outright. I can cite continuing biphobia expressed by many lesbians and gays, through direct hostility, or through failing to acknowledge the existence or presence of bisexuals. I have my doubts about this ever changing, especially now that a mainstream element has virtually seized control of organizations and media, bent on assimilating into middle-class conformity. The result is a split in queer life where the liberationist and radically creative impulses are purposely marginalized, if not openly demonized. Bisexuals, like the transgendered, upset the drive for acceptance. Widely welcoming us would only derail the train toward assimilation.

Of course, there are conservative middle-class elements within the Hindu community, especially among South Asian immigrants influenced by the Anglo-Indian Puritanism induced by colonialism. But Hinduism per se is not an erotophobic or homo/biphobic religion. Many of the divinities worshiped are so polymorphous and pansensual as to defy Western categories of gender or sexual orientation. And Hindu tolerance allows a large space for dissenting or nonorthodox religious sects and practices to coexist relatively peaceably. Faced with the mounting emptiness I feel within my former primary community, every

day I take more and more solace and comfort from my growing identifi-
cation as a Hindu. Besides my discomfort with growing lesbian and gay
conservatism, I am alienated by other aspects of the life I formerly so
strongly identified with. After more than two decades "in the life," I've
come to the angering conclusion that the assimilationist lesbian and gay
community will never go beyond mere lip service and breast beating to
actually address racism and religious bigotry. I suspect there is more
segregation here among heterosexuals, and that all the rain-
bow-waving talk about diversity is exactly just that–talk. Any feminist
or queer liberationist stance against outmoded sex roles, erotic repression, ageism, or patriarchalism seems shunted aside as personal ads address people as commodities: gay men are as obsessed with youth as
ever, lesbians power-broke, and everyone tries deciding who's a top or
a bottom. I seriously ask myself why I stay. Is the dance finally over?

Yet I remain. Somehow there persists that deep connection I sense
and feel between my spirituality and my sexuality. Maybe it is my
karma to be wedged between these two communities, undecided
whether to leave one for the other. But that would mean the dance is far
from over. When I ponder this, it seems to be what my Beloved wants.
For Shiva, as Tandava, the Eternal Dancer, is the Source and Reconciler
of apparent "opposites." As a follower of Lord Shiva I see the flow of
life and everyone within it as really another aspect of him, the Actor and
Dancer, who, along with his Consort, the Divine Mother, plays out as
everything which is this universe. It seems they have placed me here,
forever between worlds, for it is only when I am between that I feel most
alive. Therefore I suspect the tension of my dilemma itself is part of the
Dance.

I had been *brahmachari*, or celibate, for over a year before undertak-
ing to write this. Originally I thought there was some weighty life decision I had to make. I had even been thinking about escaping the tensions
of my dilemma via an arranged marriage. My alienation from queer life
had been that strong. I planned to go to Kashi, or Benares, the sacred
city of Shiva in India, for a yatra, or religious pilgrimage, or maybe an
escape from my disillusionment. Again and again I have looked to my
Beloved for an answer. And once more the answer was not in the
obvious.

One evening, during an ecumenical spiritual ceremony at an area
Metropolitan Community Church, I read to those assembled the story of
Shiva's love affair with his fellow god Vishnu. Despite the latter's pro-
testations that the love between two male deities could not be fruitful,
Lord Shiva seduced him just the same. Then Vishnu trans-sexualized

into the Mohini, a divine enchantress, and gave birth to the divinity Ayyapa. This god, the offspring of a homosexual union and trans-gendered birth, went on to triumph over the asuras, or demons, of igno-rance and negative passions. The more I pondered this story the more it resonated within me. The gods had wrought the possible out of the im-possible. Maybe that is what my Beloved is telling me: conflict, inner conflict most of all, leads to its own sort of recreation of the new and vi-brant and vital. The apparently same and the different are really not op-posites. It is our hesitation about living life on life's often-ambiguous terms that keeps us from taking true creative advantage of it. We want an easy road map for our spirituality and sexuality, a painless, tearless means for evolving new sorts of community. We create irreconcilable opposites often as an excuse. Yet the missteps, the stumbling, the fa-tigue, and the falls are part of Life's Dance too. If we just give up, if I just give up, opting for a kind of unilateral safety, hiding myself in the false security of resignation, I cut myself off from what life wants of me. The dance, life, my Beloved are inviting me to birth all the possibilities for living out of those very same projections of the impossible which I myself created from past failures, fears, hurts, and resentments.

No way am I stepping out of your Lila, your Dance, my Beloved. I am staying right here, forever in the creative middle with you.


## NOTE

1. Reprint from *Blessed Bi Spirit: Bisexual People of Faith*, Debra R. Kolodny, edi-tor, 2000, New York/London: Continuum.

# The Sparrow Sings

*Angus West*

Available online at http://www.haworthpress.com/web/JB
© 2005 by The Haworth Press, Inc. All rights reserved.
doi:10.1300/J159v05n02_32

[Haworth co-indexing entry note]: "The Sparrow Sings." West, Angus. Co-published simultaneously in *Journal of Bisexuality* (Harrington Park Press, an imprint of The Haworth Press, Inc.) Vol. 5, No. 2/3, 2005, pp. 275-281; and: *Bi Men: Coming Out Every Which Way* (ed: Ron Jackson Suresha, and Pete Chvany) Harrington Park Press, an imprint of The Haworth Press, Inc., 2005, pp. 275-281. Single or multiple copies of this article are available for a fee from The Haworth Document Delivery Service [1-800-HAWORTH, 9:00 a.m. - 5:00 p.m. (EST). E-mail address: docdelivery@haworthpress.com].

**SUMMARY.** An ambivalent young man explores the potency and tenderness of his own desires for men and women while living as a member of a traditional Pennsylvania Dutch enclave. *[Article copies available for a fee from The Haworth Document Delivery Service: 1-800-HAWORTH. E-mail address: <docdelivery@haworthpress.com> Website: <http://www.HaworthPress.com> © 2005 by The Haworth Press, Inc. All rights reserved.]*

**KEYWORDS.** Bisexuality, bisexual men, Pennsylvania, personal transformation, Amish, Mennonite communities, sexual exploration, heterosexual women

I awake to the singing of sparrows, the typical Amish alarm clock. The early rays of sunshine fill my room as I slowly dress myself. Opening the bedroom door, I feel a cool breeze coming from the adjacent hallway. The space is dark, and out of habit I feel for the light switch and then retract my hand. Old habits run deep. There is no electricity. I descend the long staircase and open the door that leads to the kitchen. An infant child is in a high chair eating cereal. The sound of a diesel engine roars in the background. A potpourri of eggs, bacon, and propane fill my senses. A woman preparing breakfast on the other side of the room offers a quiet morning greeting. I acknowledge her and proceed to the bathroom. The view outside the bathroom window is breathtaking. I want to lose myself in the scene. A man and teenage boy bid a hearty good morning to me in the bathroom. When finished, we return to the kitchen and sit down.

The woman is dressed in a very modest, light blue dress. A black apron is pinned around her waist. It is a homemade garment, but certainly does not lack precision. Her hair is pinned up with an ornate organdy head covering that symbolizes her place in this community. The man and boy are dressed exactly like me: black broadcloth pants held up by suspenders. Our button-up shirts are brightly colored, but lack outside pockets or stylish design.

The signal is given and we bow our heads in silent prayer. Thoughts about my family back home and the upcoming day race in my mind. The man exhales and prayer ends. I eat my breakfast quickly, once in a while adding to the conversation. As I gobble down the rest of my toast, I grab my straw hat and go outside.

June is the time we harvest strawberries. I do not adore picking berries, but it is part of the process. I start picking at the far end of the field.

I like the isolation, as it gives me a chance to think and daydream. Mothers, sons, daughters, cousins and friends all arrive to pick and package strawberries. Like me, the visiting workers are all dressed according to the rules of the church.

A girl my age, nineteen, walks up to me and greets me with a shy hello. She is a beautiful girl; her smooth lines and fair complexion shine in the sun. I am attracted to her, but I always feel that I need to be on guard. Our relationship is dictated by the strict guidelines of the church. We chat about my recently ended first year of college. She is curious about my non-Amish family back home in suburban Massachusetts. I enjoy her company, but I always feel strange around her, as I have no experience with women. I am sexually attracted to her, but I am also attracted to men.

The picking lasts for several hours until a large pickup arrives. The truck driver is dressed in jeans, a T-shirt, and a Marlboro baseball cap. He has a full beard and large, bushy moustache that covers his upper lip. He looks out of place among us, but it seems no one notices except me. I am drawn to his beard and moustache, mesmerized by the quality and structure it shows over his face. We load the trays of strawberries into his truck and he heads off to auction. I wish I could go with him. The thought of riding in his truck and spending time with him excites me. I still have my license due to my parents' insistence that I keep it, but do not own or operate a car, as it is not permitted by church regulations. Instead, the horse-drawn carriage is the accepted mode of transportation, and a striking defiance of modernism. This is the life I want. I want to remain here and become a member of the Old Order Amish church. To achieve this I must learn hard work and dedication and Christian ideals, and be attracted solely to girls.

My next chore is to buy a few dozen eggs from a neighbor's farm. I find myself elated at the idea of getting off the farm and running an errand alone. As I make my way under the railroad bridge and onto the main road, the isolation turns into excitement and adventure. The sun shines heavily upon the asphalt highway as a steady stream of cars swerve around me. A horse and buggy passes me on the other side of the road. Even after a month, the sight of a buggy still moves me. The older, long-bearded driver of the buggy gives me the characteristic Amish wave and I smile. The man has no idea that my own grandfather, probably around his age, drives around town in a Lincoln Town Car. The entire modern world turns at a pace that clashes with that of the Amish community.

As the driveway to the egg farm approaches to my left, a bearded, leather-clad biker passes me on his motorcycle and gives me a hearty wave and smile. I feel helpless. I cannot help but be attracted to the biker's ruggedness. Seeing his bushy beard makes my heart beat faster. I feel as though I am in two worlds at once, the center of one world and the fringe of another. Walking down the long driveway, I feel nervous to meet the young family who recently took over the egg farm. After all, it is not every day that these people experience an outsider who has come into their community based on his own free will and personal conviction. Their church does not send out armies of missionaries to convert the masses; it is a quiet assembly where the idea of evangelism is as distant as the idea of driving a car.

The house, located behind a huge kitchen garden that is further hidden by elaborate grape arbors, appears suddenly. Three small children play in a sandbox. A large dog hitched to a post spots me and starts barking, causing a man to open the barn door and peek out. He looks sweaty, and has a thick blond beard that lacks a moustache in accordance to Amish rules. He immediately greets me and starts speaking the German dialect of Pennsylvania Dutch. Somewhat surprised when I answer him in English, he quickly switches to English without hesitation. He is slim, attractive, and smells of fresh sweat. His odor, so natural and honest, arouses me, and I feel slightly guilty enjoying it. He gives me a few dozen eggs in a Dairy Queen bag, and I leave. As I head back up the driveway, he yells, "See you in church on Sunday!"

I just smile and answer, "Sure thing–see you then." By the time I reach the main road, my mind is preoccupied with the church service on Sunday and my attraction to the egg farmer. I arrive home just in time for lunch. The menu this afternoon consists of roasted chicken, mashed potatoes, creamed peas, and homemade bread. The lunch is quiet, with the clutter of Pennsylvania Dutch dishes dancing around the table. It is truly a sing-song of English-flavored German.

After lunch, we separately finish chores and prepare for market the next day. We sell produce and goods at the large farmers' market in northern Lancaster County. I thoroughly enjoy going to market, as it provides a necessary change of pace. Also, in the back of my mind, I know there will be many blue-collar men to admire.

Everyone has a specialty; mine is to prepare fifty gallons of homemade root beer. It is hot work, but a refreshing change from the physical labor of the farm. Sparkling gallons of root beer slowly fill the shelves of the milk room. I take my time bottling the root beer; I am in no hurry.

This is my last project of the day aside from loading the trailer for the morning journey to market.

I retire to bed early. The crickets and tree frogs outside orchestrate a chorus of awesome proportion. The night is otherwise still and quiet, untouched by the glare of television or radio. The only event of the evening we share with the rest of the world is the sharp darkness of the night and the faint glow of a full moon.

*   *   *

It has been a few years since I lived with the Amish, yet they are still a part of my life. In my own way, I still have daily interactions with them and struggle with life outside of a sectarian society. For so many years, I lived within two worlds. After finishing graduate school and starting my professional career, my life became less focused on Amish teachings, and for the first time, I found myself living according to my own ideals and beliefs. This was not always easy, as there was great comfort in giving up my individuality for the protection of a community. My search for peace and fulfillment has not ended, but rather has taken on a different form. Perhaps I was just hiding from my own sexuality, and the Amish allowed me to live in a world of separation. In the past two years, I have come out of the closet, had male lovers, attended gay events, and made new friends.

I still find many women sexually attractive, and often wish to experience intimacy with them. Because of this, I call myself bisexual. I have a difficult time explaining my sexuality, as it is diverse. Although it might seem ideal, I cannot have a relationship with both a male and female. I often wish I had stayed with the Amish, married a woman, and kept my feelings for men secret. Other times I feel liberated, and thankful I did not make that decision. I often wonder why I chose the path I did, considering what I have given up or gained. I gave up most of my earlier life, but I feel as though I have gained something extraordinary. I feel lucky having had some very unique and interesting experiences. I respect the validity of both worlds, but unfortunately I can physically live only in one.

Two years ago, while attending graduate school in New York City, I rented a small cottage near the shoreline in Connecticut. By then, I had been in relationships with both men and women. My first male relationship had just ended and I struggled again with my sexuality. I was certain I made a huge mistake continuing school and leaving the Amish.

Shortly after, I remember pulling into the driveway of my cottage and noticing a nest of sparrows in the tall bushes that lined the sidewalk. I felt completely humbled at seeing them in their simple home. I could accept myself as the man that I am, even though I did not understand completely what that was. The world was peaceful and full of opportunity, and I knew I could embrace my individualism, education, spirituality, and sexuality.

The young sparrows in the nest sang, and a tear rolled down my cheek. At that moment, I learned a little more about my place in this world.

# Beyond Bisexuality

*Marco Vassi*

Available online at http://www.haworthpress.com/web/JB
doi:10.1300/J159v05n02_33

[Haworth co-indexing entry note]: "Beyond Bisexuality." Vassi, Marco. Co-published simultaneously in *Journal of Bisexuality* (Harrington Park Press, an imprint of The Haworth Press, Inc.) Vol. 5, No. 2/3, 2005, pp. 283-290; and: *Bi Men: Coming Out Every Which Way* (ed: Ron Jackson Suresha, and Pete Chvany) Harrington Park Press, an imprint of The Haworth Press, Inc., 2005, pp. 283-290.

**SUMMARY.** The second, concluding section of the famous deceased author's treatise, including diagrams, on sensuality beyond gender, fully attaining all aspects of femininity and masculinity through coincident sexual union with men and women. Excerpted from "Beyond Bisexuality," in *The Erotic Comedies* by M. Vassi, 1981.

**KEYWORDS.** Bisexuality, bisexual men, ritual Tantric sexuality, transcendental eroticism, personal transformation, heterosexual women, polyamory, sexual exploration, spirituality

Sex is a key to doorways of knowing. For me it has been a yoga through which new qualities of self evolved. Like the alchemist who works with a potion for decades and in the process brings about a transmutation of his essence, I spent all my conscious life since the age of eight mixing elements in the crucible of sex, sifting enormous amounts of material to produce a few grams of pure substance. I had fucked or been fucked by over five hundred different women, and twice that many men, in circumstances ranging from brief gaspings in alleys and whorehouses to lengthy relationships. I had gone through all the possible scenarios. And with the suddenness of total change, I became a different kind of person.

At the far edge of bisexuality I realized that all that had gone before was but the task of perfecting the instrument, the mindbody that is myself. My adventures had served a single purpose: to exhaust all the subjective aspects of the sexual act. The many modes, which had been challenges, areas of exploration, were now my tools–homosexuality, heterosexuality, bisexuality, abstruse psychosexual states and practices, the so-called perversions, the many masks of libidinal displacement . . . these were now at my command, to be used the way a director uses a cast of characters to realize a vision.

Having no term which encompassed the totality of my erotic awareness and function, I found it necessary to coin a new word, and thus formulated the concept: METASEXUALITY.

\* \* \*

Metasexual consciousness is born once one has healed the internal male-female duality. Strictly speaking, only those who have attained that state are capable of understanding it. But in the same way that the Buddha nature inheres in every living thing, and enlightenment is simply a waking up to what we have been all along, metasexuality is manifested in all human beings whether they know it or not. But to see this involves at least an intellectual effort, that of making the distinction between metasex and sex itself.

Sex is that activity which takes places between one man and one woman who are fucking to make a baby. Metasex is everything else. This is gone into in full detail in *The Metasexual Manifesto*, so I won't elaborate here.

In this essay, I would like only to suggest some of what is uncovered once that crucial distinction is made. For once we cease applying the laws of sex to metasex, metasex reveals itself as a rich and unexplored territory.

The most blatant example of confusion between the two vehicles lies at the core of every historical civilization–and a metasexual awakening challenges this principle head on–and consists of the prejudice that *two* is the *natural* number for the erotic encounter. This is obviously valid for the sexual realm but proves completely erroneous in the metasexual worldview. The assumption that *two* allows the most perfect erotic union is a misconception rooted in primitive bisexual consciousness.

When one transcends male-female dualism, eroticism becomes susceptible of a more subtle mathematical understanding. For each number, there is a different and unique quality of consciousness, and no one is intrinsically superior to any of the others.

*One*, the single point, metasex of no dimension. This is the realm of masturbation, that poorly understood activity, usually considered to be an aberration, but actually a powerful vehicle in its own right. To masturbate to full orgasm (not merely ejaculation or clitoral twitching, but full vegetative release) is a sublime and solitary act, requiring capacity for fear and awe. To bring about one's own orgasm, without the company of others, without fantasies to mask the facticity of the deed, requires great inner resources.

*One* has certain shadings, for a person can masturbate in the presence of others and vary the nature of the experience. Masturbating while another assists, giving positive reinforcement, kissing, stroking, speaking, is a profound means of grasping the reality of self and other. How many couples, thinking themselves uninhibited, are unable to masturbate in one another's presence? It is not going too far to suggest that unless an individual has come to terms with *one*, he or she will lack full capability in the higher numbers.

*Two* is the official sexual model of our civilization, entrenched in our archetypal mind. It is, however, from a metasexual viewpoint, nothing more than the metasex of a single line, the metasex of one dimension: it is totally flexible since a line can assume an infinity of curves, but it always remains in one dimension.

A ————————————— B

With *two* accepted as the ideal, the "natural" way of doing things, the other numbers get relegated to the categories of sin, crime, perversion, or diversion. Even many sophisticates measure their orgies against an unconscious norm. Again, this is because they have not dealt with the internal bisexual split.

The enforced exclusivity of the number even damages the couple-form itself. As people try to squeeze all erotic exploration into that single format, it suffers from a fatal overload. It is as though, with the integral calculus available to us, a law was passed forbidding us to do anything but count on our fingers and toes.

*Two* has its uses, its value, and its delights, as well as its limitations. Biologically, it is the vehicle of procreation. And it possesses a certain classic purity of line which makes it attractive to radicals as well as traditionalists. Perhaps its major appeal lies in its comparative simplicity.

*Three* is the first number in the metasex of two dimensions, metasex of the plane. *Three* must be understood as more than the addition of one more to the basic two. It involves a whole new quality of consciousness, something which cannot come about with people who are still thinking in male-female terms.

The fact of the new dimension becomes clear when one sees that within a triangle, the twosome is but one element of the greater vehicle. In a triangle, in fact, there are seven elementary constituent parts:

individuals: A, B, C; couples: AB, AC, BC; and the overall form: ABC.

In theory, the triangle is equilateral; in practice, there are many functional variations. For example, using the situation with Robert and Diane, with Robert as A, Diane as B, and myself as C, Robert and Diane, a mated pair-bond, represent a stronger energy than either Robert and myself or Diane and myself; thus, AB will be shorter than either AC or BC. But that is only within one category. Since Diane and I are in a pair-formation situation in terms of our biological sexuality, our metasex will have an intensity greater than what happens between her and Robert in the pair-maintenance situation.

In this triangle, BC will be shorter than either AB or AC. In a third context, since Robert and I have cocks and Diane a cunt, the AC bond will possess an idiosyncratic quality which neither AB or BC can manifest, thus giving yet another shape to the basic triangle.

It is possible to go on, showing how differences in body type, ages, astronomical factors, genetic determinations, and so forth, each produce a new triangle. It is the constant tension between the complexity of human dynamics and the inherent properties of a given number which gives the metasexual act its defining nature. The amount of energy available gives it its scope. This can be stated as a general principle: any metasexual act is a function of energy, personality, and geometry.

*Four* is a difficult number. From one angle, it is two squared. Thus, many couples attempting different numbers before having come to terms with the bisexual split, go to *four*, where they do nothing more than intensify their basic dualistic bias.

In another sense, *four* is the next two-dimensional figure after three, having one more side than a triangle. As such, it offers fifteen elementary units! As follows:

individuals: A, B, C, D; couples: AB, AC, AD, BC, BD, CD; triangles: ABC, ABD, ACD, BCD; and the overall form: ABCD. The richness of this structure is grasped when one realizes that not only are all of these sub-units operating simultaneously, but all personality components are functioning, and at the high energy level four people can generate. This gives a strong, continually changing, multi-leveled reality which only a very few are capable of experiencing and integrating.

But further, *four* is the first number which yields three dimensions:

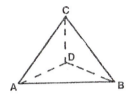

a pyramid with a triangular base. To answer the question as to what makes the difference in any given group of four between a plane with four sides and this pyramid is outside the scope of this article. But one can see that the reality of a metasexual fourth dimension, a spacetime of Einsteinian eroticism, would be the next step in this direction.

I am not personally qualified to discuss the numbers from *five* upward since I have not experienced them, except in gatherings of swingers who had not yet realized their metasexual nature and were piling on bodies without changing the essential consciousness of the act.

It is also fascinating to wonder at *zero*, or metacelibacy seen not as a renunciation, but as an embrace, of all metasex.

There was a time when it seemed to people that the sun revolved around the earth, a view enshrined in the Ptolemaic model of the solar system. Now, with a less parochial view, we have developed a new understanding signaled by the introduction of the Copernican model.

The introduction of the metasexual paradigm is no less a shift in the history of our evolving understanding. The vast majority of the species has not seen past the conditioned strictures of the number *two*. And even those in the vanguard, having their orgies, still operate from the standpoint of a male-female dualism. The most sophisticated among them proclaim themselves bisexuals, not aware that this is the dead-end of that particular tunnel vision. The only way out is to go within to heal the internal split. A monad has no gender.

The question now presents itself: what form does the metasexual lifestyle take?

I won't presume an answer. As for myself, I currently allow circumstances to guide me. Having no prejudices, no preconceptions, I am open to whatever is possible, to whoever wants to dance with me. Yet, if this is a genuine satori, as I practice the living awareness of it, a specific form may evolve. It is possible that I might one day accept a simple pattern to express my true nature: perhaps an uncomplicated heterosexual linear bond, or perhaps a gay threesome, or a life of introspective masturbation. For, if one has subsumed all forms, then one is free to manifest in any form whatsoever.

Beyond bisexuality, externals take on a different meaning than when one is caught in the male-female duality. Even the most stereotyped act is permeated with a brilliant awareness that transforms the perception of reality. To paraphrase the Zen masters:

> *Sucking cock,*
> *Fucking cunt,*
> *Empty and marvelous!*

## NOTE

Excerpt from *The Erotic Comedies* by Marco Vassi; sections 3-5, Sag Harbor: Permanent Press, 1981. See *Bi Guys* (Haworth Press, 2005) for sections 1-2.

# Liquid Ritual

*Chuck Greenheart Bradley*

Available online at http://www.haworthpress.com/web/JB
© 2005 by The Haworth Press, Inc. All rights reserved.
doi:10.1300/J159v05n02_34

[Haworth co-indexing entry note]: "Liquid Ritual." Bradley, Chuck Greenheart. Co-published simultaneously in *Journal of Bisexuality* (Harrington Park Press, an imprint of The Haworth Press, Inc.) Vol. 5, No. 2/3, 2005, pp. 291-304; and: *Bi Men: Coming Out Every Which Way* (ed: Ron Jackson Suresha, and Pete Chvany) Harrington Park Press, an imprint of The Haworth Press, Inc., 2005, pp. 291-304. Single or multiple copies of this article are available for a fee from The Haworth Document Delivery Service [1-800-HAWORTH, 9:00 a.m. - 5:00 p.m. (EST). E-mail address: docdelivery@haworthpress.com].

**SUMMARY.** The author honors his fluid sexuality with a ritual derived from ancient Celtic traditions. He examines his own personal experiences as a seeker of sexual and spiritual enlightenment and integrates them into his ritual practice. *[Article copies available for a fee from The Haworth Document Delivery Service: 1-800-HAWORTH. E-mail address: <docdelivery@haworthpress.com> Website: <http://www.HaworthPress.com> © 2005 by The Haworth Press, Inc. All rights reserved.]*

**KEYWORDS.** Bisexuality, bisexual men, nature rituals, neo-Celtic ritual, Bear subculture, personal transformation, sexual exploration, spirituality

"I am descended from a long line of drunken Irish sailors," is a line I spring on friends to describe certain unexpected behaviors. Unexpected because, although my usual demeanor is soft-soften and gentle, I need an excuse for the occasional flurry of colorful language and raw humor that escapes my lips, as well as my delight in imbibing spirits.

The excuse has some elements of reality. My father was half Irish, and my mother is half Irish, so I consider myself all Irish with my paternal grandmother's Polish-ness and my maternal grandfather's Lithuanian-ness swallowed up in the shamrocks and leprechauns that follow in my wake. And my maternal grandparents did own commercial fishing boats that docked at the New Jersey state marina. I will leave aside their drinking habits out of respect for my elders.

What has any of this to do with bisexual men? The mission statement of the Bisexual Resource Center says: "We believe in a world that acknowledges people as whole and indivisible and where they should not have to leave any part of their heritage and identity at the door." In light of that, I am a bi man whose exploration of religion and mysticism are a profound part of what makes me tick. Continued visits to the New Jersey shore and boat rides on my grandparents' boats have deeply impressed the mystical value of the ocean on me. I am not the only one in my family who feels this way: two relatives have had their ashes spread out in the ocean, and that is my own wish for myself and another living relative's wish. For my family, the ocean is a good place to spend an eternity or two.

The more deeply I swim into mystical territory, the more my Irish heritage speaks to me; I am fascinated with Celtic Christianity, the pre-Christian Druids, the inspiration of *fáiths* (seers or prophets) and bards, and with deeper unrecorded tribal animism. These days, when I have something to pray about or meditate on or celebrate, I create my own rituals based on what I have learned about ancient Irish rituals.

Today, I wish to celebrate being a bisexual man. The reason I consider being bisexual something to celebrate will emerge from the memories I will meditate on. I use a ritual based on the myth of the Four Treasures of the *Tuatha Dé Danaan* (Tribe of the deities of Danu/Ana). The Tuatha Dé Danaan was a tribe who inhabited Ireland before the Irish. When the Tuatha Dé Danaan, who were descendants of *Danu* or *Ana* (their term for Mother Earth), arrived in Ireland, they brought with them their four greatest treasures: the Spear of *Fios* (Knowledge), the Sword of *Cath* (Battle), the Cauldron of *Bláth* (Plenty), and the Stone of *Séis* (Song). I will visualize these treasures during my ritual. Each treasure activates a function that a tribe must have in order to survive.

As for tools for my ritual, nothing could be simpler, because I have chosen only two. The first is a rock, small enough to hold with one hand but large enough to have some weight so I will not forget I am holding it. The rock, like most magickal tools, will be polyvalent, representing more than one thing. The other tool is the venue itself: the ocean. Each part of the ritual will have four divisions: action (what I am doing), visualization (what I am imagining), words (what I am saying) and meditation (remembering how I have come out as a bisexual man).

*Action:* I walk out into the ocean at Revere Beach, a short bus ride from my apartment, until I am waist deep in the water. I am clutching the rock with my non-dominant hand (in my case, my left hand) and holding it towards my chest; I am careful not to let the rock touch the water. I am facing the east.

*Visualization:* Despite its being past midday, I imagine what the sun looked like as it rose.

*Incantation*: Every Good Spirit of Land, Sea and Sky
                I seek your blessings during this fine jewel of a day
                Ancestors and Teachers who long ago did die
                I invite you to stand with me in the water to pray
                And Shining Ones to whom I now cry
                Stand with me, you members of the Tuatha Dé

*Meditation:* I place the rock in my right hand, still not letting it touch the water, and plunge my cupped left hand in the water. I concentrate on the sensation of my right hand touching the rock. It is hard, inflexible, unyielding, like my past religious beliefs and my opinions about sexuality. Next, I concentrate on my left hand in the water: moist, smooth, refreshing, flowing.

*Action:* I raise my left hand above water level and switch the rock from my dominant right hand to my non-dominant left hand, again making sure the rock does not touch the water. I point the index finger of my right hand in front me of as a makeshift magick wand, turn clockwise three times and continue an extra 180 degrees so I am facing west. Again I switch the rock, left to right, and extend my left hand out, palm upwards, as if preparing to receive something just beyond me.

*Visualization:* In my visioning third eye, I see a spear coming from the sky and hovering above the water. Carved on the spear handle is the image of a boar. The spear is coming towards me slowly as one might expect a precious gift to be given. I understand the spear is filled with fios/(knowledge).

*Incantation:* My gratitude goes to you
       Lord of Illumination, Lugh
       Your spear to me will show
       How it is that I know what I know

*Meditation:* Lugh (the *gh* is silent) is the member of the Tuatha Dé Danaan to whom the spear belongs. One of his epithets is Samildánach, which means "Many-Skilled" because he is a builder, a champion, a harpist, a warrior, a poet, an historian, a mage, a physician, a cupbearer and a metalworker. In other words, Lugh is highly skilled and has much knowledge.

Now I go deep into my memory to ask, how did I know I was bisexual?

For many years I desired women and men without knowing the term for such a thing. I do not remember having sexual desire or even a rudimentary knowledge about sex as a child. But now I remember when I first heard the words "gay" and "lesbian." I was in second grade, and my father was superintendent of an apartment building in Plainfield, N.J., that had problems with bats flying through hallway windows sometimes left open by neglectful tenants. I asked my father, "where do the bats come from?" He responded, "Have you ever heard of 'bats in your belfry'?"

I answered, "That means 'you're crazy'."

Dad explained that sometimes bats in the belfry are a literal problem: the Episcopal Church across the street had bats in its belfry. But Dad explained that God had cursed that church with bats because they allowed gays and lesbians to worship there.

I had no idea what in the world a "gay" or a "lesbian" was. But neither did I ask. My six- or seven-year-old mind filled in the details. Obviously a gay or a lesbian must be a type of monster. Why else would a loving

God, who probably had better things to do, go to the extreme of cursing a church with bats because of their presence?

I do not remember hearing the words gay or lesbian again until high school. By that time I was aware of being attracted to girls and boys. I did encounter the word homosexual before high school in a book on childcare lying around our apartment. The author was quick to assure new parents that if they saw homosexual inclinations among their children, they should not be too worried, since homosexuality is an immature form of sexuality, which resolves itself naturally into acceptable heterosexuality. That made sense to me since I never saw a female couple or a male couple; I only saw couples that had "one of each." My childhood was undisturbed by my homoerotic feelings; after all, it was just a phase, destined to disappear by adulthood. No need to bother anyone about it now.

My mother had remarried after my father's death when I was twelve. When I was fourteen, I noticed I still had crushes on both boys and girls. I wondered why this phase was not ending. Around then I heard the word "gay" applied to a class of people for the first time since my father had used it. This time it was directed at an openly gay boy in my high school. I met this fellow because we both sang in the choir (clichéd, but true). He seemed to have an abrasive wit that contrasted with my goody-two-shoes way through life. I took an immediate dislike to him and never considered that his meanness was a logical strategy for an openly gay boy in a suburban New Jersey high school in the early 1980s, who went through every abuse from light taunting to routine beatings by straight kids. Still, I thought, if this fellow is gay, then I, with my manners, shyness and eventually two (consecutive) steady teenage girlfriends, was decidedly not gay.

Also, I was reintroduced to the word "lesbian." One of my stepsisters complained that she was at a party and a lesbian flirted with her in an unwelcome manner and soured her evening. I asked my stepsister when she became part of the drama club.

"I haven't joined the drama club. Why do you think that?" my stepsister asked.

"Well didn't you just say an actor was being fresh with you?" I asked.

"No," my stepsister said, "You are thinking of a thespian. A lesbian is a gay woman. I have nothing against gay people, but she was being rude."

"Oh," I said, "I understand." But, in a way, I did not. Rumors about the gay boy at school led other students to inform me that all gays liked sex "up the butt" and try as I might I could not see how two women could do that. But if lesbians were gay, they must be "into that."

Unfortunately, confusion and ignorance led to where it oft leads, to prejudice. I was a teenage homophobe for a short while. Religious people whom I respected described gays and lesbians as deliberately trying to destroy families. I accepted this attitude from people I trusted. Looking back, I do not see the churchgoing people who were so influential to my youth as intentionally hateful. Rather, they held their religious attitudes in the same manner as I now hold this rock. Their attitudes were like this rock: cold, hard, and rigid. However, if it was church people who led me to homophobia, it was other church people who shocked me out of it for a while.

When I was sixteen, the summer between junior and senior year, I enrolled in a summer program at Berklee College of Music in Boston. This was the first time I was away from New Jersey for more than a week and the first time away from my parents. I was always interested in religion and liked to spend time in religious book and gift shops. The Arlington Street Church, a Unitarian Universalist church in Boston, had a bookstore. Visiting the store, I saw a button that made my inexperienced sixteen-year-old mind go blank. The button said, "Nuke a Gay Whale for Christ." Satire and sarcasm were unknown to me, so after several minutes, when my mind came back, I was plagued by the most ridiculous thoughts: "How do they know which whales are gay? Isn't nuking them going way overboard? How is this church going to get nukes? Why do these people think Christ approves of either weapons or harming animals?" Finally, the catalyzing thought, "This church is weird; I should leave right now before anyone tries to convert me to this gay animal nuking church!" My initial thoughts were so strange because I had no context in which to make sense of the button. But when I went home, I decided to not judge people I did not understand and eventually made steps towards being a friend with the one openly gay fellow in my high school.

Still, I was concerned. I understood gay to mean sexually attracted to the same sex and not to the opposite sex. So, what did that make me, desiring both? And what of the notion of it being a phase? I could no longer take comfort in the thought that my sexual peculiarity was a phase, since I began to doubt that. Still, the word "gay" didn't fit with its exclusion of heteroerotic desire, and that left me with no term to identify with. But that was soon to change.

Another student at my high school was snickering about the name of a decade-old, but still popular, rock group. I asked him why the band's name was so funny, and he asked if I knew what it meant. Images of batteries and electrical outlets came to mind until he whispered in my ear. I cannot recall what he whispered, but I recall my first thought. "Wow. I'm AC/DC!"

It was not until college that I heard the term bisexual and then, I had knowledge that I was a bisexual man.

*Action:* I turn 90 degrees clockwise. I face north. My left hand is again held in a receptive fashion.

*Visualization:* I imagine a sword hovering above the water, coming down from the sky and then towards me. The sword has the image of an eagle carved on the blade. I acknowledge the sword to be filled with cath/(battle).

*Incantation:* Nuada with the silver arm
                Your sword will protect me from harm
                Defender of your divine tribal race
                Show me the battles I may have to face

*Meditation:* Nuada, who for a time had a silver arm, is the owner of the sword of the Four Treasures. He is thus a powerful warrior figure.

Coming out as bisexual made me go through some battles. Some I was prepared for. Others, I was not.

Although raised Roman Catholic, I became Eastern Orthodox after high school, and returned from New Jersey to Boston, this time for seminary to become a priest. Though I understood I was bisexual and that it wasn't a phase, the church acknowledged sexual activity as only having a place within marriage, and marriage was a sacrament uniting one man and one woman. Thus I viewed my homoerotic feelings, which I believed could never be fulfilled, as a divine curse. I pleaded again and again with the Christian God to show me why I should be cursed. I received no answer.

I kept my sexual identity hidden, for fear I would never be made a priest if I became public. I told only two good friends, a priest who was my spiritual director, and, when I met a woman I wanted to have a long-term relationship with, I told her prior to any sexual involvement.

The spiritual director seemed not to pass judgment on me. However, only days later, I found myself in his car traveling to an event with him and other spiritual charges. The others started to talk about two gay men in Boston who were physically assaulted. The seminarians agreed that the victims deserved to be attacked because of their publicly displayed affection. The priest, who was my spiritual director, agreed completely. I was shocked to find out that he could believe such a thing, that his heart was as hard as the rock I now hold as I remember the conversation.

Afterward, I continued to be afraid not only that something would call my sexuality into question, but, once again, that I was cursed. Even when I came out to the woman who I eventually married, I explained my bisexuality in these words: "I am damaged on the inside."

My wife had also attended seminary with me, and the Orthodox Church allows married men to become priests. But I never became a priest, and my wife and I divorced after seven years of marriage. Though I was out as bisexual to her before we married or even engaged, and though we were monogamous and I never cheated on her, today when people hear I am bisexual and divorced, they automatically assume one has everything do with the other, as if no exclusively heterosexual marriages ever fail. My marriage failed for the same reason a lot of marriages fail: intrusive in-laws, fiscal irresponsibility, lack of compatibility and so on. Trying to explain that a mixed orientation marriage is not automatically doomed remains a constant battle.

It was while I was engaged that I ceased to view myself as a cursed bisexual. One of the male seminary friends I came out to had a younger brother who was a devout Orthodox Christian, a historian devoted to academics and openly gay. This young man taught me that same-sex unions had being happening in the Christian church since the third century, and were still happening in rural, mountainous parts of Greece and Albania where the western notion of homophobia had not yet been imported. The same man told me the names of various same-sex coupled saints through history. (This exchange happened a few years before *Same-Sex Unions of Premodern Europe* was published posthumously by Yale University scholar John Boswell.) I came to believe that God did not leave anyone aside because of their sexuality and that many holy people were in some way queer. But still I lived in fear of the seminary's attitude about sexuality, and it remained a battle until I realized I could not remain in the Orthodox Church. I left it soon after I was divorced and fifteen years after having converted to it in the first place.

The battle I did not expect, but which was the saddest and most despicable, was the battle I faced when I was divorced and out of seminary and started to come out to everyone I met in Boston. I had not realized that many gay people wish to exclude bisexuals. For awhile, I did use the word gay to describe myself, afraid of the backlash from newly made gay friends who lectured me on how bisexuals were untrustworthy, deceptive, underhanded, and just plain confused. Some people I met thought bisexuality simply did not exist (which made me feel as if I had been called a liar).

So I began to call myself gay until I realized that I had left one closet just to enter another! Even as an out bisexual, there are still battles to be fought. The second Pride parade I marched in was a wonderful event, but afterwards I had the misfortune to attend an outdoor block party with a tank top that said, "Bisexual Pride." One gay man shouted, "I hate bisexuals!" so loud into my left ear, I was deaf for the rest of the evening. That was the worst thing that happened to me at that event, at which I was also spit upon by another gay man and pushed against a wall by another (this time drunken) gay man as he ridiculed my tank top.

The battle continues. It is not, however, a battle between bi men and gay men. I have been blessed to meet many bi-friendly gay men and lesbians. The battle is between the entire gay, lesbian, bisexual, transgender, intersex, and queer-identified community and every harmful spirit that would make a lie of our claims of honoring diversity and inclusivity. Such baneful spirits include the spirits of racism, sexism and ageism. Such spirits are all intertwined.

Other battles I have faced are not only with biphobic gays but also with biphobic straights. I have in mind certain straight people who appear to be accepting of gays and lesbians, but who are heavily invested in the notion of a solid dividing line between straights and gays, with little tolerance for anyone who blurs the line, which might force them to reexamine their own sexuality. All of this biphobia from both gays and straights points to rigidity around how people conceive sexuality. This rigidity of thinking, once again, reminds me of the rock I hold.

Before I turn away from the north, the place of battle, I remember my own struggle with my appearance. Fat, hairy and masculine-appearing, I could not identify with the standards of male beauty set by either mainstream society or the gay community. I have been successful in that battle, and I thank the goddesses and gods for the day I stumbled into the porn section of the local gay bookstore.

Whenever I visited Glad Day, a gay bookstore that used to operate in Boston, I was diligent not to wander into "the other side" of the bookstore, the porn side, and stuck to the more acceptable literary offerings on the "safe side." But wander I did, and I found a centerfold that amazed me. Hairy, large belly, and, unbelievable to my eyes, naked and loving it! "This cannot be," I thought, "he looks like me and has the audacity to think he is sexually desirable." Suddenly, the phrase "Law of Supply and Demand" came to me. I realized he must be desirable to someone and that there would not be such a magazine if there were no audience for it. In awe, I flipped to the cover of the magazine, which I discovered was entitled *Bear*. These days I consider myself a member of both the bi community and the bear brotherhood. More importantly, I know that, although not everyone will find me sexy, there will always be someone who does, and I am determined not to be caught by surprise when that happens.

*Action:* I turn 90 degrees, again clockwise, and face the east. Left hand is again ready to receive.

*Visualization:* With my visioning eye, I see a great cauldron descend from the sky and rest just above the water. An image of a salmon is carved on its side; I recognize that this cauldron is filled with *bláth* (plenty).

*Incantation:* Fat Father God of Abundance, the Dagda by name
   I seek the prize that you possess, the wealth that gives you fame
   Where might my treasure lie? Where might it be?
   Show me riches I already have, but do not clearly see

*Meditation:* The Dagda is a father figure in Irish myth, ever generous because his cauldron is never exhausted. This feature is lucky, because the Dagda is always voraciously hungry for food. With his sizeable girth and perky demeanor, the Dagda is also voraciously hungry for sex. Fat, jolly, and horny, some suggest that the Dagda is a "perverted Santa Claus." Though some may find such a description unsettling, bear events make me wonder if I have not encountered this god many times over!

The cauldron usually is connected to material goods, but I feel coming out as a bisexual man has given me riches in the form of friends. Living as an openly bi man in Boston, I have come to look forward to a twice-monthly Bi Brunch. There the bisexual agenda becomes manifest: omelets, pancakes, waffles, bacon, sausages, corn muffins, biscuits, orange juice and coffee. If such an agenda sounds ordinary, even boring, let me assure you, it is radical to me. Sitting, talking, and laughing with a group of people who will not force you into one of two small boxes labeled "straight" and "gay" is liberating. Getting to know people from every conceivable background with whom I never have to play the "pronoun game," covering up the gender of a lover, or of a potential lover, is a rare experience. Never having to be called "confused" over something I am so sure of is a welcome change.

But as I still clutch the rock, I remember how rigid my views were when first getting to know the greater Boston bi community. When I first learned the term polyamory as a term for responsible and honest non-monogamy, I recoiled in judgment. The same reaction occurred when I learned how many new friends were into BDSM (Bondage,

Domination, Dominance, Submission, Sado-Masochism, Sex Magick). Many hardened, rigid attitudes melted when I saw the level of acceptance for all lifestyles in the bi community, as well as the respect not to force anyone to embrace a lifestyle that would not work for them personally. I now see myself as polyamorous in inclination, though not partnered with anyone. As for BDSM, I have not availed myself the opportunity to explore this way of being, but I could be called "kink-curious."

I am grateful to have found a "cauldron of riches" in the form of friends in the bi community. I furthermore feel gratitude for the patience shown me by the community during times I was more rigid in my thinking and less accepting.

*Action:* I turn, clockwise once more, another 90 degrees. I now face the south. The left hand is turned palm down as if to reach out and touch something

*Visualization:* I visualize a great stone rising from the water. I know it is filled with séis (song) that I do not yet hear, but am confident I will soon. On the stone is an etching of a stag.

*Incantation:* Great Mother, your works amaze.
                What's this I spy through the mist and haze?
                To touch the stone, do I dare?
                And then listen closely to what may be to hear?

*Meditation:* Knowledge, courage in battle and plenty of wealth were the three functions that Celtic tribes needed to survive. Surviving, however, is not the same as flourishing. If a tribe expanded its territory, but their collective soul remained puny, what true gain would there be? Moving from the west with its function of knowledge, and then to the north to face battle, and further to the east to embrace abundance, the tribe must make total peace with the land they reside on. The tribe does this in the south where song, music, and inspiration are found.

For me, the more I am honest with myself and with the world, about not only my sexuality but indeed all my formerly secret longings, the more I tap in to a well of inspiration.

I joke that I came out of the closet to my mother on three different occasions and received three different responses. People wonder how that is possible. A few summers ago I went to New Jersey, telling my mom and her brother that I was bisexual. Though my mother shed tears, she told me she loves me no matter what, and even expressed interest in talking more about it the next day. I am sure coming out as bi did not change who I was in her eyes; I am the son she always loved and will continue to love.

The following summer, I came out again, and was not quite as well received. But it was a totally different "coming out." I have a few tattoos hidden by my clothes that I decided to tell her about. She grumbled, "You're going to the dogs."

The next summer, if only to prove to myself that I had gone beyond coming out and was in full TMI (too much information) mode, I told her I go to nude beaches and that I was just at such a beach in Sandy Hook, New Jersey. Without batting an eyelash, she said, "Oh, that beach is still open?" and seemed entirely unconcerned.

Being "out" as a bi man has led me to being open and unafraid of admitting any curiosities I was previously scared of being judged for. Trading in a rigid understanding of mysticism and sexuality has taught me what the ocean has been telling me my whole life, even when I was not open to hearing. The ocean said, "You think being solid as a rock is powerful, but I am not solid; I am fluid and more powerful than a rock." Now that I have heard that voice, my mysticism is fluid; I do not limit myself to established doctrine which shuts down my creativity, my zest for life and my acceptance of my whole self: bisexual man, queer bear, multi-religious mystic and whatever else I may discover in the future. Also, my view of sexuality is fluid. Though some may see themselves fixed at a point, whether totally gay, totally straight or somewhere fixed in between, I see myself as fluid and ever changing in my sexuality. This does not scare me. Actually, I celebrate it. When people ask what my sexual orientation is, I tell them I do not have one. Rather, bisexuality is my sexual disorientation!

With this new openness, I want to discover new areas of myself, and bring songs and music out. Writing music is becoming easier than it was before I came out. I am drawn to do more divination work, and want to study bodywork, both massage and energy healing. In short, coming out as a bisexual man was the starting step to finding inspiration inside myself.

*Action:* I turn clockwise 270 degrees to face the east one last time, but I do not stare into the east. Rather, I look down to see the center of the imaginary circle of energy. I grab the rock with both hands. The rock up to now has been held over the water. Now I plunge it in the water, step on it, and begin to chant a line from the 78th chapter of the *Tao Te Ching* by Lao Tzu. I leave the rock behind, walk out of the water and prepare to go home.

*Visualization:* As I plunge the rock in the water, I imagine it transfiguring in mass and value. The rock ceases to be the symbol of limited rigidity it has been. Now the rock becomes the stone of the Four

Treasures, the stone in the south that gave inspiration. The transformed rock has become the gift of the goddess known as Lady Sovereignty, who alone determined the rightful king of Ireland. As a tribe must "marry" the land to be in harmony, so the true king must be accepted by Lady Sovereignty as her lover. She indicates this by making the stone cry out in joyful song as a sign of the true king.

The final act of this ritual is to claim sovereignty, that is, responsible and proud ownership over my sexuality. This visualization is hardest of all, because it envisages a paradox: when stepping on the rock, I am bonding with the stone that chooses me, and allow the ocean's energy to flow through me.

I am liberated to go on further travels with my bisexuality as a vital part of my life as a man. Aware of the ceaseless flow of embracing, owning, and letting go of my bisexuality, I complete the celebration.

*Incantation* (from *Tao Te Ching*):

> Nothing in the world
> Is as soft and yielding as water.
> Yet for dissolving the hard and inflexible,
> Nothing can surpass it.
>     The soft overcomes the hard;
> The gentle overcomes the rigid.
> Everyone knows this is true,
> But few can put it into practice.

*Meditation:* For some, ritual is a waste of time. I am sure what many people saw on the beach today was a hirsute, thirtysomething fat guy, carrying a rock for some inexplicable reason, who splashed in the water and "did the Hokey Pokey and turned himself around" before he came back out of the water sans rock.

For me, ritual is joy. Arriving at the end of my ritual, I offer thanks as I receive the greatest gift of sovereignty: its balance, harmony, and healthy sense of pride lead me on a path of serenity.

# Is That Me Up There?

*Wayne Bryant*

Available online at http://www.haworthpress.com/web/JB
© 2005 by The Haworth Press, Inc. All rights reserved.
doi:10.1300/J159v05n02_35

[Haworth co-indexing entry note]: "Is That Me Up There?" Bryant, Wayne. Co-published simultaneously in
*Journal of Bisexuality* (Harrington Park Press, an imprint of The Haworth Press, Inc.) Vol. 5, No. 2/3, 2005,
pp. 305-312; and: *Bi Men: Coming Out Every Which Way* (ed: Ron Jackson Suresha, and Pete Chvany) Harrington Park Press, an imprint of The Haworth Press, Inc., 2005, pp. 305-312. Single or multiple copies of this
article are available for a fee from The Haworth Document Delivery Service [1-800-HAWORTH, 9:00 a.m. -
5:00 p.m. (EST). E-mail address: docdelivery@haworthpress.com].

**SUMMARY.** The author investigates the history of negative representations of male bisexuality in Hollywood and foreign films and its impact on his personal development as a bisexual man. Arguing that bisexuality is everywhere in modern films but is never called bisexuality, the author asks whether it has become the sexuality that cannot speak its own name. Portions of this essay appeared previously under the title "Stereotyping Bisexual Men in Film," published in *Journal of Bisexuality* 1: 2/3, 2001. *[Article copies available for a fee from The Haworth Document Delivery Service: 1-800-HAWORTH. E-mail address: <docdelivery@haworthpress.com> Website: <http://www.HaworthPress.com> © 2005 by The Haworth Press, Inc. All rights reserved.]*

**KEYWORDS.** Bisexuality, bisexual men, coming out, bisexual representations in cinema, bisexual invisibility

When I was growing up in the 1950s and early 1960s, there simply weren't images of bisexual men on the silver screen. Of course, growing up in a small town meant that the "silver screen" was usually a black and white television set that mainly showed films from the 1940s. It was a real treat when my dad would take my sister and me to the drive-in to see a current film. There was something particularly exciting about seeing films with Rock Hudson, Cary Grant, James Dean, Marlon Brando, Sal Mineo, and Montgomery Clift. The treats nearly ended when my mom discovered that he had had the good taste, but bad judgment, to take us to Alfred Hitchcock's *Psycho*, starring Anthony Perkins.

Despite all those great bisexual male actors, there were no bi characters in any of these films. This was because in 1934, Hollywood had introduced the Motion Picture Production Code as a self-censorship mechanism to head off proposed Congressional action that would have imposed even stricter limitations on the film industry. Among other things, the Code banned any depiction of same-sex attractions or relationships. From the 1930s until the early 1960s, the Code effectively prevented any bisexual characters from appearing in Hollywood films. Nazi censorship and the postwar devastation had a similar effect on German films during this period.

The rest of the media was just as silent on bisexuality because during the McCarthy era, the right wing quite effectively associated gays and bisexuals with Communists. With no bisexual role models available, it is easy to see how boys my age could swallow the "it's only a phase" explanation for their same-sex attractions. For the lucky ones, that phase ended in the aftermath of Stonewall. Those less fortunate often spent their years in bad marriages or ended them by swelling the suicide statistics.

Once McCarthy was exposed for the fraud and bully that he was and the Motion Picture Production Code went by the wayside, bi film characters began appearing, first in underground and foreign movies and then in Hollywood productions. But in almost all cases, the bi character on screen was not the sort of person you hoped to grow up to be.

The history of male bisexual characters in film has been one of negative stereotyping. This is not surprising, since the same can be said of the Hollywood depiction of almost every oppressed group. Take African-American men, for instance. From the rapist in *Birth of a Nation* to the dimwitted, shuffling Stepin Fetchit character to the highly sexed criminals in blaxploitation films of the 1970s and beyond, racist stereotypes of African-American characters have been the norm.

Look at any Disney film and the evil character will be the one with the dark complexion. It is interesting, then, that from the 1930s through the 1950s, Hollywood enforced special restrictions preventing the release of films which negatively stereotyped Latin American characters. The reason was not that stereotyping is wrong. After all, Blacks, Asians, and women were regularly derided in films from that period. The reason was that the powerful fruit companies, who were making millions in Central America and the Caribbean, pressured Hollywood (via Washington) to make sure nothing in their films would cause riots, boycotts, work stoppages, or even hard feelings against "American interests."

Bisexual and gay men had no such powerful lobby in Hollywood. For about the first sixty years, bisexual men were almost entirely absent from films made in Hollywood and most of the rest of the world. Leading bi female characters, often played by bisexual actresses, appeared in such films as *Pandora's Box* (1929), *Morocco* (1930), and *Queen Christina* (1933). However, bi male characters were difficult to find. Oliver Hardy's character in the comedy *Their First Mistake* (1932) can be read as bisexual, but no leading males played bisexuals in any U.S. drama before the 1960s.

Two European films proved to be the exception. In 1916, Swedish bisexual director Mauritz Stiller released a film called *Vingarne* (*The Wings*). Based on a story by gay writer Herman Bang, the film was about the life of a sculptor and his relationship with a male student who later leaves him for a woman. The story was remade by Carl Theodor Dreyer in Germany in 1924 using the title *Mikaël*.

Two films from the '40s–*Gilda* (1946) and *Rope* (1948)–had suggestions of male bisexuality, but nothing explicit. In both cases, the men involved were criminals. Bisexuality was implied again in *Rebel Without a Cause* (1955) and *Compulsion* (1959). On the eve of the '60s, Joe E. Brown's character in *Some Like It Hot* (1959) does not withdraw his marriage proposal, even when he discovers that his girlfriend is really a man.

In the early 1960s, with the end of the Code, the floodgates opened–not simply for films with bisexual characters, but for the stereotyping that accompanied them. Bi male stereotypes came in a variety of forms. A common theme was that bisexual husbands always hide their sexuality from their wives. A young Robert Redford stars as just such a bisexual man in *Inside Daisy Clover* (1965). Bi men who beat their wives were also frequently seen, as in *Petulia* (1968).

Another frequent trope was the bisexual victim of extortion. A good example can be found in *Advise and Consent* (1962). Senator Brig Anderson is extorted for his vote on a key issue by opposition leaders who have discovered that he once had a relationship with a gay man. The revelation is so devastating that Anderson commits suicide. *Victim* (1961) was an English film that also used this theme, except that the victim in this case fought back rather than cave in to the extortionists.

The bisexual man who can't deal with his same-sex attraction is the theme in John Huston's *Reflections in a Golden Eye* (1967). Marlon Brando plays an army officer whose wife (Elizabeth Taylor) is carrying on an affair with another officer. Brando, meanwhile, is attracted to a young soldier who enjoys riding horseback in the nude (the original barebacking movie?). Brando's character can't seem to get a grip on his desires and murder predictably follows.

In the 1970s, the switch-hitting criminal became part of the bisexual lexicon. In *Dog Day Afternoon* (1975), Al Pacino stars as Sonny, a married man who robs a bank to pay for his boyfriend's sex change operation. By the early '80s, the bi male criminal stereotype was elevated to murderer with *Deathtrap* (1982). Michael Caine enlists the help of boyfriend Christopher Reeve to kill Caine's wife. This stereotype escalated into the realm of the psycho-killer with David Lynch's *Blue Velvet* (1986), in which Dennis Hopper plays a sadistic murderer who proudly proclaims, "I fuck anything that moves!"

Of course, the "anything that moves" theme is recurrent in bisexual filmography. Terrance Stamp's bisexual angel sleeps with everyone in the family in Pasolini's *Teorema* (1968). In *Angel, Angel, Down We Go* (1969), an obnoxious bisexual singer named Bogart Stuyvesant sleeps with a father, mother, and daughter (played by Holly Near). A bi male character in *Burglar* (1987) reportedly "gets more ass than a toilet seat."

In *The Naked Face* (1984), Rod Steiger's police officer summed up Hollywood's view of bisexual men quite succinctly with the line, "A bisexual is a fag with a family." Basically, the '80s gay stereotype of bisexual men prevailed. Bisexuals were considered men who were really homosexual, but were afraid to come out.

The 1990s brought the stereotype of the bisexual man who spreads AIDS to straight women. In *Together Alone* (1991), Brian is a man who has just had unprotected sex with a gay man named Bryan. Brian, who refuses to disclose his HIV status, finally admits that he has never been tested. Yet he never wears a condom if he can get away with it, and only reluctantly reveals that he is married, has a child, and that his wife is pregnant. *Les Nuits Fauves* (*Savage Nights*, 1993) is another film in which a bisexual man has unprotected sex with others. In this case, he does so knowing he has AIDS.

In 1997, the landscape began to change. Bisexual men were popping up everywhere. They were just regular characters, neither perpetrators nor victims. In *The Fifth Element*, flamboyant journalist Chris Tucker has a sexual encounter with a flight attendant and exclaims, "This is the most fun I've ever had . . . with a woman!" David Cronenberg's frighteningly bizarre film *Crash* featured several characters who have sex with both women and men, but the unifying theme is car crashes. One might think of the action in the context of certain S/M communities in which the particular fetish carries more importance than the gender.

When it was released, *Chasing Amy* was one of the most talked-about films in queer circles. The most obvious bisexual character is Alyssa, who is identified by others as a lesbian, but who has a romantic/sexual history with men and begins a relationship with Holden. More central to the film, however, is the relationship between Holden and Banky. They are childhood friends who identify as heterosexual but are deeply in love. Banky's jealousy over Holden's relationship with Alyssa is a driving factor in the plot. Even the minor characters get in on the act. Jay and Silent Bob, repeat characters from *Clerks*, are ostensibly straight and, at the same time, a humorous parody on an "old married couple." Is there more going on here than meets the eye? Perhaps in *Clerks*, when Jay screams out, "I'll fuck anything that moves," he means it, after all. Director Kevin Smith says that he doesn't use the b-word because "it's so politically charged." More insight into Jay's complex sexuality is revealed in *Dogma* (1999).

One of the best films of 1997, Peter Greenaway's *The Pillow Book*, reinforced the director's reputation for stunning visuals, brilliant music, and meticulously crafted editing. It includes a number of characters who have sex with both men and women, most importantly the key men in Nagiko's life–her father and her lover.

The curious thing that all of these films have in common is that none of the characters actually identify as bisexual. Another example is Gregg Araki's film *Nowhere*, in which almost every character is attracted to both men and women. Araki, a gay film icon, has been dating a woman who plays a bisexual character in the film. "Young people today don't want labels for their sexuality. Who needs it?" Araki says. "You're going to see this more and more in movies from now on because that's what's happening out in the real world, whether people want to recognize it or not."

This trend continues in 2004 with the release of *A Home at the End of the World*. The film has sex, drugs, and polyamory, but it doesn't have a man who calls himself bisexual. Nonetheless, Bobby (Colin Farrell) and Jonathan (Dallas Roberts) are sleeping with each other, as well as their wife, Clare (Robin Wright Penn). When Clare first gets a crush on Bobby, she asks Jonathan whether his friend is gay. He answers, "Bobby's not gay. It's hard to say exactly what Bobby is." It's always hard to say "bisexual" in a movie.

The storyline centers on Bobby and Jonathan, who grow up very differently in the same Cleveland suburb. They become close friends and, eventually, lovers despite their differences. When Jonathan moves to New York City to spread his wings and meet men, Bobby follows and becomes involved with Clare, Jonathan's roommate/lover. The three decide to move to Woodstock as a family and make plans to have a child together. The movie's tagline is "Family can be whatever you want it to be," but the real challenge is getting agreement on what that is. The question becomes, is this threesome up to the task?

The screenplay for this film was written by Michael Cunningham, based on his novel of the same name. Cunningham's earlier novel *The Hours*, which won the 1999 Pulitzer Prize, also explored bisexual themes and was released on film in 2002. One of the producers, Christine Vachon, has had a hand in a number of bi-inclusive films, including *Velvet Goldmine, Swoon, Go Fish*, and *Far from Heaven*, and the trans-themed movie *Hedwig and the Angry Inch*.

While many of the bisexual male stereotypes we have lived with for the past several decades are still with us, the most prevalent trend as we enter the new century is the inability of bi men to utter the word "bisexual." When a younger version of me looks at the screen today, he can find himself, but that self he sees is reluctant to identify as bisexual. In Hollywood, as well as independent and foreign films, it has become the sexuality that dares not speak its name.

## NOTE

Portions of this essay appeared previously under the title "Stereotyping Bisexual Men in Film," published in *Journal of Bisexuality* 1: 2/3, 2001, The Haworth Press, Inc.

# Acknowledgments

[Haworth co-indexing entry note]: "Acknowledgments." Co-published simultaneously in *Journal of Bisexuality* (Harrington Park Press, an imprint of The Haworth Press, Inc.) Vol. 5, No. 2/3, 2005, pp. 313-316; and: *Bi Men: Coming Out Every Which Way* (ed: Ron Jackson Suresha, and Pete Chvany) Harrington Park Press, an imprint of The Haworth Press, Inc., 2005, pp. 313-316. Single or multiple copies of this article are available for a fee from The Haworth Document Delivery Service [1-800-HAWORTH, 9:00 a.m. - 5:00 p.m. (EST). E-mail address: docdelivery@haworthpress.com].

The editors wish to thank Fritz Klein, MD, who offered invaluable editorial advice. We also owe a great debt to Bill Palmer, Rob Owen, Rebecca Browne, Regina Reinhardt, Tracy Sayles, Julie Ehlers, and all the incredibly supportive folks at Haworth.

We offer our gratitude to Martha Stone, who eagerly agreed to review and fact-check the text, and Jeff Shaumeyer, who reviewed and commented on sections of the manuscript.

We cannot imagine having compiled this anthology without the help of the community of bi folks and GLBTIQA writers. Significant among the people who offered advice and support for this book are: Franklin Abbott, Felice Picano, David Bergman, Michael Bronski, Greg Wharton and Ian Philips, Paul Willis and Greg Herren; the Saints & Sinners "Beyond Monosexuality" panel: Patrick Califia, T Cooper, and Elyn Selu; Tristan Taormino, Rachel Kramer Bussey, and Sharon Bear Bergman; Robyn Ochs, Bill Burleson, Kuwaza Imara, and the 8ICB "Bi Bears" discussion group; Matt Rice, Bobbi Keppel, Lani Ka'ahumanu, Loraine Hutchins, Marshall Miller and Dorian Solot, Sheeri Kritzer, Vance Briceland, Tom Aloisi, Luigi Ferrer, Chris Byrne and Ric Kasini Kadour, Richard Schneider, Jim Marks, Les Wright and Bob McDiarmid, Chris Griffith, Steve Klarer and Don Galbraith, Keith Rodwell, and Van Waffle.

During the process of editing *Bi Men* and *Bi Guys*, Ron underwent cancer surgery and radiation therapy, and he wishes to acknowledge his immense gratitude for the health care providers and friends who compassionately guided and supported him through this challenge: Dr. Anthony Barone, Dr. Deborah Wu, Dr. K.S. Tsay, Dr. Michael Raizman, Dr. Tim Cavanaugh, Dr. John Mazzullo, Dr. Mike LeRoux, Dr. Scott Triedman, Drs. Richard and Christina Spagnuolo, Dr. Ann Sousa, Dr. Arnie Klein, Stephen Harrington, Ken Leavett, Jim Brennan, Wayne Cotnoir, Jim Fenter, Jerry Cornish, Michael Downs, Russell Richards, James Buescher, Meir Amiel, Adam Steg, Dale Irvin and Dave Johnson, Todd Smith, Joe Banks and John Gardner, and Tony and Rose Monti.

With all his heart, Ron thanks his partner, Rocco Russo, for his endless love, understanding, and support.

Pete would like to thank his families: Alan Hamilton, Roland "Woody" Glenn, Barbara "Pepper" Greene, Peter Jon Chvany, Elena Chvany and Isaiah Landers, Alec and Heather Chvany, and Steve Chvany, for their encouragement and love.

## REPRINT PERMISSIONS

The editors offer their thanks to reprint the following essays:

"Coming Out Successfully in The Netherlands" by Koen Brand. Excerpt: *Journal of Bisexuality* 1:4, Binghamton, NY: Haworth Press, 2001. Used by permission of the publisher.

"Loving without Limits" by Bob Vance. Excerpt: *Men and Intimacy: Personal Accounts Exploring the Dilemmas of Modern Male Sexuality*, Franklin Abbott, ed. Freedom, CA: The Crossing Press, 1990. With 2005 update from Bob Vance. Used by permission of the author.

"Bicurious Husbands Online Discussion Group." Excerpt: *Bisexual & Gay Husbands: Their Stories, Their Words*, edited by Fritz Klein, MD, & Thomas Schwartz. New York/London/Oxford: Harrington Park Press, 2001. Used by permission of the publisher.

"Whereto, My Beloved?" by Ganapati S. Durgadas. Excerpt: *Blessed Bi Spirit: Bisexual People of Faith*, Debra R. Kolodny, ed. New York/London: Continuum, 2000. Used by permission of the author.

"Choosing Not To" by Michael Ambrosino. Excerpt: *Bi Any Other Name: Bisexual People Speak Out*, Loraine Hutchins & Lani Ka'ahumanu, eds. Los Angeles/New York: Alyson Publications, 1991. Used by permission of the publisher.

"It's a Life: Eriq Chang/Jim." Excerpt: *In Your Face: Stories from the Lives of Gay Youth*, Mary L. Gray, editor. New York/London/Oxford: Harrington Park Press, 1999. Used by permission of the publisher.

"Beyond Bisexuality" by Marco Vassi. Excerpt: *The Erotic Comedies* (Sections III–V), by M. Vassi, Sag Harbor, NY: Permanent Press, 1981. Used by permission of the publisher.

Portions of "Is That Me Up There?" by Wayne Bryant appeared previously under the title "Stereotyping Bisexual Men in Film," published in *Journal of Bisexuality* 1: 2/3. Binghamton, NY: Haworth Press, 2001.

# Selected Bibliography

[Haworth co-indexing entry note]: "Selected Bibliography." Co-published simultaneously in *Journal of Bisexuality* (Harrington Park Press, an imprint of The Haworth Press, Inc.) Vol. 5, No. 2/3, 2005, pp. 317-320; and: *Bi Men: Coming Out Every Which Way* (ed: Ron Jackson Suresha, and Pete Chvany) Harrington Park Press, an imprint of The Haworth Press, Inc., 2005, pp. 317-320. Single or multiple copies of this article are available for a fee from The Haworth Document Delivery Service [1-800-HAWORTH, 9:00 a.m. - 5:00 p.m. (EST). E-mail address: docdelivery@haworthpress.com].

Abbott, Franklin, editor. *Men and Intimacy: Personal Accounts Exploring the Dilemmas of Modern Male Sexuality*, Freedom, CA: The Crossing Press, 1990

Alexander, Jonathan, & Karen Yescavage, editors. *Bisexuality and Transgenderism: Intersexions of the Others*. Binghamton, NY: Harrington Park Press, 2004

Angelides, Steven. *A History of Bisexuality*. Chicago/London: University of Chicago Press, 2001

Appleby, George Alan, editor. *Working-Class Gay and Bisexual Men*. New York/London/Oxford: Harrington Park Press, 2001

Beemyn, Brett, & Erich Steinman, editors. *Bisexuality in the Lives of Men: Facts and Fictions*. New York/London/Oxford: Harrington Park Press, 2001

Besen, Wayne. *Anything But Straight: Unmasking the Scandals and Lies Behind the Ex-Gay Myth*. Binghamton, NY: Harrington Park Press, 2003

Boykin, Keith. *Beyond the Down Low: Sex, Lies, and Denial in Black America*. New York: Carroll & Graff, 2005

Brent, Bill, & Carol Queen, editors. *Best Bisexual Erotica*. Volume 1, 2000; volume 2, 2002. San Francisco: Black Books; Cambridge, MA: Circlet Press

Bryant, Wayne. *Bisexual Characters in Film: From Anaïs to Zee*. New York/London: Harrington Park Press, 1997

Burleson, William E. *Bi America: Myths, Truths, and Struggles of an Invisible Community*. Binghamton, NY: Harrington Park Press, 2005

Buxton, Amity Pierce. *The Other Side of the Closet: The Coming-Out Crisis for Straight Spouses*, revised & expanded edition. Hoboken, NJ: Wiley, 1994

Driggs, John H., & Stephen E. Finn. *Intimacy Between Men: How to Find and Keep Gay Love Relationships*. New York: Plume, 1991

Garber, Marjorie. *Vice Versa: Bisexuality and the Eroticism of Everyday Life*. New York: Touchstone, 1995

Gray, Mary L., editor. *In Your Face*, New York/London/Oxford: Harrington Park Press, 1999

Hutchins, Loraine, & Lani Ka'ahumanu, eds. *Bi Any Other Name: Bisexual People Speak Out*, Los Angeles/New York: Alyson Publications, 1991

Jones, James H. *Alfred C. Kinsey: A Life*. New York/London: Norton & Co., 1997

*Journal of Bisexuality*. Binghamton, NY: Haworth Press, 2000

King, J.L. *On the Down Low: A Journey into the Lives of "Straight" Black Men Who Sleep with Men*. New York: Broadway Books, 2004

Klein, Fritz, MD. *The Bisexual Option*, 2nd edition. New York/London/Norwood, Aus.: Harrington Park Press, 2001

Klein, Fritz, MD, & Thomas Schwartz, editors. *Bisexual & Gay Husbands: Their Stories, Their Words*. New York/London/Oxford: Harrington Park Press, 2001

Kolodny, Debra R., editor. *Blessed Bi Spirit: Bisexual Spirit of Faith*, New York/London: Continuum, 2000

Leddick, David. *The Secret Lives of Married Men*. Los Angeles: Alyson, 2003

Nestle, Joan, Clare Howell, & Riki Wilchins, editors. *GenderQueer: Voices from beyond the Sexual Binary*. Los Angeles: Alyson Books, 2004

Ochs, Robyn, & Sarah Rowley, editors. *Getting Bi: Voices of Bisexuals Around the World*. Boston: Bisexual Resource Center, 2005

Queen, Carol, & Lawrence Schimel, editors. *PoMoSexuals: Challenging Assumptions about Gender and Sexuality*. San Francisco: Cleis Press, 1997

Silverstein, Charles, MD, & Felice Picano. *The Joy of Gay Sex*, 3rd edition. New York: HarperResource, 2003

Suresha, Ron Jackson. *Bears on Bears: Interviews and Discussions*. Los Angeles: Alyson, 2001

Thompson, Keith, editor. *To Be a Man: In Search of the Deep Masculine*. Los Angeles: Jeremy P. Tarcher, 1991

Tucker, Naomi, editor. *Bisexual Politics: Theories, Queries, & Visions*. New York/London: Harrington Park Press, 1995

Vassi, Marco. *The Erotic Comedies*. Sag Harbor, NY: Permanent Press, 1981

# Resources
# for Bisexual Men

Available online at http://www.haworthpress.com/web/JB
© 2005 by The Haworth Press, Inc. All rights reserved.
doi:10.1300/J159v05n02_38

[Haworth co-indexing entry note]: "Resources for Bisexual Men." Co-published simultaneously in *Journal of Bisexuality* (Harrington Park Press, an imprint of The Haworth Press, Inc.) Vol. 5, No. 2/3, 2005, pp. 321-325; and: *Bi Men: Coming Out Every Which Way* (ed: Ron Jackson Suresha, and Pete Chvany) Harrington Park Press, an imprint of The Haworth Press, Inc., 2005, pp. 321-325. Single or multiple copies of this article are available for a fee from The Haworth Document Delivery Service [1-800-HAWORTH, 9:00 a.m. - 5:00 p.m. (EST). E-mail address: docdelivery@haworthpress.com].

## THE BISEXUAL FOUNDATION

The nonprofit Bisexual Foundation advocates for and achieves better understanding and visibility about bisexuality through education, training, and media outreach, raising awareness about sexual-orientation diversity. The organization provides conference sponsorship, including the biannual International Conference on Bisexuality, bisexuality research project funding, and speakers on bisexuality for colleges, universities, and LGBTIQA organizations, including speaker training. The Foundation also underwrites, develops, and monitors the following Websites:

<www.bimagazine.org>

BiMagazine.org is an innovative global online magazine that advocates increased understanding and visibility for bisexuality, with an emphasis on the expression of bisexuality through the arts. Features include nonfiction articles and essays, fiction, poetry, visual arts (photography, painting, and sculpture), music, and animation.

<www.bisexual.org>

Bisexual.org is "bringing bisexuals together" as the main Website of the Bisexual Foundation and is dedicated to the support of bisexual individuals and the education of the public at large about the various bisexual communities.

## *BISEXUAL RESOURCE CENTER*

P.O. Box 1026, Boston, MA 02117-1026 USA; 617-424-9595
http://www.biresource.org

The Bisexual Resource Center (BRC) is a nonprofit organization that envisions a world where everyone's love is celebrated, regardless of gender(s), a world that acknowledges people as whole and indivisible, and where they should not have to leave any part of their heritage and identity at the door. Oppression based on sexual identity is intertwined with all other oppressions. The BRC publishes the *International Bisexual Resource Guide* and supports local, regional, national, and international organizing.

## BINET USA

4201 Wilson Blvd. #110 Box 311, Arlington VA 22203-1859
USA; 1-800-585-9368
http://www.binetusa.org

A nonprofit umbrella organization and voice for bisexual people,
BiNet USA facilitates the development of a cohesive network of bisexual communities, promotes bisexual visibility, and collects and
distributes educational information regarding bisexuality. To accomplish these goals, BiNet USA provides a national network for
bisexual organizations and individuals across the United States,
and encourages participation and organizing on local and national
levels.

## AUSTRALIAN BISEXUAL NETWORK

PO Box 490, Lutwyche, Queensland, Australia 4030;
within Australia: 07-3857-2500, outside Australia:
61-7-3857-2500
http://members.optusnet.com.au/~ausbinet/

The Australian Bisexual Network (ABN) serves bisexual women, bi
transpersons, bisexual men, partners and friends of bi people, and bisexual and bi-friendly groups and services. ABN does not claim to represent all bisexual-identified or bisexually active people but does offer a
voice for people united by their sexuality, as diverse as their lifestyles
may be. ABN cooperates and interacts with a range of groups and
services nationwide.

## BI.ORG

http://www.bi.org

Bi.org serves the worldwide bisexual community by providing free
or by-donation Internet presence for bisexual individuals, groups, and
nonprofit organizations, and extensive resource listings of groups, organizations, magazines, Internet newsgroups.

## *BICAFÉ*

http://www.bicafe.com

An online café and social spot for bisexual people worldwide, offering personals, mailboxes, forums, and fiction.

## *THE NATIONAL MEN'S RESOURCE CENTER*

PO Box 1080, Brookings, OR 97415-0024
http://www.menstuff.org

Working since 1982 to end men's isolation, the Men's Center offers support services and information resources for men dealing with relationships, sexuality, health, fatherhood, and prostate and testicular cancer awareness.

# Index

# BOOK ORDER FORM!

Order a copy of this book with this form or online at:
http://www.haworthpress.com/store/product.asp?sku=5703

## Bi Men
## *Coming Out Every Which Way*

___ in softbound at $19.95 ISBN-13: 978-1-56023-615-3 / ISBN-10: 1-56023-615-9.
___ in hardbound at $34.95 ISBN-13: 978-1-56023-614-6 / ISBN-10: 1-56023-614-0.

**COST OF BOOKS** _____

**POSTAGE & HANDLING** _____

US: $4.00 for first book & $1.50
for each additional book.
Outside US: $5.00 for first book
& $2.00 for each additional book.

**SUBTOTAL** _____

In Canada: add 7% GST. _____

**STATE TAX** _____

CA, IL, IN, MN, NJ, NY, OH, PA & SD residents
please add appropriate local sales tax.

**FINAL TOTAL** _____

If paying in Canadian funds, convert
using the current exchange rate,
UNESCO coupons welcome.

❑BILL ME LATER:
Bill-me option is good on US/Canada/
Mexico orders only; not good to jobbers,
wholesalers, or subscription agencies.

❑**Signature** _____

❑**Payment Enclosed: $** _____

❑ **PLEASE CHARGE TO MY CREDIT CARD:**

❑Visa ❑MasterCard ❑AmEx ❑Discover
❑Diner's Club ❑Eurocard ❑ JCB

**Account #** _____

**Exp Date** _____

**Signature** _____
*(Prices in US dollars and subject to change without notice.)*

| PLEASE PRINT ALL INFORMATION OR ATTACH YOUR BUSINESS CARD |
|---|

Name

Address

City                    State/Province                    Zip/Postal Code

Country

Tel                                    Fax

E-Mail

May we use your e-mail address for confirmations and other types of information? ❑Yes ❑No We appreciate receiving
your e-mail address. Haworth would like to e-mail special discount offers to you, as a preferred customer.
**We will never share, rent, or exchange your e-mail address. We regard such actions as an invasion of your privacy.**

Order from your **local bookstore** or directly from
**The Haworth Press, Inc.** 10 Alice Street, Binghamton, New York 13904-1580 • USA
Call our toll-free number (1-800-429-6784) / Outside US/Canada: (607) 722-5857
Fax: 1-800-895-0582 / Outside US/Canada: (607) 771-0012
E-mail your order to us: orders@haworthpress.com

**For orders outside US and Canada,** you may wish to order through your local
sales representative, distributor, or bookseller.
For information, see http://haworthpress.com/distributors

*(Discounts are available for individual orders in US and Canada only, not booksellers/distributors.)*

The **Haworth Press** Inc.

**Please photocopy this form for your personal use.**
www.HaworthPress.com

BOF05